Contents

Preface	vii
Welcome to "Lose Your Faith 101"	1
Part I: Eastern Religions	**21**
Hinduism	23
Buddhism	31
Confucianism	37
Taoism	45
Part II: Western Religions	**55**
Judaism	57
Christianity	99
Islam	155
Part III: Taking a View	**179**
Judgment Day	181
Bibliography	207
Appendix: The Development of Writing	209
Timeline	211
Index	**217**

For my mother, Ruth Gabrielle;
Uncle Dan, Christina, and Johan; Batman and Joker;
and all of my other friends and students who asked for a book they could understand. With special thanks to Brianna and other sharp-eyed students and friends who helped to reduce the number of errors in the text.

Preface

• • • • •

You shall not act dishonestly in rendering judgment. Show neither partiality to the weak nor deference to the mighty, but judge your fellow men justly.
—Dt 19:15

Education is an admirable thing. But it is well to remember from time to time that nothing that is worth knowing can be taught.
—*Oscar Wilde*

I began teaching "Introduction to Religious Studies" in 1988. For most of my career, I have used Huston Smith's *The World's Religions*. I liked the simplicity and directness of his approach to the nature of the different religions; I disliked the lack of chronological order in his exposition, his allusions to art, poetry, drama, and history that were too far removed from the experience of my students, and his use of technical terms without adequate definition in the text. *The World's Religions* was a great book for me, given the closeness of my age and cultural experience to that of Smith, but it was not a great book for my students.

I have also become more critical of the supposition that religion can be treated from a neutral standpoint. I am not neutral. I am a priest in the Roman Catholic tradition, and a member of the Society of Jesus (also known as "the Jesuits"). I accept everything that the Church teaches. In Vatican II (1962-1965), the 21st ecumenical ("worldwide") council in the Roman Catholic tradition, the Church stated her belief that "Humanity forms but one community," and that "All share a common destiny, namely God":

> Men expect from the various religions answers to the unsolved riddles of the human condition, which today, even as in former times, deeply stir the hearts of men:
> What is man?
> What is the meaning, the aim of our life?
> What is moral good, what sin?
> Whence suffering and what purpose does it serve?
> Which is the road to true happiness?
> What are death, judgment and retribution after death?
> What, finally, is that ultimate inexpressible mystery which encompasses our existence: whence do we come, and where are we going?[1]

The Church does *not* teach that only Catholics go to Heaven, and that everyone else goes to Hell; she does *not* teach that there is no truth, wisdom, or holiness outside the boundaries of the Church. On the contrary, the Church teaches that Catholics have an obligation to recognize truth and honor goodness, wherever they are found.

> The Catholic Church rejects nothing of what is true or holy in these religions. It has a high regard for the manner of life and conduct, the precepts and doctrines which, although differing in many ways from its own teaching, nevertheless often reflect a ray of that truth which enlightens all men and women. … The Church, therefore, urges its sons and daughters to enter into collaboration with members of other religions. Let Christians, while witnessing to their own faith and way of life, acknowledge, preserve and encourage the spiritual and moral truths found among non-Christians, together with their life and culture.[2]

This view of world religions has a basis in Scripture. When preaching to the Roman soldiers in the household of Cornelius, Peter said, "In truth, I see that God shows no partiality. Rather, in every nation whoever fears him and acts uprightly is acceptable to him" (Acts 10:34-35).

I propose to consider "the spiritual and moral truths found among non-Christians" in this book. Many—even those who reject His authority—will quote Jesus: "Judge not lest ye be judged" (Mt 7:1). I am morally certain that Jesus was not saying, "There is no religious truth; no one can tell the difference between good and evil; you are on your own in figuring out who God is; all beliefs are equally worthy of honor." I take this saying as a reminder that I am not God, and that I cannot presume to say who is in God's favor and who is not. I judge that Jesus is "the Way, the Truth, and the Life," and that no one comes to the Father except through Him (Jn 14:16);

---

[1] "Nostra Aetate," 1; reformatted to highlight the list of questions.
[2] "Nostra Aetate," 2.

I judge all other religious traditions in the light of that truth, while leaving judgment about the final destiny of the adherents of those religions—and myself—in God's hands.

Gender-Neutral Language

In our present culture, professional writers have an obligation to use inclusive terms. I hold myself and my students accountable to this standard. I will not say "man," when I mean "men and women," nor will I use "he, him, his" as generic references to the human being. I will let the old language stand when quoting from sources.

Etymology

Etymology (Greek, *etymon*, "true sense" + *logos*, "word, reason, logic") is the study of the original meanings of words. The meaning of words change over time. I often find it helpful to think and speak about the original meanings from which the process of development began. Recognizing the relationships between the roots of words can help us to grasp associated terms and concepts that have evolved from a common ancestor, as well as to understand how original meanings may differ from later connotations.

Some Preliminary Vocabulary

These are terms that I find useful when trying to sort out the various types of religions found around the world. The first group are based on ***theos***, the Greek word for "god."

- **theism**: generic belief in some kind of god.
- **atheism**: belief that there is no god.
- **monotheism**: belief that there is only one God.
- **polytheism**: belief in many gods/goddesses.
- **pantheism**: belief that "all (*pan*) is god," with no distinction between Creator and creation.
- **pantheon**: collection of (or temple for) all gods/goddesses.
- **theology**: reasoning (*logos*, logic) about God; "God talk."

The second set of terms are derived from ***deus***, the Latin word for "god."

- **deism**: Western Enlightenment image of God as the Great Clockmaker; God creates the laws and machinery of the universe and sets it all in motion, but is otherwise not personally involved in our daily life.
- **deity**: synonym for "God" or "Divine Being."

- **divinity**: much like "deity." May also suggest "the state of being a god."

The final pair comes from a Greek word for knowledge, ***gnosis***.

- **gnostic**: someone who does know or who claims to know.
- **agnostic**: someone who says, "I don't know."

This last root appears in "ignorance," "diagnosis," "prognosis," "cognition," "precognition," and "recognition." It also entered into the formation of "knowledge" (*gno-* from the Greek became transliterated into *kno-* in English).

BC and AD: Calendric Incorrectness

Dionysius Exiguus ("Dennis the Short," "Dennis the Humble," or, as I like to think of him, "Denny the Dwarf"; c. 470-c. 544 AD) invented the system of counting the years "Before Christ" (BC) and "Anno Domini" (AD; Latin, "*annus*," year, + "*Dominus*," Lord). Up until then, the Roman calendar system counted the years "ab urbe condita" (AUC)—from the time that the city of Rome had been founded.

Denny was a monk, and for him, as for most Christians, it makes perfect sense to divide all of time into these two periods. Both BC and AD honor Jesus, and make a religious affirmation: that Jesus is **"the Christ"** (see page 146) and that He is **"Lord"** (see page 70). Those who disagree with these two claims about Jesus sometimes take offense at having to use these religiously loaded terms just to express a date. They have invented other terms:

BCE: "Before the Common (or Current or Christian) Era"
CE: "Common (or Current or Christian) Era"
BP: "Before the present" (often used by scientists)

I think I am a Christian (other Christians may disagree with me about this). Consequently, I believe that it is proper to call Jesus both Christ and Lord. I will, therefore, use the terms from my tradition to tell the story of the history of the universe from the Catholic standpoint. Students should understand the issues involved, and may use the convention that they prefer.

Jews have a very different calendar. For them, time begins with creation on Rosh Hashanah (see page 77), 1 Tishri of year 1, which—according to contemporary calculations—corresponds to 7 October 3761 BC in the Julian calendar. In English, the abbreviation for a date on the Hebrew Calendar is "AM," which stands for "Anno Mundi" (Latin, *annus*, "year" + *mundus*, "world" = "year of the world"). The Jewish calendar has an entirely different definition of days, months, and years from the Christian calendar; it is used by observant Jews to determine the proper days to celebrate their annual festivals and holy days.

A Note on Style

Although I give credit where credit is due by using footnotes and page references (a very important part of formal writing), I am not adhering to all of the other standards I set for my students in their formal essays. I will use "you" (second person), contractions, a conversational tone, and the occasional rhetorical question. Students must not take the informal tone in this book as an excuse to avoid learning how to write in the formal, academic style.

Welcome to "Lose Your Faith 101"

• • • • • •

An Unassailable Truth

Relativism is a very popular philosophical outlook in our culture. It suggests that there is no truth; and that, therefore, no one should "impose" their idea of truth on other people; all that we have are a range of opinions, and everyone should choose the interpretation of life that seems best to them.

I am going to state a proposition to which no one can reasonably reject:

People disagree.

Anybody who opposes this statement *proves my point by disagreeing with what I said.* Therefore, we may be certain that this proposition is true. We may agree that people disagree with each other. This leads to a second proposition:

People can agree with each other.

These are two small indicators that the relativist position is false. A third, and related, indicator is to recognize that relativism is *self-refuting*. The claim that "there is no truth," or that "no human being can know the truth" is a truth-claim. If it is thought to be true by the person who makes the claim, then it provides immediate evidence that it is false. No one can consistently say, "I know that it is true that there is no truth."

Dedicated and sophisticated relativists—the kind of people whom you are likely to meet on college campuses—never expose the idiocy of their views by putting the matter that bluntly. They express their commitment to relativism indirectly rather than directly, perhaps by asking questions, making jokes, raising an eyebrow, or murmuring in distaste when someone claims to know something. Their sole **dogma** (authoritative teaching) is that there *is* no dogma. "Everyone has the right to their own opinion. You must not inflict your interpretation on others. Diversity is beautiful. It is better to ask questions than to answer them."

Notice that the prohibition of certainty is an imposition of the speaker's opinion on all other human beings. The person who says, "No one may argue that their view is superior to anyone else's view" is expressing a view that is superior to all other views—the speaker's view is that there is no truth, and that therefore, all argument is nonsensical.

It is a fact that people disagree. We disagree with each other on philosophical and religious grounds. As we will see, all of the religions of the world tend to break up into splinter groups on the basis of such disagreements. The sophisticated relativist may even make an argument for relativism on the basis of this fact:

> If there were truth, people would agree with it. But people disagree about what is true. Therefore, there is no truth.

The problem with this argument is the assumption it makes about "people" in general. If it were true that all human beings are equally capable of reasoning, and if it were true that all human beings are equally willing to follow where reason leads, then the premise of the argument would be strengthened. One would also have to assume that the truth has been expressed in such a way that people can—and should—be expected to understand and accept it. In other words, the reasons why people disagree may not be that there is no truth, but that the truth has not been expressed well, or that the people who disagree reason poorly, or are unwilling to accept the conclusions to which reason leads.

I am at peace with the fact that "people disagree." I am not surprised that the majority of people disagree with my commitment to the truth of Catholicism. I believe that where truth is found, everyone *should* accept it, but I understand that there are barriers to the expression and reception of truth, some more innocent than others. That's life.

Using Philosophy as an Instrument in Religious Studies

In the high Middle Ages (13th century), it was common to say that "philosophy is the handmaid of theology." **Philosophy** comes from the Greek for love (*philos*) of wisdom (*sophia*). A very simple definition of philosophy is that it is thinking about thinking or reasoning about reasoning.[1] People

---

[1] My definition is inspired by Bernard J. F. Lonergan's slogan: "Thoroughly understand what it is to understand, and not only will you understand the broad lines of all there is to be understood but also you will possess a fixed base, an invariant pattern, opening upon all further developments of understanding" (*Insight*, xxviii; emphasis removed).

can do philosophy almost unconsciously, making choices about how to make up their minds when they are confronted with new questions, new ideas, or new information. Not everyone is equally adept at identifying and expressing their own philosophy or entering into extended philosophical discourse. It is part of the Jesuit tradition, which, in turn, is part of the Catholic tradition: to honor what we can discover, simply by the use of human reasoning. This is why studies in philosophy are part of the core requirements in most Jesuit colleges and universities.

Scientists use mathematics as a common language to express their findings, even though mathematics is a discipline in and of itself. So, too, everyone who studies a religion—either from the inside (as a **theologian** [Greek, *theos*, "god" + *logos*, "word, reason, logic"])—or from the outside (as a scholar in Religious Studies) will *use their own philosophy as a tool to investigate the meaning and significance of religious beliefs*. Philosophy can provide a common ground for constructing, debating, and judging differences of opinion.

We cannot think about *anything* unless we have at least an implicit view of what we think thinking is. When we think about our own religion or the religions of the world, we bring our own philosophy to bear on those issues. The better we are at thinking about thinking, the better the odds are that we will think rightly about religion.

Epistemology: How Do We Know What We Know?

Epistemology (Greek, *epi*, "upon" + *histhemai*, "to stand" + *logos*, "word, reason, logic") is the study of understanding. "How do you know that?" is one of the favorite challenges of our age to claims made by religious traditions. In a sense, there is no greater question that we can ask of others or of ourselves. Confucius said, "Shall I teach you what knowledge is? When you know a thing, to recognize that you know it, and when you do not know a thing, to recognize that you do not know it. That is knowledge" (*Analects*, II, 17).[2]

John Henry Newman (1801-1890) was an Anglican priest who converted to Roman Catholicism. In both parts of his life, he defended the idea that faith is a reasonable choice. In his *Grammar of Assent*,[3] he made some observations about how our minds work that I find very useful in understanding the academic study of religion.

Newman identifies four operations of the mind. The first he calls **notional apprehension**, which means grasping ideas, concepts, theories, definitions, plans, or the like. After we get an idea in our minds, then we are capable of **notional assent**, which means "making up our minds one way or the other" about the idea. Although "assent" means "to agree," Newman says that accepting

---

[2] All of my quotations of Confucius are from Arthur Waley's translation and annotation of *The Analects of Confucius* (New York: Vintage Books, 1989). I give the book and number of the particular saying in parentheses immediately after the quotation. When I quote Waley's notes, I give his name and the page number of the reference.

[3] The full title of the book is *An Essay in Aid of a Grammar of Assent*; 28-30.

or rejecting an idea is essentially the same act of the mind; when we *reject* one thought, we *accept* (assent to) a contrary notion.

Besides understanding ideas, the mind can also understand realities. Newman defines **real apprehension** as understanding some reality or other. **Real assent** means to accept or reject a reality. There may be an unfortunate misinterpretation of Newman's terms. He is not contrasting "real" with "unreal" in his definition of terms; notional apprehension and notional assent are just as "real" as real apprehension and real assent. In using the word "real," he is trying to distinguish between the mental world and all of the things that go *beyond* our mental world. Such things are what they are, whether we know them or not.

In both his philosophy and religion, Newman believed in realities that go beyond the physical world. The technical term for those realities is **"metaphysical"** (Greek, *meta*, "beyond" + *physis*, "nature," the root of our word "physical"). Not surprisingly, some people disagree (e.g., Carl Sagan—see page 187) that there are any metaphysical realities we can or should worry about. As a general rule, most religions make some kind of claim about metaphysical realities; there are some religions and/or spiritualities that downplay the value of trying to apprehend or assent to metaphysical claims.

Metaphysics raises questions about whether there are realities *beyond* those dealt with by the senses: truth, beauty, goodness; spiritual realities; a supernatural origin for the universe (the unmoved Mover, the uncaused Cause, the Intelligence that orders all things; see page 195); origin and destiny of the human person; life after life; Heaven, Hell, Purgatory (see page 142); existence of gods and goddesses; and so on. *Metaphysical questions, by definition, cannot be settled by laboratory experiments.* Note that that last sentence is a metaphysical claim that cannot be proved or disproved by any scientific observation or lab experiment. Either you see the truth of the statement or you don't. For those who believe that all truth must be determined by scientific experiments, metaphysics is just bunk. (Of course, the thought that "all truth must be determined by scientific experiments" is a metaphysical statement itself, so, by the standard set in that proposition, it, too, must be judged as bunk.)

In order to define Newman's terms, I had to take them one at a time, following his own order of exposition. Once we understand his terms (exercising our power of notional apprehension by grasping his definitions), we can use them freely and in a different order to analyze how we know what we know.

Once upon a time, a long time ago in a different century and millennium, a friend of mine asked me how I liked Big Macs. I didn't know what he was talking about. He explained in general terms that it was a hamburger sold by McDonald's. Since then, I've learned that the definition of a Big Mac is "two all beef patties, special sauce, lettuce, cheese, pickles, onions on a sesame seed bun." That is just the *idea* of this kind of hamburger. I know that this is true (I assent to this definition), because I have seen the commercial countless times, and have just verified the ingredients by checking an article in Wikipedia.

	Ideas	Things (*realities*)
	Notional Apprehension	**Real Apprehension**
Understanding	• **understanding ideas**, definitions, blueprints, formulas, words, concepts, theories (scientific, theological …), abstractions, images, maps • gaining information about mental constructs	• **recognizing a reality** • personal experience • sense knowledge of physical things • religious, moral, intellectual experience of spiritual (*metaphysical*) realities • gathering information about extra-mental realities
	Notional Assent	**Real Assent**
Choosing	• **agreeing to an idea** • (*or agreeing to its opposite*) • deciding whether an idea is true or false • making up your own mind about theories	• **embracing a reality** • making a commitment • deciding to take ACTION • personal behavior

John Henry Newman (1801-1890), *Grammar of Assent*

Knowing the definition of a Big Mac is one kind of knowledge. The more important kind, from one point of view, is to know what it is by actually eating a Big Mac. That is real apprehension—knowing what a Big Mac is by personal experience. In order to gain that kind of knowledge, I had to find a McDonald's restaurant, pay for the burger, and make the decision to eat it. That is an example of real assent. Only by making the decision to eat a Big Mac could I gain real apprehension (personal experience) of what a Big Mac is.

A few weeks after writing this section, I opened a pack of Wrigley's Extra Classic Bubble Sugarfree Gum. Under the cover, it said, "Try explaining the taste of bubble gum to someone who has never tasted it." Real apprehension (personal experience) is very different from just hearing someone describe something verbally (notional apprehension).

Architects who dream about building proceed from notional apprehension to notional assent and then from real assent to real apprehension, if they can get the resources they need to build the building they have designed. First comes the apprehension of an idea: "I wonder if I could build a mile-high building?" The architect then starts drawing plans and explores the science of structures and materials. Many such studies have been done, and, as far as I can tell, there is a consensus (notional assent) that such buildings are possible. No one has invested the time and money to build such a building (real assent), so we cannot yet experience (have real apprehension of) a mile-high building as a physical reality. For now, the theory that such buildings *can* be built (notional assent) has not been tested by experience (real apprehension of such buildings).

By contrast with these first two examples, science as we now understand it generally begins with observation of a thing or a process (real apprehension). On November 11, 1572, Tycho Brahe noticed a new star in the sky. (Let us pause for a moment to praise the astronomers of centuries past who knew the sky so well that they could recognize *one* extra star just by gazing heavenward on a clear, dark night!) Tycho checked and double-checked his observation, then exercised real assent by judging that this was happening in the universe, and that his perception of a new star was not just a figment of his imagination.

The behavior of this star was strange compared to all the other stars in the sky. It appeared unexpectedly, brightened, then disappeared. The astronomers of that time had no theory (notional apprehension) of what could cause that kind of behavior. We now know that scientists could not explain novas ("new stars") and supernovas until they understood the law of gravity (in the 17th century) and the nature of nuclear fission and fusion (20th century). Only then were the right ideas available to understand what causes novas and supernovas.

Newman's distinctions about the four fundamental operations of the mind can be applied in various ways to the study of religion. In Christianity, the first generation of believers had real apprehension of Jesus of Nazareth. The author of the first letter of John claims to know what "we have heard, what we have seen with our eyes, what we looked upon and touched with our hands" (1:1). That group of people could make up their minds about Jesus as a person (real assent) and about His teaching (notional assent) by way of conversation with Him (notional and real apprehension). Some of them saw for themselves that He was dead, and later claimed to have seen for themselves that He was risen from the dead (real apprehension and real assent).

As a general rule, subsequent generations of Christians cannot personally verify the claims (ideas, doctrines, definitions, propositions) made by the first generation. We have no way to see Jesus' death and resurrection for ourselves—we cannot have personal experience, real apprehension, of His death, or of the events at the tomb a few days later. Faith in subsequent generations begins with hearing the gospel preached (notional apprehension) and accepting the trustworthiness of the preachers (a blend of notional and real assent); the believer makes a personal decision to accept the realities (real assent) revealed by the testimony, and then may or may not have some interior experiences (real apprehension) that confirm and strengthen the act of faith. (See page 116 for a longer discussion of whether the apostles were trustworthy witnesses.)

Some Implications of Newman's Epistemic Observations

I want to reflect on four ideas that follow from recognizing the four fundamental operations of the mind. I do not claim that this is an exhaustive list. There may be other morals to the story that I haven't noticed. At the end of my oral examination for my master's degree, Quentin Lauer, SJ, said: "Let's assume that what you have said is true. So what? What difference does it make?" That is the question I want to address in this section.

1. Because *understanding* and *accepting* are two different operations of the mind, **we can understand (*apprehend*) what we do not accept (*assent to*)**. Aristotle is said to have said, "It is the mark of an educated mind to be able to entertain a thought without accepting it."[4] We do not have to *be* a member of a religion to understand something about what the religion *teaches*. I understand Hitler's theory that humans are just animals and that, as a consequence, the ordinary principles of animal husbandry should be applied to the human animal (breed for desired characteristics, and kill off those animals that have undesirable characteristics); I do not accept his theory because I think humans are more than just another animal species.

2. I think there is general agreement in our culture that **we *should* understand what we do not accept**. This is the principle of open-mindedness. People who make up their minds without understanding the issues involved are prejudiced, ignorant bigots who make themselves unworthy of being given a hearing in reasoned discourse. They, of course, are free to think and act as they choose, but others are under no obligation to pay attention to their rantings, or to treat them with any special respect. By exhibiting "contempt prior to investigation"[5] they discredit themselves.

Expanding the range of what we understand is the primary objective of a college education. Readings and lectures are all intended to provide students with new ideas and call their attention to new realities that they have not previously understood. Even atheists and agnostics *should* understand something about the religions of the world; believers in one religious tradition *should* understand something about the religions that they do not accept.

There is, of course, a limit to how much information we can take in at any time in our lives. We have to make choices about what we consider worthy of our time and attention, and let go of other things. I have not kept up with contemporary music since 1970 or thereabouts. The consequence of choices like this is that we give up our right to form judgments about those areas that we have decided not to investigate. I know that I don't know enough about popular music to

---

[4] I have not been able to trace the source of this quotation further. Whether or not Aristotle said it, I think it captures the essence of Newman's distinction between notional apprehension (entertaining an idea) and notional assent (accepting or rejecting it).

[5] Bill Wilson, "Spiritual Experience," *Alcoholics Anonymous*, 3rd ed., 570.

name the genres (kinds of music) properly, let alone determine which artists and works are great, and which are contemptible. I have no theory to guide my selection. I just cruise the radio dial at random and change stations when I am not pleased with what is on the air.

3. **We can accept what we do not understand.** Although the ideal of knowledge is to understand what we take to be true, there are many aspects in science and religion where assent precedes apprehension. Tycho saw the new star. He knew that it was something real. He had to accept the truth of his observations without being able to explain how such things could happen. He died centuries before the theories of gravitation, fission, and fusion developed that could make his observations fully intelligible (when some stars burn up the readily available nuclear resources for fusion, gravitation causes the star's material to collapse upon itself and ignite one last violent explosion).

Even where theories and observations coincide, there still can be areas where facts resist our questions, or where our theories seem to run amok. In the present state of particle physics, Heisenberg's Principle of Uncertainty states that we cannot know the position and momentum of the same particle at the same time. Determining where the particle is destroys the information about where it was going, and vice versa. We are *certain that we cannot be certain* about both. It is a very perplexing situation, but I accept that this is how reality is when looked at with the instruments and methods currently at our disposal. To measure the position of a quantum particle and determine its vector require interaction with the particle; the interaction that yields information thus changes the state of the particle itself.

I do not have a totally open mind about whether scientists can come up with tools that can get around this fact. At some point, they come up against the smallest distance we can measure (a Planck meter) and the smallest time interval we can distinguish (a Planck second). Both of these units are related to the quantum nature of light (another stubborn fact that I accept without understanding it!) which means that there is a limit to how small the smallest wavelength of light can be. Right now, scientists don't have a better tool than wavelengths of light to use as a ruler to measure space and time. For now, I'm going to bet than they won't find a better ruler, but I won't be surprised if they surprise me and prove me wrong. That's how science has grown over the last five or six centuries.

As a Christian, I accept many things that I do not understand and that I know I cannot understand in this lifetime (and possibly in the next as well). We will return to this theme when we talk about **Trinity, Incarnation,** and **Atonement** (see page 114 andpage 139).

4. **We can accept what we cannot prove.** I have not precisely defined what I mean by "proof," nor have I specified what Newman means by the word. That's because I understand that logicians and mathematicians disagree about the proper definition. If the people whose lives are devoted to proving things in the abstract can't define the term, I'm not going to beat them at that

game. I'm using "proof" in an informal, everyday sense. We take something to be proved when we feel that it would be against the essence of reason itself to deny the proposition—and we expect that any other reasonable person would agree with us. The whole idea of Newman's *Grammar of Assent* was to explore the question of when it is proper for us to assent to ideas or realities. When we are confronted with proof, we *should* assent to what has been shown to be true, real, good, or beautiful.

The kind of proof needed varies with the issue at hand. Logical and mathematical proofs only need the proper mental constructs and operations; proof about various kinds of realities require various methods (repeatable observations, lab experiments, statistical surveys, exploration of art and literature, spiritual insight, religious or mystical experience, etc.).

I cannot prove in the abstract that I exist. I find it absurd for me to think that I don't exist, because as Descartes said, "*Cogito, ergo sum.*" The fact that I am thinking proves *to me* that I exist. Every thought that passes through my mind implies the existence of me and my mind. I judge that the same is true of every human being and every human mind, but I know that I do not personally experience other minds in the same way that I do my own. For me, my trust in the existence of other people and other minds is an act of faith, and one that I consider extremely reasonable, but I don't consider it as proven beyond the shadow of a doubt. It's a reality that I *see* as a reality, but can't completely translate into words and formal operations.

I cannot prove that I am the child of the man and woman who claimed to be my parents. Every document about my birth could be forged. DNA testing would only show a family resemblance; I could be the son of my uncle on my father's side and the woman who says she is my mother, or an aunt on my mother's side and the man who claims to be my father. Although I was present at my birth (of that I am totally certain on purely logical grounds), I didn't have the capacity at that time to recognize and remember the woman who gave me life. Since I did not exist until I was conceived in her womb, I never had the opportunity to observe for myself who fathered me. I have to take Mom's word for that.

Even though I don't have "perfect proof" of who my parents are, I am morally certain that Mom was my mother and Dad was my father. I am convinced that I *should* assent to that proposition, even though I know that the lines of evidence fall short of ideal proof.

Most of the things that we know about the world around us fall into this category. It is proper for us to take information on others' say-so. We cannot personally verify all the facts of history, geography, or science by direct observation (real apprehension) or logical argument (notional apprehension), but we would be cut off from a vast reservoir of knowledge if we resolved never to take anyone else's testimony about what is true.

5. We do not need a complete theory of knowledge (notional apprehension) to know some things (notional and real apprehension). I was interested in epistemology before I knew what it was. I chose St. Thomas Aquinas as my confirmation saint in 1965, and started thinking about his Five Ways to recognize God's existence (see page 195). I know that not everyone shares my enthusiasm for philosophical and theological abstractions. People can go through their whole lives without thinking about how it is that they know what they know, even though they know many things, and possess skills that earn them and their families a good living. There are some who are content to just enjoy their relationship with God without raising questions about how they know what they know about God. More power to them!

A Car in Pieces is Not a Real Car

I call the introductory course in Religious Studies "Lose Your Faith 101," because the study of what humans believe can cause us to lose our capacity for faith. Ronald Knox, a British Catholic author from the early 20th century, said that "the study of comparative religions is the best way to become comparatively religious."[6] The sins of people who claim to be religious give religion a bad name. Trying to come up with theories that explain religious assent raises a host of questions that may be difficult or impossible to answer. Thinking about thinking is harder than it sounds at first, and some of our general philosophical convictions may lead us astray when we try to think about religious thinking.

In 1965, when I was in eighth grade, I bought a used 1954 Pontiac Star Chief with an inline eight-cylinder engine for 15 dollars. It had been licensed and on the road the year before and still was in running condition, although it was a bit of an eyesore—because it was painted with stolen orange bridge paint. I knew enough about mechanics to start taking pieces out of the engine compartment, cleaning them up, repainting them, and reinstalling them. All went well with the project, until I reassembled the master cylinder for the brakes. I couldn't get the brake fluid to go into the reservoir, and without brake fluid in the system, the brakes wouldn't work at all. Without brakes, I couldn't drive the car any more, and it sat rusting away, until I paid a tow truck driver to haul it away in 1973, just before I entered the Jesuit novitiate in Syracuse, New York.

Years later, I learned the secret. To get fluid into the lines, someone has to open the bleeder valve at each wheel, one at a time; a second person pours fluid into the top of the master cylinder; a third person sits behind the wheel pumping the brakes, until the person at the bleeder valve reports that there are no more air bubbles coming out of the line. It's not a hard concept to grasp, but it is a lot of work to get it right—and it is well worth it to get it right if you plan to drive the car in hilly territory!

I knew enough to take my car apart. I did not know how to put it back together. All the pieces of my car were unbroken, but a car in pieces is not a real car. So, too, it is easy to take faith apart by various kinds of analysis, but faith in pieces is not real faith. The components need to be reassembled correctly for the faith to come alive again.

---

[6] Kreeft, *Fundamentals of the Faith: Essays in Christian Apologetics* (San Francisco: Ignatius Press, 1988), 74.

People who know how to take things apart and put them back together can do amazing things. They can make old cars, motorcycles, houses, airplanes, and the like as good as, or even better than, new. I appreciate the philosophers and theologians who equip us to do the same with faith, but I realize that some students will almost certainly leave the course with their faith in disarray. On balance, I think it is better to take that risk than to remain with a childish faith that has never asked or answered the tough questions that arise in Religious Studies. Paul said, "When I was a child, I used to talk as a child, think as a child, reason as a child; when I became a man, I put aside childish things" (1 Cor 13:11). A childish faith is perfect for children; it is not adequate for adults. It is not hard to show what is wrong with childish forms of the faith; it is not easy to make the transition to mature faith.

The essence of baby faith is to believe everything that an adult says. Children pass through a stage of magical thinking that predisposes them to believe in Santa Claus, the tooth fairy, the Easter bunny, and all kinds of fairy tales like *Harry Potter*. In order to grow up, they have to learn how to question what they have heard, and to determine for themselves what is real and what is merely a figment of human imagination. Baby faith is good for babies; it is not good for grownups.

Academic and Religious Freedom

In the courses I teach, I intend to grade students solely and only on their *notional apprehension* of the material presented in the course. They must demonstrate that they have grasped the names, dates, definitions, and relationships that characterize the religions considered in the course. I respect and honor the freedom of the students to make up their own minds about what is true, real, good, or beautiful, and to decide for themselves how those core beliefs will affect their behavior (real assent).

The Definition Game

If Socrates, a Greek philosopher (470-399 BC), didn't invent this game, he was certainly a master at it. The "Socratic method" consists of asking students a series of questions designed to bring out what the students already know, to show them that their beliefs are confused, or to reveal their ignorance. The presupposition of the definition game is that if we cannot define the terms we are using, then we literally do not know what we are talking about; the task set in the definition game is to define the terms first, and then use them in that defined sense for the rest of the dialogue. To use a word or term in two contrary senses in the same argument is to commit the sin of "equivocation," that is, treating two things that are not the same as if they were the same.

I'm all in favor of helping students to clarify what they mean when they say something. This is a fundamental task in education. Clarity of thought, like the clarity of gemstones, allows light to pass into the heart of the matter and create brilliant flashes that please the eye of the mind. If you have ever been caught in a blinding snowstorm or a smothering fog, you know what a relief it is to emerge from the cloud and enter the clear light of day again. The task of writers and speakers is to provide all that is necessary for the reader or audience to *see what they mean*.

Although I love clarity, I see that the demand for clarity can be taken to ridiculous extremes. St. Augustine (354-430 AD), one of the great philosophers and theologians of the **patristic era** (see page 136), said, "I know well enough what time is, provided that nobody asks me; but if I am asked what it is and try to explain, I am baffled."[7] We have a problem putting what we know (notional or real apprehension) into words. Michael Polanyi (1891-1976 AD), a philosopher and scientist, said, "We know more than we can tell."[8] **Lao Tzu**, the Chinese sage whose poetry inspired the development of **Taoism** (see page 45), said, "The **Tao** that can be put into words is not the real Tao."

If we take the definition game too seriously, we will ask something like "What is the correct definition of religion?" and then press for a definition of every term used in the first answer, and then demand definition of every term used in the second answer, and so on, until we come to the point at which we find that we have no precise definition for "definition," "word," "meaning," "language," "speaking," or "thinking." We may even reach the point of saying, "That depends on what the definition of 'is' is." The evil Socratic genius, also known as a **relativist**, will then conclude (without defining any of the terms used in stating the skeptical conclusion) that it is certain that nobody can say anything certain about *anything*.

I would prefer to place a different interpretation on the outcome of the game. I suggest that the absurd outcome of demanding precise definitions for every term used in discourse shows that the demand is absurd—not that we don't know what we mean by the words we use. Aristotle, a student and critic of Plato, said, "It is the mark of an educated man to look for precision in each class of things *just so far as the nature of the subject admits*; it is evidently equally foolish to accept probable reasoning from a mathematician and to demand from a rhetorician scientific proofs."[9]

The sub-terms that come into play when we try to define religion are things like "God," "sacred," "profane," "supernatural," "transcendental," "mystical," "numinous" (awe-inspiring), "good," "evil," "beautiful," "true," "meaningful," "spiritual," and so on. None of these terms has a self-evident definition; the meanings associated with them vary by culture, and even within the same culture

---

[7] *Confessions* XI, 14, 64.

[8] *The Tacit Dimension* (New York: Doubleday and Company, 1966), 4. My PhD dissertation was on Polanyi and Newman; it was published as *Personal Catholicism: The Theological Epistemologies of John Henry Newman and Michael Polanyi*, with foreword by Avery Dulles (Washington, DC: The Catholic University of America Press, 2000). I also had the privilege of helping to coauthor the first full-length biography of Polanyi with William T. Scott: *Michael Polanyi: Scientist and Philosopher* (Oxford University Press, 2005).

[9] *Nicomachean Ethics* I.1094b24 (*Wikiquote*). Emphasis added.

over the course of time. There is no perfect definition of "religion" or any of its associated terms that fits every culture at every time in history, nor every use of the word by the members of the same culture.

That's life. There is also no perfect definition of "perfect", "definition," "culture," "history," or "time" that fits every culture and every author at every time in history. I blame the French mathematical and philosophical genius, René Descartes (1596-1650 AD), for kindling the fire of perfectionism in the early days of the **Enlightenment** (see page 170); he invented the system of assigning coordinates to points in the plane (x, y), which, in turn, allowed geometry to be linked to algebra—we call these pairs "Cartesian coordinates" in his honor. Descartes recommended that we take all of philosophy apart by systematically doubting everything. His goal was to find "clear and distinct ideas" along the lines of a geometer's definitions of point, line, plane, angle, intersection, etc., so that, like the geometer, we could rebuild a system of truths based on undoubtable axioms and perfectly logical operations. In this fashion, he hoped that we would come to know *exactly* what we know; everything known would be strictly proved, and anything not strictly proved would be treated as unknown and uncertain.

The Cartesian program in philosophy sounds perfectly reasonable. It is easy to state, and it arouses great enthusiasm for the project of finding out exactly what we know, defining it precisely, and separating real knowledge from the uncertainties of mere opinion. The problem is that there is no "clear and distinct idea" of what a "clear and distinct idea" is. The best that can be said is that such ideas are *like* the definitions and operations of mathematics—but comparisons using "*like*" are notoriously slippery, and get us into a world of hurt when we try to specify all of the similarities that matter, and set aside the differences that don't matter.

I suggest that we need to resist perfectionism, and as best we can, put it in its proper place. It is splendid when we can give definitions that promise to last for the ages. I love Newton's definition that "force equals mass times acceleration" ($F = ma$) and Einstein's proposition that matter may be converted into energy, and vice versa ($E = mc^2$). I use the Pythagorean theorem ($a^2 + b^2 = c^2$) all the time in various carpentry projects. Such breakthroughs are magnificent, and are deserving of the highest honor we can give to those who made these discoveries.

Most of the time, and with most terms at our disposal, we don't have that kind of clarity. We can get along with definitions that are "close enough for government work." What we need are tools of expression that we can use to achieve our own purposes when we write and speak. That is all anyone can ask of us, for they are in exactly the same boat that we are. What they do to us in demanding perfect precision in every term can be done unto them, with exactly the same results: If we must have perfect definitions, then we must conclude that no one knows anything for certain.

For myself, I have taken a phrase from Tibor Horvath, SJ, one of my teachers in my seminary days in Toronto. He founded a journal called *Ultimate Reality and Meaning*. That phrase has stuck with me for more than a quarter of a century. Religion has something to do with "ultimate reality and meaning." Of course, the players of the definition game respond that there are many antireligious, irreligious, or atheistic philosophies that also would be included under that definition. I accept that as a consequence of using a very broad understanding of "religion." For me, any system of thought that deals with religious questions is religious, even if the proponents of that system deny that their view is religious.

The definition that I've argued for so far, "**Religion is a body of beliefs that deals with ultimate reality and meaning,**" does not explicitly mention that certain types of behavior follow (or should follow) as a consequence of adopting the fundamental vision of reality in the religion. For me, it seems clear (get back, Descartes! I mean "relatively clear"!) that ideas have consequences, and that actions speak louder than words. Some visions of reality lead to church-going and regular participation in sacred rituals; some do not. The activities that humans have engaged in as a consequence of their belief systems cover a huge spectrum, from ritual murder and suicide to self-emptying love in the highest possible degree, from temple prostitution to Holy Communion, from violent self-mutilation to mystically peaceful self-possession.

"Actions speak louder than words" because they reveal our deepest commitments. An improved definition would have to include the understanding that a religious worldview is linked to a way of life. Peter Kreeft says that any religion can be understood in terms of its **creed** (set of basic beliefs), **code** (ethical guidelines), and **cult** (public religious rituals).[10]

For the most part, I will ignore the details of ritual behavior, except insofar as here or there they cast light on the vision of reality that they embody. Other Religious Studies scholars take a different tack, as is their right. I don't like their books and they undoubtedly won't like mine. "People disagree," and Religious Studies scholars are, first and last, people, too.

Spirituality vs. Religion

Some people in Alcoholics Anonymous and other Twelve-Step programs like to say that they are spiritual, not religious. While this is a perfectly valid choice for them to make, it may give the impression that there is some intrinsic opposition between spirituality and religion. From my point of view, that is not the case. Those who press the distinction seem to me to be operating from a hatred or resentment of "organized religion" (see page 182). I guess that disorganized religion seems more appealing, because it is—by definition—free from any public or objective standards by which a believer's attitudes or actions could be judged by others. From this standpoint, the affirmation of spirituality as an alternative to religion functions as a big "Leave me alone" sign.

---

[10] *Fundamentals*, 288. Many Religious Studies textbooks create a grid along these lines and mechanically plow through every religion, making sure that every box in the grid is filled in for each religion. That kind of book makes my eyes glaze over. I prefer to take a historical view of the origin and development of the religions, and to tell only as much about the creed, code, and cult of the religions as interests me.

For my purposes in this book, I will use the term **spirituality** to mean a body of practical wisdom advocated by a person or a tradition as *a guide to making good decisions in life*. Although the word itself is based on "spirit," I am not suggesting that all spiritualities are based on a metaphysical commitment to a spiritual dimension to life, a supernatural order, or divine or quasi-divine spirits (God, gods, goddesses, angels, demons, saints, ghosts, and the like). Every vision of reality, even materialism or atheism, will inspire an awareness that there are practical consequences to one's own outlook on life. Every human being who is capable of thinking and choosing will have some kind of spirituality, whether they call it by that name, and whether they are themselves conscious of the patterns that they habitually use to decide what to do next.

For me, spiritualities are the means by which religious worldviews enter the practical order. I cannot imagine a spirituality without religion, or a religion without spirituality; other people clearly can imagine such things.

"What is truth?" (Jn 18:38)

Trying to define truth is one of the most vexing forms of the definition game. We know that the question has troubled full-time, professionally educated, and thoroughly certified philosophers in the Western tradition for nearly three thousand years. I'm going to offer some of my answers to the question. I aim to stand in the tradition of Aristotelian realism, as refined by Thomas Aquinas (1225-1274 AD) in the Middle Ages.

- Truth is what our minds hunger for. We *want* to know the truth; we do not want to be hoodwinked by untruths (myths, legends, mere opinions, lies, fictions, hoaxes, figments of our imagination, etc.).
- What is true is the opposite of what is false. "True" means "not false" and "false" means "not true."
- To know the truth is to judge of what is that it is and of what is not that it is not. To know is to be *conformed* to reality.
- Judgments are *expressed* in sentences (also known as propositions).
- We cannot, at the same time and in the same sense of the words, affirm a proposition and its contrary. It is ***self-referentially inconsistent*** to deny these two basic propositions of logic:

Principle of Identity: $a = a$
Principle of Non-Contradiction: $-(a = -a)$
  or $a \neq -a$

These principles suggest that a thing is what it is (identity) and that a thing is not what it is not (non-contradiction). Anyone who tries to deny these basic principles must *use* them in order to specify what is being denied, and what, by contrast, is being affirmed; it is hypocritical to *say* one thing ("The principle of identity is false") and to *do* another (use the principle of identity to specify what is being denied).[11]

- The **Principle of Excluded Middle** says that there is nothing in between "true" and "false." Linguistic constructs that are neither true nor false are not "propositions"; they may be interrogatory, meaningless, accidental, imaginary, hypothetical, poetic, comic, surrealistic, random, or fictitious).
- I have a moral obligation to accept what is true, and to reject what is false. If you can show me that I am mistaken in my epistemology, I *ought* to change my mind about these basic beliefs that guide my thinking.
- Reality is what it is, whether I know it or not (except for the special class of mental realities associated with my personal consciousness—so, for example, I can only know that I'm awake when I'm awake).
- To say that something is true is to say that it is true for all who adopt the same standpoint and terminology of the speaker. Einstein's formula, $E = mc^2$, is a claim about how all energy and matter in this universe are related to each other. He did not intend to say that it was true "just for him"; it is true (or false) for everybody who understands the terms and symbols used in the formula.

We will come back to the question of the importance of passing judgment on religious assertions in a later chapter (see page 181). The purpose of this section was just to give an indication of what I mean when I speak of knowledge, truth, judgment, and reality in the rest of the book.

Critical Thinking

It is easier to define uncritical thinking than it is to define critical thinking. People who are uncritical take things at face value. They accept the first thought that pops into their minds as

---

[11] For those who are interested in philosophy, I note that in the Jesuit tradition, accusing an opponent of self-referential inconsistency is known as *retortion* (or, in Europe, *retorsion*), because the essence of the argument is to turn the opponent's position against the opponent by *retorting*, "You have just done what you said is impossible, immoral, or unreasonable to do. It is hypocritical to say one thing and do another. You should be ashamed of yourself." Those who have eyes to see and ears to hear will notice how often I use retortion in this book. My master's research was on this topic, and the first two articles I ever published presented the results of my study: "Retortion: The Method and Metaphysics of Gaston Isaye," (*International Philosophical Quarterly* 27 (1977) 59-83) and "The Role of Retortion in the Cognitional Analyses of Lonergan and Polanyi," (*Self-Reference: Reflections on Reflexivity*, 218-38. Dordrecht: Martinus Nijhoff Publishers, 1987).

reality, and cannot step back and question their own presuppositions and line of reasoning that led them to their convictions. They may be gullible when listening to others, or they may be as suspicious as a scientist, but they assent or object to what they hear on instinctive—rather than intellectual—grounds. They may or may not have native gifts of intelligence, but they use what intelligence they have to extend the realm of their prejudices, rather than to learn something new.

Critical thinkers, by contrast, are able to question their own view as well as that of others. The critical questions are related to the issues raised in the last section, and depend on an implicitly realist epistemology. Of things in our experience, we may ask the questions suggested by Aristotle:

- Is this real?
- What kind of thing is it?
- What caused it to be what it is?
- What is its purpose (if any)?

Of judgments made by other people, we may ask:

- Are they right?
- Do they know the truth?
- Are they telling the truth?
- Have they made a good case for their view?
- Does the evidence support their argument?
- Is there evidence against their position?
- Is their argument coherent and logical?
- Are they being objective? Or is their judgment clouded by self-interest?
- Have they dealt with all of the important and relevant questions?
- Have they presented their case in an appealing and persuasive fashion?

The television show, *Mythbusters*, and a host of sites like Snopes (*http://snopes.com*) exist to help sort out fact from fiction. Most people don't like to be taken in by hoaxes or counterfeit images. We do not want to be fooled. We want to know what is real, true, and credible.

Last, but not least, critical thinkers question themselves along exactly the same lines as they question others:

- Am I right?
- Do I know the truth?
- Am I telling the truth?
- Have I made a good case for my view?

- Does the evidence support my argument?
- Is there evidence against my position?
- Is my argument coherent and logical?
- Am I being objective? Or is my judgment clouded by self-interest?
- Have I considered all of the important and relevant questions?
- How shall I present my case in such a way that it will persuade others?

In every academic discipline, scholars strive to develop theories that fit the facts in evidence.[12] In such cases, the critical questions are:

- Does this theory (notion, idea) account for all of the facts (real apprehension)?
- Is there any way to test it?
- Can it be verified or falsified?
- What kinds of observations (real apprehension) would be needed to sustain and vindicate the theory? What kinds of observations would overturn it?

Asking questions is the essence of critical thinking. I suppose that all of the questions suggested above might be reduced to just a handful:

- What is real?
- What is true?
- What is trustworthy?
- What do we know for certain?
- How do we tell the difference between knowledge and delusion?

In personal relationships, the critical questions are:

- How can I evaluate what I'm being told?
- Who is telling the truth?
- Whom should I trust?

---

[12] Since scholars are people, and people disagree, I know that some academics will complain that my theory of what scholarship is doesn't fit the facts of what they do. I know from long experience with such types that no amount of friendly discussion will persuade them to notice that their denial of my theory about theories upholds my theory. People say and do the darndest things.

People make mistakes. People sometimes deceive themselves or deceive others. We cannot immediately (stupidly) accept everything we ourselves think or that others tell us. In order to have a chance to think things through, we need to ask the relevant critical questions.

Asking questions is such a powerful tool that some people get carried away and claim that asking questions is more important than answering. This is a very romantic and appealing slogan, but please note that it is a statement, not a question, and that it is therefore a self-referentially inconsistent dogmatic assertion. People who say things like that are talking nonsense. They give the illusion of openness while, in fact, having a closed mind about what is most valuable in life. I question whether asking questions is more important than finding answers; my answer is "No." Asking questions is a very useful tool, but it is not the be-all and end-all of thinking. Those who over-exalt questioning are like a young boy with a hammer; everything in the house (including younger siblings) looks like a nail to him. Questions, like hammers, have a useful purpose in our mental toolbox, but there are other useful tools available that are far better than the hammer for dealing with things that aren't nails.

The name of the great game we are all playing is: "You Bet Your Life." We cannot call a timeout from time while we make up our minds about reality. Life forces choices on us all. We all have our own philosophy of reality and our own personal epistemologies, even if we never say those words aloud. In Newman's terms, we each need some "grammar of assent" that will help us to decide what to accept and what to reject—some guidelines to help us find our way in life.

Judge rightly. Your life depends on it. Making "contact with reality"[13] is the gift that gives all other gifts. People who are in touch with reality make sound decisions and see good fruit come from them; people who are out of touch with reality are fools "full of sound and fury, signifying nothing" (*Macbeth* 5:5). We are each responsible for what we choose to believe about reality. All of the actions we take come from our own vision of reality. It is good to be able to think critically. We shouldn't believe everything we hear from others, or everything we read (especially on the Internet!). While skepticism has its place in the development of our minds, it is also good to know what constitutes a reasonable doubt and what does not.

---

[13] "Contact with reality" is a major theme in the works of Michael Polanyi: "Yet personal knowledge in science is not made but discovered, and as such it claims to establish *contact with reality* beyond the clues on which it relies. It commits us, passionately and far beyond our comprehension, to a vision of reality. Of this responsibility we cannot divest ourselves by setting up objective criteria of verifiability—or falsifiability, or testability, or what you will. For we live in it as in the garment of our own skin" (*Personal Knowledge*, p. 64; emphasis added).

Part 1

Eastern Religions

Hinduism

• • • • • •

Unlike the other religions considered in this book, Hinduism has no definite beginning and no one person or group of people that could be thought of as "founders." Hinduism is not one religion in and of itself, but a combination of hundreds—if not thousands—of local beliefs, stories, ritual traditions, and tribal or regional customs from the Indian subcontinent that stretch back to time immemorial. There is no single leader of "the" Hindu religion; there are no creeds defined by councils, by which one might judge that another has ceased to be Hindu, and no Hindu has the authority to excommunicate another Hindu. It is somewhat misleading, then, to speak as though Hinduism were a single religion. The advantage in doing so is that this abstraction allows us to think about some of the key features that the thousands of particular forms of Hinduism have in common.

Sanskrit developed a written form around 1500 BC, and is one of the dominant religious languages in the Hindu tradition. Unless otherwise indicated, the foreign language terms introduced in this chapter are Sanskrit. The earliest written traditions are in the **Vedas**, four collections of curses, blessings, chants, ritual scripts, stories, and speculation; *veda* means knowledge, so we might think of the Vedas as something like an encyclopedia of Hindu religious knowledge. The **Upanishads** are an enormous collection of other writings that have been collected over the millennia.

The Good News of Hinduism: We Can Have What We Want

For Hindus, the entire universe appears (to use the language of Western fables) as a wishing well or as a fairy godmother that will give us everything we ask for. This is a thrilling prospect: "Ask and you shall receive!" Neville Goddard (1905-1972 AD), a British citizen who founded his own religion, shared this premise with Hinduism: "The universe says: Your wish is my command."

Many contemporary self-help and business management books affirm this vision. They recommend the power of positive thinking,[1] and teach that we all should fill our minds with images of ourselves succeeding in life. Athletes often practice that kind of upbeat psychology, too, visualizing themselves hitting the winning home run, clearing the high bar, taking the perfect golf swing, or edging the other runners at the tape.

The bad news of Hinduism is in the **law of karma**. "Karma" means action and all of the consequences of action; in an extended sense, it may mean "fate" or "destiny." It is essentially a principle of perfect and immediate justice. Do good, get good; do evil, get evil. There are proverbs in Western culture that capture the karmic outlook: "What goes around comes around." "As you sow, so shall you reap" (Gal 6:7). "Sow the wind, reap the whirlwind" (Hos 8:7). "Be careful what you ask for; you might get it!"

The story of "The Monkey's Paw," by William Wymark Jacobs, illustrates the law of karma perfectly. The monkey's paw grants three wishes. An English couple obtain the paw and make a wish for wealth; they receive it through the insurance settlement for the tragic death of their son in an industrial accident. They then wish for their son's return—but when he comes back to life in the horribly mutilated state caused by being crushed in the machine, they wish—without thinking—for him to go away. The lesson is clear: we can have what we want *but we get what we choose*.

In all three wishes, the couple gets *exactly* what they chose, but they do not get what they wanted: *happiness*. This points toward a great truth: *Every choice we make in life is ultimately motivated by our desire to be happy; there is no higher human motivation.*[2] We are built for bliss. You are reading this book now, because doing so means that it will help you to be happy. Even if your motivation is solely to get good grades in Lose Your Faith 101, the reason you want the grades is that you understand that they can be a means to happiness in life.

The law of karma operates immediately, as well as over the long run. The first victim of the decision to do evil is the evildoer. We cannot act outside of ourselves. In order to injure someone else, we first must injure ourselves. There is no such thing as an action without consequences for the actor. Every choice we make is a step toward our ultimate bliss or a step away from it. Good people benefit from their own good actions immediately ("Virtue is its own reward"), and bad people suffer from their evil actions immediately (that's what we mean by "poetic justice").

---

[1] A slogan and movement inspired by the Rev. Norman Vincent Peale's book, *The Power of Positive Thinking*.

[2] The Western philosopher, Aristotle (384-322 BC), used the Greek word, *eudaimonia*, "good spirits," for this greatest good that we seek in every choice we make.

Reincarnation: Try, Try Again

Hindus believe that the principle of life inside of us (**jiva**) can take on any living form in successive **reincarnations** (Latin, *re*, again + *in* + *carne*, meat, flesh = becoming embodied again). People find this an immensely attractive idea, perhaps because of the cyclic nature of the seasons, or noticing the cycle of life, in which the same materials and nutrients pass from the earth into plant and animal life, then return to the earth through decomposition. Plants draw from the soil; animals eat the plants; other animals eat the plant-eaters; all die and become food for later generations. The sweet, long days of summer die in the fall, and darkness reigns in the winter—but only for a season, since spring sets the whole cycle in motion again.

The Hindu concept of "jiva" should not be translated as "soul." Jiva is like a driver in a car; there is no causal relation between the identity of the driver and the kind of vehicle that the driver occupies. When one vehicle is destroyed, jiva moves into another higher or lower vehicle, according to the law of karma. The Western concept of "soul" comes from Aristotle, and is related to his distinction between form and matter. "Soul" in this sense means that which forms or informs the body, giving it its own life and identity. In Aristotelian thought, plants and animals (including, of course, the human animal) have souls that are inextricably related to the bodily life of the organism. A plant soul can only form plants; a horse soul can only form horses; a human soul can only form human beings. Jiva is metaphysically supernatural to the living forms that it inhabits, while soul, in the Western tradition, is that which gives a living thing its particular nature.

The Sanskrit word for the totality of everything that comes into being and then passes away is **samsara**. As we move from one embodiment to another, we move from lower forms of life to higher forms, just as much as our actions deserve such a reward; or from higher forms of life to lower forms, just as much as our actions deserve punishment.

The law of karma provides a perfect religious justification for the **caste system**. There are four large classes (castes) in society:

seers (**Brahmin**)—teachers, scholars, priests
administrators—royalty and warriors
producers, traders
followers, workers

These four groups are furthered subdivided into about three thousand different classes. People live their whole social life within the level of the society into which they were born, and generally marry within that same level. Their fate in life (karma) comes from their actions (karma) in their previous life.

The lowest level of society consists of those who are "**untouchables**." They are so far down the scale that they do not even have a caste. English has borrowed the word "**pariah**" from one large group of untouchables; many of the lowest classes have adopted the term "Dalit" (which means "oppressed"). They did—and do—the most wretched manual labor in society, and are often treated as if they were not fully human. **Mahatma Gandhi** (1869-1948), the George Washington of India who led a successful nonviolent revolution against the British colonial regime, inspired the new government to outlaw discrimination against the untouchables. As with the civil rights movement in the United States (whose principles of truth-telling and nonviolent resistance were largely inspired by Gandhi), simply putting laws on the books does not change hearts overnight. It will take time for both cultures to live up to the high ideals of equal rights for all human beings.

Because we have infinitely many lifetimes to achieve happiness, Hindus can, in theory, be calm and at peace about the social condition and personal behavior of other people. In a sense, it doesn't matter what they choose to do in this lifetime. If they do well, they will ascend the scale of goodness; if they do poorly, they will descend and suffer the just punishment for their wrongdoing. Sooner or later they will get the idea of where true happiness lies. As the existentialists said, "No one else can take a bath for you." Either we see for ourselves, or we see nothing. All of us make our own choices and personally enjoy or suffer the consequences. With infinitely many chances to get it right, everything should work out well in the long run, even if someone is heading in the wrong direction in this lifetime. Someone who works out their karma as a pariah in this lifetime will ascend the social scale in their next incarnation; for now, they have to realize that they brought this upon themselves.

The *Bhagavad-Gita* teaches this kind of trust in karma. It is a short excerpt from a much longer epic poem (74,000 verses and almost 2 million words!) composed, as far as scholars can tell, over a period of about 1200 years, from around 800 BC to around 400 AD. The title means "Song [*gita*] of the Divine One [*Bhagavan*]" or "Song of God." At the outset of the *Gita*, a great battle is about to take place, pitting one part of a tribe against the other part. **Arjuna**, a young warrior, is depressed about the upcoming battle, in which he will have to fight against his blood relatives and his teacher. He tells his chariot driver, **Krishna**, to drive to the center of the battlefield so that he can look on both sides and mourn the bloodshed to come.

Krishna first lectures Arjuna on his obligation to fulfill his karma as a member of the warrior class. When a warrior kills in battle, he is doing the work of Shiva, the Destroyer. Jiva, the inner principle of life, is indestructible, so it simply passes on to another form of life under the law of karma. Arjuna's feelings of sorrow are therefore based on a misunderstanding of the spiritual realities involved. He is a victim of maya, the deceptive outward appearance of samsara, the changing world.

After this reminder of the basic principles of reincarnation, Krishna reveals to Arjuna that he himself is not an ordinary human, but an **avatar**, a manifestation or incarnation of a god in human form—and not just any old god, but the one and only God. This is an example of Nirguna Hinduism (see page 78). Everything is part of God, and God is part of everything. Krishna is Brahma, the Creator; Krishna is Vishnu, the Preserver; Krishna is Shiva, the destroyer; he is all that is. Arjuna sees a multitude of visions of Krishna in his glory.

The term in Religious Studies for the self-revelation of a god is "**theophany**" (Greek, *theos* + *phanos*, "shining forth"). The *Gita* ends with this theophany. Krishna instructs Arjuna to be devoted to him. By devotion (***bhakti***) to Krishna, Arjuna will find a sure path to his destiny.

Finding Happiness

Hindu theologians suggest that there are **four basic kinds of appetites** in each of us, ordered from lowest to highest in the following table:

Dialectics of Desire	
1. Pleasure	Path of Desire
2. Success	
3. Duty	*Path of Renunciation (sannyasa)*
4. Moksha (liberation)	

I talk about these desires as **dialectical** (Greek, *dia*, "through" + *logos*, "word, speech" = "by dialogue, by investigation") because the conviction is that we will move from one level to the next on our own initiative when we personally realize the limitations of the lower levels. "Dialectics" is a term from Western philosophy that was made popular by Georg Wilhelm Friedrich Hegel (1770-1831) and Karl Marx (1818-1883). In a dialectical process, we keep making changes in our philosophical outlook or our social structures until we find what we are seeking.

The fairy tale about Goldilocks illustrates the dialectics of desire. She burglarized the home of the three bears and found what she was looking for by testing the bears' breakfast, chairs, and beds. She was not content to remain with the first thing she found, but kept trying other alternatives, until she found the one that was "just right." In the terminology of Johann Gottlieb Fichte, we begin with a *thesis*, then explore the *antithesis*, and, if all goes well, work out a *synthesis* that combines the best of the first two alternatives. The synthesis itself then becomes a thesis for further investigation ("dialogue") that may be opposed to an antithesis and resolved in a higher synthesis. Hegel believed that a dialectical process along these lines would lead everyone to reach his idea of the Absolute. Marx predicted that the dialectics of history would lead to the perfect form of leadership, the dictatorship of the proletariat.

Our natural instinct when we are told that we can have infinitely many lifetimes just like this one is to focus on pleasure. Hindus are, in principle, tolerant of people who dedicate their lives to sex, drugs, and rock 'n' roll. They expect that over the course of thousands of lifetimes, the pleasure-seekers will realize that *they themselves* are not satisfied by pleasure. Pleasure is good, but it is not good enough to make us happy.

The second part of the Path of Desire is success. In order to succeed in life, we have to strive to please others, not just ourselves. There is no way to rise to the top of a profession without self-sacrifice—no slackers need apply. If people spend a few thousand lifetimes seeking and enjoying success, they will realize *for themselves* that success in the world of changing things, samsara, is not enough to make us happy.

The third stage of exploration is duty. Here we embark on the Path of Renunciation. We are no longer concerned with our own pleasure or success, but are oriented toward other people's needs. Policemen, judges, lawyers, soldiers, social workers, politicians, teachers, and doctors exemplify this kind of dedication to the good of others. But even though there can be great joy in this kind of selflessness, it is still not good enough for real happiness.

For Hindus, what we really, really, *really* want is **moksha**, liberation from samsara. We want to break out of the cycle of reincarnation, and attain an everlasting happiness that is not interrupted by returning to the ever-returning world. Paradoxically, it is by **renunciation** (**sannyasa**) of samsara that we gain all of our heart's desires. The finite world is just too small for us. We want **sat** (infinite being), **chit** (infinite understanding), and **ananda** (infinite bliss). The good news is that the universe is prepared to give us what we want, because **"Atman is Brahman"**: *my true self is God*.

We cannot fully attain and enjoy our godhood in this finite form of existence. From this point of view, everything in samsara is **maya**: tricky, illusory, deceptive. Everything in this world of reincarnation may *seem* to be good, especially in those moments when we are tasting the good fruits of pleasure, success, and duty, but the thought that we could keep on returning to finite goods infinitely many times would lead us away from our destiny, our karma, to become divine.

There is a conflict between our small, deceived self, and atman, true self. In the West, we may use the word "ego" (Latin, "I") to stand for the mistaken self that resists and blocks our desire to leave samsara forever and pass on to greater things. We need to cultivate **samadhi**, God-consciousness, the awareness of who we really are inside, underneath the deceptive veil of appearances, in order to overthrow the little self.

How Many Gods and Goddesses Are There?

At first glance, Hinduism seems to be **polytheistic**. The custom, from time immemorial, has been for Hindus to accept all of the gods and goddesses of all religions into their **pantheon**. For them, it is natural to think that Jesus is God—so is the Buddha and Confucius and Martin Luther King Jr. and Moses and Muhammad—and you and me and everyone we meet!

Those Hindus who uphold the polytheistic tradition treat each god and goddess as separate, real, divine realities. When another human reaches the summit of life, the number of gods and goddesses increases by one. This is **Saguna Hinduism**.

Nirguna Hindus, by contrast, argue that there is really only one divine being of whom everyone and everything is merely a manifestation. This is a kind of **monotheism**, since it affirms that there is just one divine reality, all appearances to the contrary notwithstanding. The appearance of multiple persons is maya, deception. I am you and you are me and we are they, and of everything we see we may say, "*Tat tvam asi*": "That thou art." All is one and one is all. This kind of **pantheism** is distinct from the monotheism of Judaism, Christianity, and Islam, all of which hold that we are created by one God, but are not "part" of God (see page 201).

There are some gods (or manifestations of the one God) that are known, if not necessarily worshipped, by all Hindus: **Brahma**, the Creator; **Vishnu**, the Preserver; and **Shiva**, the Destroyer. Each of the three has at least one goddess as a partner and consort, so efforts to compare the three chief divinities of Hinduism with the three persons of the **Trinity** (see page 139) break down very quickly. Nirguna Hindus see all the millions of gods and goddesses (and billions more in the making) as aspects of a single divinity; there is no special three-in-one (tri-unity, trinity) in their theology.

Many Paths to Happiness

In the thousands of years that Hindus have been thinking about the human condition, they recognized that there are different personality types, and therefore, different **yogas** (disciplines) that may be helpful in attaining moksha. All of the higher levels employ **hatha yoga**, bodily discipline, which involves a multitude of exercises to keep the body limber, to train oneself to breathe deeply and calmly, and which allow the **yogi** (disciplined person) to place the body in a calm state while the mind is at work in the great quest for transcendence. The most famous posture in hatha yoga is the **lotus position**, with the ankles placed over the knees. Those who have gained or never lost the flexibility to take the lotus position can find a balance point, breathe deeply, and sit still for hours on end.

The higher mental, emotional, and spiritual disciplines are **jnana, bhakti, karma,** and **raja yoga.** Jnana yoga appeals to intellectuals, and involves reading, writing, and thoughtful discourse. This is the kind of interior discipline that would probably appeal to most college professors. "Bhakti" means "devotion." It is for people who enjoy social activities, temple visits, religious rituals, fasting, feasting, processing, going on pilgrimage, and the like. Karma yoga appeals to those who like to be active and see results—builders, artisans, engineers, or other people with a practical bent who like to see a job well done.

The fourth discipline, raja yoga, is "royal yoga." Please make a mental note that this is the kind of yoga that was practiced by the man who became the **Buddha** (next chapter). Raja yoga involves experiencing spiritual truths for oneself by doing interior mental and spiritual exercises or (in a loose sense) religious experiments.

Besides the variety of choices available for different kinds of spirituality, the Hindu thinkers also noticed that most people go through **four stages of life**. They begin as **students** under the authority of others. Eventually, they become **householders** who exercise authority over their own family. It is not uncommon (nor is it required—we're talking about general tendencies here) for someone who has fulfilled their duties as a householder to become a **forest dweller**, a person who leaves home to seek spiritual fulfillment. There is no particular "forest" to which they go; the term applies to all who leave the comforts of home in order to journey toward a greater destiny.

The final stage of life is **sannyasa**, renunciation of samsara, and the people who make the great renunciation of this ever-changing world are called **sannyasin**. They return to society clothed in prison garments—saffron robes—in order to show that they recognize that the cycle of reincarnation is a prison, and expressing their conviction that they will break out of this prison and attain what they (and we) all want.

Ramakrishna (1836-1886) was a sannyasin whose teachings on the essential harmony of all religions are very popular. In his view, the goal of reaching godliness may be compared to climbing a mountain. Everyone who climbs the mountain of god reaches the very same summit. Therefore, it doesn't matter whether they begin their ascent from north, south, east, or west. As the title of a short story by Flannery O'Connor, an American Catholic author, says, "everything that rises must converge." Ramakrishna and his followers exhibit great tolerance for all world religions, and are not troubled by the differences between them. If Hinduism is correct, we are all ascending the same mountain and all will arrive at the same summit. If we resist this upward movement, karma will see to it that we suffer the just consequences of our small-mindedness.

One of my students said that the creed of Hinduism might be compressed into a single word: "whatever." Whatever you want to think, think; whatever you want to do, do. It doesn't really matter. Karma will get you in the end.

Buddhism
(Hinduism Continued)

• • • • • •

Siddhartha Gautama of the Sakyas (563-483 BC) is the man who became the **Buddha** (literally, "the one filled with light" from Sanskrit, *bodhi*, "light"), and therefore, became the founder of **Buddhism**, which, perhaps, we might call "the religion of light" or "the religion of enlightenment." Siddhartha was a Hindu living in India, and his life story may be understood completely and fully as the fulfillment of the promise of Hinduism: that we can have what we want, and that we will get what we choose. As we follow the story of Siddhartha and his quest for fulfillment, we learn more about Hinduism.

Escape from the Pleasure Palaces

Legend has it that when Siddhartha was born, his father, an important Indian prince, asked a seer about his son's destiny (karma). The seer could not decide. "He will either be the greatest king that India has ever known, or else he will be a monk."

Siddhartha's father knew which outcome he preferred. He constructed a special home for his son that, like Disneyworld in our own day, was as close to Heaven on earth as he could make it. All who served in the palaces were young, beautiful, healthy, and well behaved. Thousands of servants catered to Siddhartha's needs and desires. When he traveled from one palace to another, servants went ahead of him to clear the path he would travel. Despite his father's orders and the vigilance of the staff, Siddhartha escaped from the pleasant prison, both physically and mentally. When he was outside the walls his father had thrown up about him, he saw **The Four Passing Sights: sickness, age, death, and renunciation (sannyasa).** The disturbance caused by the recognition that he, too, was prey to suffering and death shattered the illusion (maya) that he could find happiness on the path his father had chosen for him.

Siddhartha had already passed through the first two stages of life, from being a student under the authority of others, to taking on the responsibilities of being a householder—he was married to a beautiful princess and they had a young son. Siddhartha had lived the life of pleasure to the full, and had the best possible prospect of enjoying success as a great king. After being awakened by the Four Passing Sights, he understood that infinitely many lifetimes spent at the top of the social scale would not give him what he wanted. He abandoned his wife, his child, his wealth, power, and prestige, and became a forest dweller at age 29. All he wanted was moksha, liberation from incarnation, and the infinite satisfactions (sat-chit-ananda) to which moksha would lead.

In his quest for spiritual freedom and fulfillment, Siddhartha went to the other extreme from what he had known as a child and a young man. He became a beggar, and lived on less and less, until he was taking only six grains of rice a day for food. Starvation caused him to fall into a coma, and if his friends had not forced food down his throat, he would have died.

Siddhartha was a true dialectician. He had personally experienced the pleasures that this life has to offer. He saw that they would not make him happy, so he abandoned them all as far as he could; he dropped out of the life his father had planned for him, and broke away from the dominant forms of religion in his culture. He found out by personal experience (real apprehension) that emptying himself of all good things to the point of death did not make him happy, either. So he embarked on the **Middle Way**—meeting the needs of life without indulgence—so that his bodily condition no longer stood in the way of his spiritual quest.

The Light Goes On

For six years, Siddhartha followed the disciplines of raja yoga—just as any Hindu forest dweller or monk would have done. One evening, he sat in the lotus position under a huge fig tree, and vowed not to rise from meditation until he had found what he sought. The demon, Mara, tried to prevent him from reaching his goal by offering him his daughters, by threatening him with death, and by suggesting that he had no right to be divinized. Siddhartha sat still, and held fast to the inward path to perfect peace. His only response to Mara was to touch the earth, which roared the approval of the whole universe for his undertaking.

Something happened.

In a moment, Siddhartha awoke and received all that he desired. He was such a changed man that others called him "the Buddha." He spoke of himself as **Tathagata**, which is a complex pun and which we may loosely translate as "the guy who got it." Perhaps in English we should capitalize the word: *he got IT!* He found what Hindus saw we all want: his inner divinity. The demon returned with one last temptation: "No one will understand what has happened to you." The Buddha replied, "Some will."

The core message of Buddhism is that **we can all be Buddhas**. The Buddha explained that his **divinization** (becoming divine) shows others what they, too, may expect to receive from the great wishing well of the universe. *He got IT!*—and so can we.

They say that the Buddha sat lost in bliss for eight days, a full week, tried to stand up, then sank back into enjoyment of his awakening for 49 days, a "week of weeks." The tree under which he sat came to be known as the **Bo Tree**, which is short for "bodhi tree," the tree under which Siddhartha received the Light (Sanskrit, *bodhi*) and became the Light-Filled One (Sanskrit, *Buddha*). Then he began his compassionate ministry to the world. Besides the honorific title of "the Buddha," he also became known as **Sakyamuni**, "the great sage of the Sakyas."

The Four Noble Truths

In his 45 years of preaching after his enlightenment, the Buddha gave thousands of sermons and exhibited the principles of the awakened life in every aspect of his days. There are many *sutras* (sayings, sermons) of the Buddha; one very popular compilation is *The Dhammapada*. The core of his teaching (Sanskrit, *dharma*; Pali, *dhamma*) is found in the **Four Noble Truths**:

1. All life is suffering (**dukkha**).
2. Suffering comes from self (**tanha**, grasping, holding on to, clinging, craving).
3. **Nirvana** (literally, "being extinguished") comes from loss of self (tanha) or detachment, "letting go."
4. To achieve Nirvana, follow the **Eightfold Path**:
    1) right understanding (*4 Noble Truths*)
    2) right intention to walk the path
    3) right speech
    4) right behavior (*5 negative precepts*)
    5) right livelihood
    6) right effort to reach the end
    7) right awareness of each situation
    8) right contemplation

The essential point of these Noble Truths is illustrated in the movie *Groundhog Day*, which was written by an American Buddhist. For the sake of the movie, the cycle of rebirth (samsara) is reduced to living just one day over and over again. The movie demonstrates that it is no fun to be condemned to be born, to suffer, and to die endlessly, with no forward progress in the spiritual life. Phil, the main character, experiments with pleasure, success, and duty, but cannot escape the cycle of return until he ceases from seeking himself in any way at all. The old self (ego) is extinguished like the flame of a candle that is blown out, and then—and only then—is he able to gain liberation (moksha) from samsara. Paradoxically, when he *stops seeking* (in a grasping fashion), he finds what he desires (perfect freedom and the promise of sat-chit-ananda).

The Buddha said that he had achieved his life's goal—which is the *Hindu* ideal of realizing that "atman is Brahman," our true self is God. When the Buddha was 80, he came down with food poisoning at the house of Cunda, the blacksmith; whether it was poisoned mushrooms or tainted meat, Cunda served the food by accident, and the Buddha was struck with dysentery. He knew that he was dying, and he thanked Cunda for serving him the meal that was sending him to Nirvana. He said that he was now finished, not only with this lifetime, but with all lifetimes in samsara, and that he was happy to be coming to the end of his earthly journeys.

Subsequent Developments: Three Rafts to Cross the River

Although Siddhartha was a Hindu who lived a relatively ordinary Hindu life, passing through the stages of life (student, householder, forest dweller, sannyasin) and finding what Hinduism promises through raja yoga, the movement that began with his enlightenment under the Bo tree was countercultural to the ordinary forms that Hinduism takes. That, too, is perfectly normal. People disagree. Hindus are people. They disagree among themselves, both in theory and in practice, about the best way to find happiness. Hinduism is immensely tolerant of differences of belief and varieties of devotion, so, at least in theory, there is no reason to treat Buddhism as a separate religion; it is just one more path that Hindus may take up the mountain of divine reality.

Siddhartha's realization of the Hindu outlook on life was intensely personal. In principle, his enlightenment suggests that there is no need for outward religious forms: no temples, feasts, fasts, holy days, pilgrimages, priesthood, sacrifices, teachings, gatherings with other believers, religious art, and the like. The Buddha resisted being drawn into **metaphysical** speculation about his own philosophy and theology. When pressed to explain exactly how jiva passes through successive forms of life and how it relates to atman, true self, the Buddha exploded, "**Anatta!**"—there is no true self—and, in a sense, there is no Brahman, either! The Buddha's unwillingness to define a creed or spell out the details of his metaphysical vision leads many to call Buddhism a godless religion.

Neither scripture study nor traditional forms of religiosity turned Siddhartha into the Buddha. It was, in Newman's terms, real apprehension, direct personal experience of realities that cannot ever be put wholly into words. Such breakthroughs come from the inside out, not the outside in. From the Buddha's standpoint, people who crave verbal or conceptual representations of reality are deluded by maya, and are exhibiting the small-mindedness (tanha) that stands in the way of Nirvana.

Buddhism did have an outward form, of course; to be in this world is to be embodied. The Buddha founded communities of monks and nuns and trained them in raja yoga. The tradition that developed along these lines came to be known as **Theravada**, "the way of the elders." The name was necessary to distinguish that form of Buddhism from **Mahayana** (Sanskrit, *maha*, "great" + *yana*, "raft") **Buddhism**. The mental image suggested by "mahayana" is that a river separates samsara from Nirvana. We attain moksha by crossing that river. The claim of the **bodhisattvas** (*bodhi* + *sat* + *an extension syllable* = "infinite light being") was that they had a large raft and could ferry others across the river. In fact, unlike the Buddha, who said that this lifetime was his last and that he was finished with reincarnation, the bodhisattvas take a vow to continue reincarnating themselves until the last soul is carried across to Nirvana.

With this picture in mind, the Mahayana Buddhists scorn the **arhats** of the Theravadan tradition. "Arhat" means someone who has laid down the burdens of life, made a complete escape from samsara, and who, like the Buddha, will never return again. To the bodhisattvas, the arhats seem to lack compassion, and to care only about getting themselves into the life of bliss. They call the Theravadan tradition "**Hinayana**" (*hina*, "small" + *yana* = "little raft").

With the development of the Mahayana tradition, many of the traditional religious elements downplayed in the Theravadan tradition returned. Although the Buddha relied on no god to become the Buddha and displayed no signs of devotion, bhakti, to any god or goddess, Mahayana Buddhists treat him as a god to be worshipped and from whom graces and blessings may be expected. The **three vows of Mahayana spirituality** reflect this difference in orientation:

1. I take refuge in the Buddha.
2. I take refuge in the dharma (teaching).
3. I take refuge in the **sangha** (community).

The arhats could make a good case that this is not how Siddhartha found the light. He took refuge in no divinity; he adopted no particular philosophy or theology; he followed his own inner compass and sat alone under the Bo tree, until he made his breakthrough. The bodhisattvas might reply, in turn, that they imitate the Buddha who labored for 45 years so that others might find for themselves what he had found for himself.

One good reason for distinguishing Buddhism from Hinduism is that Buddhism found more success outside India than it did within it. These non-Indian followers of Siddhartha would probably find it very strange to be called Hindus by people in Religious Studies. What unites them is having the original Buddha as their hero and the category of "Buddha" as their leading ideal for the fulfillment of their own lives. Siddhartha was, to speak the language of the sixties, a Hindu hippie. The slogan of Timothy Leary, a devotee of LSD was, "turn on, tune in, drop out." Siddhartha tuned in to the essence of Hinduism, became Tathagata, "the guy who got it!" by meditating on what Hinduism promised, then dropped out of the Hindu religious traditions as a consequence.

An interesting and well-known variation of the non-Indian Mahayana tradition is found in Tibet, where it is called "**Vajrayana**" (*vajra*, "diamond" + *yana* = "Diamond Raft") Buddhism.

The heart of this spirituality is **tantrism**, the illuminating use of energy. Tantric practices seek to collect all of the energy available in our human embodiment and store them up until, at last, they are released in a huge burst that may, perhaps, carry us over the river into Nirvana. Evel Knievel's plan to ride a rocket-powered motorcycle across the Snake River Canyon is a perfect image of tantric spirituality.

All human powers are grist for the tantric mill: eating, drinking, praying, sexual intercourse, and use of the mind, memory, and senses. Whatever gives us energy and refreshment may be harnessed to the goal of making our escape across the river. Three notable practices may be mentioned: **mantras**, repetitive chants; **mudras**, sacred dances, in which all who perform or witness the dramatic actions strive to take on the godliness of the characters; and **mandalas**, great circular paintings that convey the Vajrayana vision of reality.

Vajrayana Buddhism is well known in the West, because of the **Dalai Lama** (Mongolian, *dalai*, "ocean" + *Lama*, "**guru**" or "enlightened teacher"), the God-King of Tibet. This bodhisattva has reincarnated himself 14 times in Tibet, after appearing as an avatar in India and China in earlier incarnations. The present Dalai Lama (born in 1935) fled from Tibet when the Communist Chinese occupied his homeland in 1959. Ever since then, he has led peaceful—but firm—protests against the occupation of his country and the violation of human rights by the Chinese government. Among dozens of honors he has received is the 1989 Nobel Peace Prize.

One further development of Buddhism is **Zen** (page 51). We will turn our attention to that after we have spent some time reflecting on the religious traditions of China, some of which contributed to the development of Zen Buddhism.

Confucianism

• • • • • •

China, like India, possesses a long, complex, and variegated history of culture and civilization. It, too, possessed a **pantheon** of divinities and a fairly comfortable accommodation to the polytheistic worldview. In addition, the native Chinese religions tended to be **animistic** (Latin, *anima*, "soul" or "spirit"). In the worldview of animism, everything is *alive* ("animated"), because it is inhabited by some spiritual force: the earth, the sea, the sky, mountains, trees, forests, rivers, storms, and so on. For them, the material world is not distinct from the metaphysical realm; it is completely penetrated by it.

Among the Chinese animists, some of the most important spiritual forces at work are our own ancestors (**Ti**), who remain close at hand after death, and who, like other spirits in the world, need to be given proper honor in order to keep them on our side, and thereby to gain health and prosperity: "When proper respect towards the dead is shown at the End and continued after they are far away the moral force (**te**) of a people has reached its highest point" (I, 9).

Kung fu Tzu ("Kung, the Master"; 551-479 BC) lived at a time when civilization had broken down into **anarchy** (Greek, *an-*, a negative prefix + *arche*, "rule" = leaderlessness). In our contemporary culture, movies like *Mad Max* illustrate the kind of tribal warfare that can emerge when central authority has broken down. We see these kinds of atrocities in Somalia, and in the gang warfare in some American cities. Where there is no law, might makes right. Thugs join forces to rape, pillage, and plunder whoever passes their way. All must arm themselves, and be on the alert at all times to rescue themselves from danger. No cavalry will ride to the rescue, because it vanished along with the central government. If you are lucky, you will have a few homies to watch your back; if you are unlucky, you will be easy pickings for the gang lords.

Dr. Kung's Diagnosis and Prescription ("Confucius say …")

Confucius (our loose transliteration of "**Kung fu Tzu**") hated the breakdown of his society. His goal was to restore a **harmonious social order** that would allow everyone to lead the good life. He studied *The Classics*, stories and teachings from an early golden age, when there had been a strong government that kept the peace and allowed the people to prosper. From these studies of times past, Confucius identified key principles essential to the formation of a wholesome civilization. These are the core of his program of **"deliberate tradition"**—the body of wisdom that people freely choose to embrace and to pass on to subsequent generations. The name that he gave to his worldview was **The Tao ("way") of the Ancients**.[1]

When Confucius's studies and distillation of *The Classics* were complete, he wanted to find a job that would allow him to demonstrate the excellence of his vision of reality. For 13 years, he tramped from place to place, offering his services to all and sundry. He got only one position—something on a par with running a county fair—but it was too small a task for his purposes. "As far as taking trouble goes, I do not think I compare badly with other people. But as regards carrying out the duties of a gentleman in actual life, I have never yet had a chance to show what I could do" (VII, 32).

He was accompanied on this **Long Trek** by some disciples. It is to them that Confucianism is indebted as the preservers of the Master's teaching. It is they who recorded Confucius's teaching, mostly in the form of anecdotes, in which the Master replied to a question or gave a short, pithy statement of his principles. ***The Analects of Confucius*** is the first collection of such sayings (Latin, *ana-*, "again" + *legein*, "to gather, collect; to speak" = "discussions" or "collected sayings"; a short definition of "analect" would be "something said again" or "something that is repeated").

The followers of Confucius studied the Master's teachings for several centuries. Confucianism eventually became the dominant religious-philosophical-political system in China (without eradicating many other religious worldviews and spiritualities) *for over two thousand years*. Civil service exams were given, to test whether applicants had memorized the Confucian teaching. When there were conflicts to be resolved, the bureaucrat was expected to remember what Confucius had taught about that issue, and to apply the right principles to the concrete situation.

In American culture, this great legacy has been reduced to the "Confucius say" (or "wise man say" or "Master say") jokes. So, for example, Confucius say:

- War not determine who right. War determine who left.
- Man who eat crackers in bed wake up feeling crummy.
- Man who leap off cliff jump to conclusion.
- Man who drive like hell bound to get there.
- Man who laugh last not get joke.

---

[1] Waley, 31.

Although most of such jokes are racist, sexist, vulgar, or otherwise offensive, they are an echo of how, in fact, the Confucian tradition developed. Confucius won people to himself who loved him and his teaching; because of their dedication to what "the Master said," China was transformed. It is a remarkable accomplishment by any standard.

Five Confucian Virtues

Huston Smith identified five key terms in Confucius's theory of what is necessary to produce a happy and harmonious social order: **jen, chun-tzu, li, te, and wen.**[2] In our language, these five precepts are called **virtues.** This word is from the Latin, *vis, viris,* which means "man." So in the original sense, "virtue" means "manliness." In an extended philosophical (and gender-neutral!) sense, it means "the qualities of character that give us the *power to achieve happiness.*"

It is good to be good. This is not something that can be proved conceptually. In the West, we say, "Virtue is its own reward." In Hinduism, the law of karma asserts that those who do good are the first beneficiaries of their own good actions, just as wrongdoers are the first victims of their own wrongdoing. "The Good Man rests content with Goodness; he that is merely wise pursues Goodness in the belief that it pays to do so" (IV, 2).

Jen literally means "kind," "gentle," "humane," and by extension, "good" or "goodness";[3] it is the virtue of human-heartedness. It is the foundation of the other Confucian ideals, and fits very well with the Western tradition of honoring all other human beings as people like ourselves. Human-heartedness causes us to curb our own desires and behaviors when they come in conflict with others. It causes us to recognize and adhere to the **Golden Rule** (a name given it in the West): "Do unto others as you would have them do unto you." Confucius expressed the same idea in slightly different terms: "Do not do unto others what you would not have them do unto you" (XII, 2).

There is something in our **first nature** that resists human-heartedness. We are born self-centered, and must be taught by our parents to take on a **second nature**: that of a person who respects the rights and individual worth of other persons. This is hard work. Watch how often parents must interfere with their children's natural drive to put themselves first and others second. To be human is to be *educated* to be human.

> (The good man) does not grieve that other people do not recognize his merits. His only anxiety is lest he should fail to recognize theirs. (I, 16)

---

[2] *The World's Religions: Our Great Wisdom Traditions* (San Francisco: Harper Collins, revised and updated, 1991), 172-180.

[3] Waley, 27-29.

At fifteen, I set my heart upon learning. At thirty, I planted my feet firm upon the ground. At forty, I no longer suffered from perplexities. At fifty, I knew what were the biddings of Heaven. At sixty, I heard them with a docile ear. At seventy, I could follow the dictates of my own heart; for what I desired no longer overstepped the boundaries of right. (II,4)

The second essential virtue is **chun-tzu**, nobility of character. Confucius recommended that we study the qualities of the highest classes of society, and freely choose to imitate the best behavior of the best people. In the West we have an understandably ambiguous attitude toward the remnants of European nobility. There is something tantalizing about kings, queens, princes, princesses, dukes, duchesses, lords and ladies, and gentlemen and gentlewomen. Such figures appear often in our literature and art. There is some remnant of admiration for a society, in which one is destined by birth for a high calling; see, for example, *The Narnia Chronicles*, *Lord of the Rings*, and even, in their own way, the Harry Potter novels. At the same time, there is contempt for the corruption that so often is found in the history of our European royal houses. "Power tends to corrupt," said Lord Acton in his study of the sins of popes against their subjects in the papal states, "and absolute power corrupts absolutely."[4]

Confucius was undoubtedly aware of the same ambiguity in the history of Chinese royalty. Nevertheless, he wanted us to imitate what was best in the lives of our social superiors. The great figures of both the Eastern and Western traditions exhibit noble self-restraint. They keep the power that they have inherited under control, using it not to serve themselves, but to serve others. The truly noble person is humble:

A gentleman is distressed by his own lack of capacity; he is never distressed at the failures of others to recognize his merits. (XV, 18)

If he finds he has made a mistake, then he must not be afraid of admitting the fact and amending his ways. (I, 85)

The true gentleman ... does not preach what he practices till he has practiced what he preaches. (II, 13)

A gentleman takes as much trouble to discover what is right as lesser men take to discover what will pay. (IV, 16)

Third, we need **li**, propriety and ritual. Our social relationships are structured. Unlike the mythology often found in American westerns, Confucius did not think that we are self-made and capable of finding the right thing to do by behaving spontaneously and on impulse. Instead, we live in an orderly universe, surrounded and supported by the spirits of our ancestors. For

---

[4] *Essays on Freedom and Power* (Boston: Beacon Press, 1949), 364.

him, authority was inherent in the elderly, the parents who gave us life, and each of us has to be trained to take our place in the family hierarchy and to express our awareness of where we stand by proper courtesy and etiquette. "Behave in such a way that your father and mother have no anxiety about you, except concerning your health" (II, 6).

The whole system of government, as Confucius understood it, was under this same obligation to act with reverence toward the all-enveloping spiritual world. Confucius endorsed the three hundred major rituals and three thousand minor rituals for which the government was responsible, acting on behalf of the whole citizenry.[5] When the Confucian system was adopted long after his death, a new ritual was added to the list. Every Chinese school began its day with a sacrifice in honor of Confucius, asking and expecting him to be active on their behalf as they carried on the tradition that he had inaugurated.

Under this virtue, Confucius also taught the doctrine of the **mean**, something that bears a striking resemblance to the Middle Way of the Buddha, as well as to the teaching of Greek philosophers of a slightly later time: "to go too far is as bad as not to go far enough" (XI, 15). The Greek slogan for this principle is that "**virtue is the mean** (the middle ground) **between extremes.**" This is something we take for granted in our contemporary culture. Every time a commentator identifies someone as an extremist, either to the right or to the left, or speaks in praise of moderates, that person is implicitly appealing to this ideal. "Pleasure not carried to the point of debauch; grief not carried to the point of self-injury" (III, 20).

In Confucius's day, the extremes were represented by the **Mohists** and the **Realists**. The Mohists were pacifists who thought that if people were just left to their own devices, their natural goodness would spontaneously bring harmony to our life together. They resemble the hippies of the 1960s and the spirituality of the Woodstock generation: "All you need is love; love is all you need" (John Lennon, 1967). The Realists, by contrast, resemble the fascists of World War II (Adolph Hitler and Mussolini) and the totalitarians (Stalin and Tojo). Their theory was that people have to be forced to behave rightly.

Confucius taught that virtue, the power to achieve happiness, is in the mean, the middle ground. Sometimes individuals and governments should leave others alone; sometimes decisive action and force need to be used to preserve the social order. "Govern them by moral force *[te]*, keep order among them by ritual *[li]* and they will keep their self-respect and come to you of their own accord" (II, 3). But he expected and hoped for sincerity in the prescribed practices: "High office filled by men of narrow views, ritual performed without reverence, the forms of mourning observed without grief—these are things I cannot bear to see!" (III, 26).

The fourth principle is **Te**, which simply means "power" in Chinese. In this context, it means the power that we all possess to elevate or destroy society. "He who rules by moral force (*te*) is like the pole-star, which remains in its place while all the lesser stars do homage to it" (II, 1). For

---

[5] Waley, 67.

Confucius, there are no isolated individuals. We are inextricably caught up in the web of social relationships so that, in a sense, there are no private actions. Everything we do affects all of our relationships. We cannot change ourselves without changing our relationships with everyone else in our lives. All of our choices affect the social realm from which we came, and to which we belong by birth.

The fifth virtue is **Wen** ("culture"), the power to bring beauty into our lives. The Chinese commitment to beauty is illustrated by the art of *feng shui* (pronounced "fung shuay," sort of), which has become somewhat popular in the West as a method for creating uplifting landscaping and interior decoration. In the Chinese tradition—and perhaps for some of the Western practitioners—the art is based on belief in *chi*, spiritual forces that can be harnessed for benevolent purposes by the physical layout of grounds, buildings, rooms, furnishings, and the like.

Even without a commitment to the metaphysics of animism, I have a great admiration for the thought that we need beauty in our surroundings in order to cultivate harmonious relationships. I say Mass in a small, dark room in a local jail from time to time. Although I know the sacrament is the same, it is a very different experience from saying Mass in a building that is designed to lift the eyes, heart, and mind upward.

The virtue of wen is exhibited in all the arts, not just landscaping, architecture, and interior design: calligraphy, painting, sculpture, song, dance, music, literature, and all of the crafts that produce beautiful things.

Religious Dimensions of Confucianism

Confucianism can be presented as a humanistic philosophy. Confucius claimed no divine inspiration, no great awakening, and no new theology, and he created no new religious rituals to displace previous practices. He studied *The Classics*—"I have been faithful to and loved the Ancients" (VII, 1); his disciples produced collections like *The Analects of Confucius*. "The Master never talked of prodigies [miracles], feats of strength, disorders [of nature], or spirits" (VII, 20). "Do I regard myself as a possessor of wisdom? Far from it. But if even a simple peasant comes in all sincerity and asks me a question, I am ready to thrash the matter out, with all its pros and cons, to the very end" (IX, 7).

> Tzu-lu asked how one should serve ghosts and spirits. The Master said, Till you have learnt to serve men, how can you serve ghosts? Tzu-lu then ventured upon a question about the dead. The Master said, Till you know about the living, how are you to know about the dead? (XI, 11)

Confucius apparently was at the other end of the scale from Siddhartha when it came to prayer and meditation: "I once spent a whole day without food and whole night without sleep, in order to meditate. It was of no use. It is better to learn" (XV, 30). From the Hindu perspective, Confucius practiced jnana yoga.

The fact that Confucius was a scholar, a philosopher, a political scientist, or a moralist is one of the factual oddities that Religious Studies scholars like to bring into the definition game (page 11). Whether we try to define religion broadly enough to see Confucius's Way as religious or else define religion narrowly so as to exclude his thought, there are problems either way. I prefer the problems of the broader definition of religion.

In defense of treating Confucianism as a religion, we may note that it took Chinese religions for granted as part and parcel of the Golden Age and the ordinary responsibilities of the government. Neither the Master nor his disciples made our distinction between "church" and "state," nor between the "material world" and the "spiritual world." Confucius used the language of Heaven, gods, goddesses, spirits, and ancestors like the people of his day. "He who has put himself in the wrong with Heaven has no means of expiation left" (III, 13).

The Master advocated a right relationship to all powers, and charged government with the responsibility to carry out the religious **sacrifices** designed to appease the powers that be; there were also prescribed rituals to try to discover what was on the mind of supernatural spirits—we call this **augury** or **divination**. "It is upon the observance of ritual that the governance of a State depends" (XI, 25).

Within the realm of the ancestors (**Ti**), there was the Ancestor of All Ancestors, **Shang Ti**; in our terms, we would call Shang Ti "God." So there is no doubt that there is an underlying religious framework to the system, despite the many evident differences between Confucius and other major figures in world religions.

Taoism

● ● ● ● ● ●

A Likely Story

This form of Chinese religion takes its inspiration from the ***Tao Te Ching***.[1] The three words mean "way," "power," and "book." Legend has it that **Lao Tzu** ("old fellow"; 604-524 BC?) lived in the same period of social upheaval as Confucius. Lao Tzu's response to the turmoil in his region was to move elsewhere. As he was departing, a border guard asked him to summarize his vision of reality before riding off into the sunset. Lao Tzu agreed, and is said to have produced the 81 poems in three days.

Scholars suggest that every element of this story (except for the horrors of the Period of the Warring States) is false. "Lao Tzu" is a description, not a name. He may well have never existed, except in people's imaginations (like Paul Bunyan, Fred Flintstone, or Homer Simpson); the author or authors of the poems may have used "Lao Tzu" as a pen name, just as Samuel Clemens chose to publish most of his fiction under the name "Mark Twain." Given that the book consists of 5000 Chinese ideograms and had to have been written in ink, it is inconceivable that it could even have been copied in three days, let alone generated from scratch on the spur of the moment by an elderly man in a poorly equipped guard shack.

The story is absurd—but it perfectly reveals the heart of Taoism. The *Tao Te Ching* teaches that happiness comes from **wu wei**, "not doing," or, perhaps, "nothing doing" or "doing nothing." All we have to do is relax, let go, go with the flow, and let the universe carry us where it will. Wu wei is exhibited by athletes who are "in the zone." They make difficult shots look easy. It seems as

---

[1] I am using the translation by Gia-Fu Feng and Jane English, with an introduction and notes by Jacob Needleman (New York: Vintage Books, 1989). I will refer to the poems by number; when quoting Needleman, I will give his name and the page number on which the quotation is found.

though they are unstoppable. Every move they make is more spectacular than the last. The rim of the basket seems to open wide for them. They see the seams of the baseball and know in a flash which way it will climb, slide, or curve. They loft long passes that fall so gently and perfectly that the receiver never has to break stride. In one of the classic sports moments, Michael Jordan changed the ball from his right hand to his left while the ball was spinning in mid-air underneath the outstretched arms of two defenders; then, at the last possible moment, Jordan softly banked the ball into the basket. He made it look easy, as if it were the most natural thing in the world.

When athletes, singers, artists, or skilled workers are "in the zone," they exhibit effortless effort. It is true, of course, that they are not literally "doing nothing," but their action seems to be given to them in such a way that it seems to come of itself—they themselves are carried along or carried away with it, just as the spectators are. The movie, *Forrest Gump*, tells the story of a natural man who simply floats on the currents of his day from childhood to old age.

The alternative to non-doing or effortless effort is exhibited by athletes who choke under pressure. They break into a cold sweat and make mistakes in judgment. The pitch gets away, and the winning run scores easily. The quarterback doesn't see the open receiver, or if he does, he misses him badly—because he is trying too hard to make something happen. A basketball player who can sink three-point shots while being double-teamed clanks free throws off the rim. An angry tennis player swings wildly at an overhead shot and plants it in the net or blows it out of the court. Players give away the game precisely because they know that they are too focused on the fact that they must *act rightly right now!*

The story of the composition of the *Tao Te Ching* may well be false, but **a story doesn't have to be true to be true.** The legend that the poetry flowed freely from the mind of a wise old man brings the essential spirituality of non-doing to mind far better than more historically accurate images of a thinker slowly assembling the collection and laboring, without complete success, to make the disparate pieces mesh smoothly with each other. Perhaps death came to the old man before he could put the finishing touches on his meditations. Then again, some of the roughness may be deliberate, and may in its own way say more about Lao Tsu's outlook than a mirror-like finish would.

Beyond All Telling

The first line of the book may be variously translated: "The Tao [*Way*] that can be told is not the eternal Tao." "The Tao that can be put into words is not the real Tao." It is a funny way to begin talking about something to say, "Everything I am about to say is woefully inadequate. I can't tell you what I want you to know. Words are useless!"

If Lao Tzu can't explain what he means, what's the point of reading what he wrote? From the standpoint of Western logic, he is self-referentially inconsistent. In a later poem he says, "Those who know do not talk. Those who talk do not know" (56). Lao Tzu seems to be condemned by his own words. At first glance, the fact that he chose to talk about what can't be put into words suggests that he literally does not know what he is talking about. We Westerners have to loosen up our minds in order to see that Lao Tzu's self-deprecating humor points to the greatness of the reality toward which he would like to direct our attention.

In his own highly compressed fashion, Lao Tzu is making the distinction between notional and real apprehension (see page 3). The Tao of ultimate reality is not the only reality that cannot be communicated fully by abstract ideas and propositional language. There are a multitude of realities too complex to be fully expressed by any sequence of sentences, any one of which can only capture a small part of the whole:

> The Chinese Taoist philosopher, Chuang Tzu …, quoted a wheelwright who appreciated that his work needed to be done at "the right pace, neither slow nor fast" and this, he observed, "cannot get into the hand unless it comes from the heart. It is a thing that cannot be put into words; there is an art in it that I cannot explain to my son."[2]

The wheelwright knew how to make wheels. As the proverb says, the proof was in the pudding—his wheels worked. But he could not transmit the skill of making sound wheels just by talking about it. His son would have to gain the skill by finding the right balance between working too fast or too slow for himself.

I know myself from the inside out. I've lived with myself for more than half a century. It is likely that I don't know any other aspect of reality better than myself, because I have been—and always will be—involved in everything I learn about anything. Despite the fact that I am a well-known reality, the me I can put into words is not the real me. I also know my friends very well, but the friend that I can put into words is not the real friend.

Philosophically, it is a tautology (something that is true by definition) that "I know what I know." But at the psychological level, I don't know what I know. I've studied English, Latin, French, Spanish, Russian, Greek, Hebrew, and have picked up a few ideas about Italian and dozens of other languages. I can't count the number of words that I know actively or passively. One night in the early 1980s, I played guitar and sang with friends at a party for five hours without once looking at any sheet music to aid in remembering the words and chords to the songs. I couldn't do that today, but I know that if I sit down and sing the songs that are easy to remember, other songs start surfacing, in whole or in part. Logically, I know all the songs that I know, but psychologically, I have no idea how much music there is in me.

I have tasted truffles twice in my life—not the chocolate candies but the extremely expensive, edible fungus that grows in the roots of trees. I know what truffles taste like. I can replay the

---

[2] Quoted by M. Oakeshott, "Rationalism in politics," in T. Fuller (ed.) *Rationalism in Politics and Other Essays* (Indianapolis: Liberty Press, 1991), 14 n. 7.

memory for myself, although it falls short of the actual experience of smelling and tasting the truffles themselves. If someone talks about truffles on TV or in an article, I know what they mean. Even with this knowledge, the truffle that I can put into words is not the real truffle. Truffles taste like mushrooms, but are much more intense and intoxicating.

The list of strange foods that I have tried goes on: tripe, elk, ostrich, frog, rabbit, rattlesnake. The taste that I can put into words is not the real taste. No matter how much I say, I will never give you the knowledge that just one bite of these foods would give you. *The taste that I can put into words is not the real taste.*

Like Lao Tzu, Oscar Wilde (a British author, 1854-1900) recognized the same difficulty of expressing our most important insights and vital experiences in mere words: "Education is an admirable thing. But it is well to remember from time to time that nothing that is worth knowing can be taught."[3] I know that I know a great deal. I know the difference between words and realities, between notional and real apprehension. I know that I can't take a bath for you. I know enough to know how little I know. I know I cannot share my vision of reality with you by spelling it out. *The vision I can put into words is not the real vision.* Either you will see it for yourself, or you won't. At some point, more words about the vision are simply a waste of breath.

May the Force Be with You

Lao Tzu believed that every aspect of reality has its own structure and logic, its own Tao. Our task is to recognize the Way that things are. To throw our lot in with the Tao of ultimate reality, the Tao of the world we see around us, the Tao of our human and personal existence, is to place all of the resources of reality at our disposal—and to place ourselves at the disposal of the whole of reality. "Become the master of the universe without striving" (57). "Use the force, Luke!"[4]

To be ignorant of or opposed to the Way is to act against our own Tao and to oppose ourselves to the totality of all that is. There is no doubt who will win that battle! When we have lost the Way, *the harder we try, the worse things get* (the "Law of Reversed Effort").

The closest concept to the Tao in American popular culture might be "Mother Nature." Everybody knows that we can't fool Mother Nature, and that things go to hell in a handcart when we try to do so. Nature (the Tao) holds all the cards. We can cooperate with nature, or else suffer the consequences of trying to go against the grain.

---

[3] "A Few Maxims for the Instruction of the Over-Educated," *Saturday Review*, November 17, 1894.

[4] *Star Wars Episode IV: A New Hope*, 1977.

Developments in Taoism

The unhistorical story of Lao Tzu dashing off the poems and then disappearing from the scene illustrates the old man's confidence that he did not have to preach his vision or hover over his disciples like a guru to see that they were making progress along the Way. In 20th-century United States, someone asked Louis Armstrong, a jazz musician, to define "swing." Armstrong replied, "If you don't know what it is, I can't tell you; if you do know what it is, I don't have to tell you." In a sense, Lao Tzu could care less about what happened to his vision. People would either get it or they wouldn't. It was really up to them to make of it what they would. His own Tao led him elsewhere.

Chuang Tzu (370-301 BC) created a kind of **Philosophical Taoism** that made the poetry of the *Tao Te Ching* more intelligible and more appealing to a large number of people. As the vision spread, it became enmeshed in the ordinary religious fabric of Chinese animism and blended with the ritual traditions, producing **Religious Taoism**, with all of the features of a garden variety religion: temples, priests, sacrifices, veneration of gods and goddesses, and a full menu of religious practices to choose from. Huston Smith calls this **magical Taoism** (204-206), and shows very little tolerance for those who try to find the Way, only to extract curses and blessings from it; from the standpoint of the original insights of Lao Tzu, the adherents of this form of Taoism seem to have lost the Way altogether. Of course, they might well defend themselves by noting that if the Tao of ultimate reality is truly polytheistic, then it follows that abiding by the Tao requires us to please all of the gods and goddesses.

At the other end of the spectrum from Religious Taoism is **Energizing Taoism**. A few people took the doctrine of inaction to heart and devoted themselves to "sitting with a blank mind" (HS, 200-204). This spirituality carries Lao Tzu's main insight to a logical conclusion: if we can't put the Tao into words, we may as well dispense with words altogether. For Taoists, the beauty of a window, a door, a cup, or a bowl is where the object is not. It is the empty space that lets light come through, a way open, or food and drink be received. Sitting with a blank mind empties the heart, and makes room for something indescribably better to fill us.

In this context, Taoists take great delight in the **yin-yang** symbol. It fits in perfectly with the view that the greatest truths cannot be put into words. Without words, the symbol says

something like this: "There are no absolutes. All oppositions contain their contraries. At the heart of yin is yang; at the heart of yang is yin." Any pair of contraries may be mapped onto this icon: light and darkness; male and female; true and false; good and evil; beauty and ugliness; being and non-being; self and other; all and nothing; knowing and not knowing; acting and not acting.

This aspect of the Eastern mind is most baffling to Westerners. Our Western **Enlightenment** is a period in history marked by the rise of scientific research accompanied by a philosophy that makes clear distinctions between true and false, proved and not proved, known and unknown. Our logic is based on **the law of non-contradiction** (see page 15): a thing is what it is, and is not what it is not; we may not say of the same thing considered at the same time under the same aspect that it *is* what it *is not*. The computer on which I am composing this sentence depends on maintaining opposition between charged and uncharged capacitors that act as the physical representation of logical ones and zeroes. In the language of mathematics and logic, 1 is not 0 and 0 is not 1. In computer science, "not" is an operation on a bit that changes it to its opposite state, so NOT 1 = 0 and NOT 0 = 1. Everything in our ordinary digital computers depends on making and preserving these distinctions. (Quantum computers are a different kettle of fish. I will pass over them in silence.)

Western science and mathematics depend on an either-or logic. In Eastern spirituality, there is a devaluation of such black-and-white thinking. Hinduism, Buddhism, and Taoism all have traditions that exhibit this kind of indifference to the principle of non-contradiction; in Nirguna Hinduism and some forms of Buddhism, things that seem contrary to each other are simply aspects of one and the same divine reality. Such things only seem contradictory because we are deceived by maya, illusory external appearances; but in reality, according to the pantheists, all is one.

Walt Whitman (1819-1892 AD), a Westerner who was attracted to Eastern spirituality, captured the flavor of the Eastern mentality in "Leaves of Grass":

Do I contradict myself?
Very well, then, I contradict myself;
(I am large—I contain multitudes.)

In the Western tradition, self-contradiction is a sign that one has made an embarrassing—and fatal—error in logic. In the East, it is a sign that one is in touch with realities too great to be forced into the little pigeonholes of our mental constructs. In the 20th century, Mao Zedong (1893-1976 AD), the leader of the Chinese Communist revolution, affirmed the Eastern view that is embodied in the yang-yin symbol: "The law of contradiction in things, that is, the law of the unity of opposites, is the basic law of materialist dialectics."[5]

Lao Tzu vs. Kung fu Tzu

Although some legends place Lao Tzu well ahead of the time of Confucius, others portray them as interacting with each other. Whether the author of the *Tao Te Ching* ever met or ever could have met Kung the Master is debatable. What is certain is that their disciples recognized that there were conflicts between the two different visions of reality; the fables about what one great thinker said to the other, even if false historically, represent the clash of the two different worldviews. Confucianism, as a general rule, emphasizes the value of the Way of the Ancients, social responsibility, human virtue in thought and deed, and collective action through ritual. Taoism, on the other hand, and again, as a general rule, emphasizes spontaneous personal expression (the tao of "the natural man"), openness to transcendent realities that baffle and frustrate rational inquiry, and a flexible and adaptive mentality toward the transient forms that culture takes.

Zen Buddhism
The Japanese Child of Indian Buddhism and Chinese Taoism

> Once upon a time, the original Buddha was walking with his disciples.
> He picked a lotus flower and held it aloft.
> He said nothing.
> One disciple smiled. At that very moment, the disciple who got the point that the Buddha was making became a Buddha himself.

This is the "**Lotus Flower Sermon,**" in which the original Buddha helped another person achieve enlightenment without saying a word. This led to the development of a particular spirituality in Indian Buddhism.

One thousand years after the Lotus Flower Sermon (~520 AD), a man named **Bodhidharma** carried this tradition into China. There he found the thousand-year-old Taoist tradition of "sitting with a blank mind." The merger of the two worldviews and spiritualities gave rise to **Ch'an** ("school of meditation"). Three hundred years later (~800 AD), this form of Chinese Buddhism spread to Japan, where the Chinese ideogram was pronounced **Zen**.

---

[5] This is the first line of Mao's article, "On Contradiction," first published in August 1937 and included in his *Selected Works*, Vol. 1 (Peking: Foreign Languages Press, 1967).

There are many other forms of Japanese Buddhism besides Zen. Just as happened with Confucianism and Religious Taoism in China, the native Japanese animist and polytheistic traditions (**Shinto**) became mixed with Hindu-Buddhist metaphysics and Buddhist-Taoist meditation practices.

Four hundred years after Zen gained a toehold in the Japanese religious scene (~1200 AD), some monks found that **koans** could help in achieving the emptiness and openness that paves the way for **satori** (the Japanese word for "enlightenment," the personal experience that changes one into a Buddha).

Koans are odd questions, statements, or parables that defy ordinary logic. There is no right answer to the puzzles posed by koans, other than to gain or exhibit satori. In one strand of the Zen tradition, the disciples will engage in **zazen**, seated meditation, while focusing on a koan to help break up our everyday patterns of thought. The disciple then shows the results of the meditation to the master in **sanzen**. If the master (the *san*) is satisfied, the disciple will be given a new koan; if not, the disciple continues to seek the great breakthrough into enlightenment as before. The disciple might spend months meditating on a single koan.

Although the use of koans is distinctive of one flavor of Japanese Buddhism, the seeds of the koan lie in the teaching of the original Buddha and the poetry of Lao Tzu. The Third Noble Truth teaches us that we will be happy *when we cease to exist*.

"Who will be happy when I no longer exist?" asks the perplexed disciple.
"You will," replies the Buddha.
"But I will be extinguished like the flame of a candle."
"Yes."
"So if I no longer exist, how can I be happy?"
"There is no 'I' in nirvana."
"Yes, there is! N-I-R ..."
"***Anatta!*** There is no true self. All appearances of self are an illusion!"

At this point, the disciple either gains enlightenment, or perhaps, bails out of the sangha. The Third Noble Truth, that we gain happiness by being extinguished, is a koan.

Lao Tzu's poetry, of course, is full of what came to be known as koans in the Japanese tradition.

> The softest thing in the universe
> Overcomes the hardest thing in the universe.
> That without substance can enter where there is no room.
> Hence I know the value of non-action.
> Teaching without words and work[ing] without doing

Are understood by very few. (43)

The yin-yang symbol is a visual koan. Like the Flower Sermon, without words, it invites the viewer to break free from the world of illusion.

There is a saying attributed to the Buddha on the Internet that is almost certainly not from Siddhartha Gautama of the Sakyas, but is instead a contemporary koan derived from elements of the eight hundred years of koans in Zen Buddhism: "The no-mind not-thinks no-thoughts about no-things."[6]

Zen and …

Zen spirituality is not confined to the meditation hall and meetings with the master. The spirituality of the Eightfold Path implies that everything we do, all day long, is part of our quest for satori. Every action and event in our days presents a fresh opportunity to acquire or exhibit enlightenment if we keep our minds properly empty and open. The principle of wu-wei combines with the virtue of wen in these practical forms of spirituality: painting, calligraphy, gardening, flower arranging, tea drinking, swordplay, archery, and a multitude of other arts and crafts. Although the Zen tradition seems to have developed independently of Vajrayana tantrism, there are some striking similarities in the pattern of building up tension as a prelude to breaking out of the old way of seeing things.

---

[6] Because I am drawn to jnana yoga, the pursuit of the intellectual life, it troubles me that I cannot find the original source of this saying. For now, I'm placing bets that it was written by an English Zen enthusiast, but I have no evidence to back up this view. From the point of view of Zen, figuring out such picayune details is about as far as you can get from *satori*, the blinding flash of enlightenment that turns people into Buddhas.

Part II

• • • • • •

Western religions

The three Western religions are Judaism, Christianity, and Islam. They form one family of religions, because they all stem from one man: **Abraham** (~1700 BC). He was born in Ur, which is now found in southern Iraq, and traveled with his family to Haran, now located in southern Turkey (Gen 11:27-31). Since Abraham was a descendant of Noah's son, Shem (Gen 9:18; 11:10-26), he and his descendants are called **Semites** (the "s" sound and the "sh" sound are represented by the same consonant in Hebrew); Abraham is also identified as a **Hebrew** (Gen 14:13), which may mean "one from across the [Euphrates] river." The three Western religions may therefore be called Semitic, Hebrew, or Abrahamic. In their developed form, all three are also **monotheistic**, but, as we shall see, it took a long time for the Western monotheistic worldview to fully detach itself from polytheism.

JUDAISM

• • • • • •

One God Created EVERYTHING

The authors of the Scriptures located Abraham in the story of the whole universe. There are two creation stories in the first two chapters of Genesis (1:1 to 2:4a and 2:4b to 2:24). A careful reading of the two stories shows that they contradict each other at the literal level. In the first story, male and female are created simultaneously, *after* everything else is created (1:26-27); in the second story, the male is created first, before all other things (vegetation, animals, the female). This is not a translation problem. The Hebrew is easy. The plots of the two stories are quite simple: in the first story, everything else is created before the human beings (1:3-25); in the second story, the creation of the male (2:7) is as far away as possible from that of the female (2:22), since the male comes first and the female comes last, with the creation of every other living being, plant and animal, separating them from each other (2:8-20). In the first story, male and female are both created by a word of command and both are "in the image and likeness" of God (1:26), while in the second story, the male is made from dirt and the female is fashioned from the rib of the male.

From a logical standpoint, two contradictory stories cannot both be true, although both may be false. I am convinced that the disagreement in the sequence of events in the two stories is a clue that they were not meant to teach us history or science. From the perspective of the theological meaning of the stories, the contradictions between the two stories make no difference in our understanding of God. The stories agree that all things come from one God.

When we contrast the two biblical accounts with the scientific narrative, it becomes clear that neither one corresponds to the actual sequence of events of the history of the universe. The scientific story of creation begins with the God Particle or Cosmic Egg, smaller than the diameter of an atom, which contained the whole of what we now experience as matter and energy in the space-time continuum. Instead of remaining as the biggest dark hole imaginable, that extraordinarily dense singularity expanded rapidly into the Big Bang. After 300,000 or 400,000 years of expansion and cooling, there was a great flash of light as the materials in the hot, dark plasma separated into protons, neutrons, and electrons, among other things, and there was room enough between them for light to travel from one thing to another.

The newborn universe was composed mostly of hydrogen, helium, and lithium, the first three elements in the periodic table. Fortunately for us, the force of gravity in some parts of the universe was strong enough to cause these extremely light gases to coalesce into first-generation stars, which eventually cooked up all of the other elements in the periodic table that make more complex physical and biological realities possible. The heavy elements were cast out of the womb of the first-generation stars when they reached the end of their lives. Everything in our solar system—the sun, planets, planetoids, moons, asteroids, meterorites, and the like—is composed of stardust from the first-generation stars. Only after the sun was created by the force of gravity acting on the stardust could its gravity capture everything else that we now see in our solar system. The beginning of life—and its development from single-celled organisms into plants, animals, and human beings—is the very last chapter of the scientific account.

The creation of light in Genesis 1:3 can be loosely lined up with the story of the Big Bang, and the general sequence of plants (1:11), birds and fish (1:20), land animals (1:25), and humans (1:26-27) bears some resemblance to the sequence of evolution, but there is no sky-dome keeping us from being drowned by the waters above the dome (1:6-7), the dry land and vegetation (1:9-12) cannot be older than the sun, the moon, and the stars (1:16), and those lights in the heavens are not "in the dome of the sky" (1:15).

The second story of Genesis is equally absurd from the scientific standpoint. Humans are a very late development in evolution, and male and female must arrive on the scene together. The claim in the second story that the male existed before plants, animals, and females is scientifically ludicrous.

A story need not be true to be true. Neither of the biblical stories can stand as science or chronology at the literal level. But both stories are inspired and sacred, because they reveal religious truths. They are not about *how* creation took place, but about *Who* created: one sovereign God, acting alone and purposefully, to create **everything.** Although both biblical accounts start with some material onstage (wind and water in the first, dirt and rivers in the second), interpreters understand that this is simply a storytelling device; theologically, we go beyond the story framework and assert that God created everything *ex nihilo* (Latin, "from nothing").

Unlike the Hindu-Buddhist worldview, which holds that the universe (samsara) just goes around in meaningless circles, all of which are illusory and deceptive (maya), the Jewish view is that time is linear. It begins with creation, and moves toward the end that God set for it in the beginning. Neither the universe nor human life is reincarnated. We get one—and only one—life, so we need to make the most of it while it lasts. For the descendants of Abraham, the belief that one God created everything on purpose gives a sense of meaning to history. In this view, the world has not lasted forever, and will not last forever. Like us, the universe has only one life to live, according to the will of the One Who created it.

The six-day story (Genesis 1) of creation emphasizes that everything God created is "good, very good" (1:10, 18, 21, 25, 31). Our goal in life is not to gain liberation (moksha) from a reincarnating world (samsara), but to find happiness in the created world:

> Go, eat your bread with joy and drink your wine with a merry heart, because it is now that God favors your works. At all times let your garments be white, and spare not the perfume of your head. Enjoy life with the wife whom you love, all the days of the fleeting life that is granted you under the sun. This is your lot in life, for the toil of your labors under the son. Anything you can turn your hand to, do with what power you have; for there will be no work, nor reason, nor knowledge, nor wisdom in the nether world where you are going. (Eccl 10:7-10)

Note the absence of a belief in a Heaven or Hell in this passage. For Qoheleth (also known as Ecclesiastes), real life and happiness is to be found here and now; any life after life is in some ghostly and empty wasteland.

> Here is what I recognize as good: it is well for a man to eat and drink and enjoy all the fruits of his labor under the sun during the limited days of life which God gives him; for this is his lot. Any man to whom God gives riches and property, and grants power to partake of them, so that he receives his lot and finds joy in the fruits of his toil, has a gift from God. For he will hardly dwell on the shortness of his life, because God lets him busy himself with the joy of his heart. (Eccl 5:17-19)

This is a radically different view of what life is all about from the Hindu belief: that no one of our infinitely many lives matters very much. Genesis 1 especially celebrates the goodness of the whole creation; Genesis 2 is focused on the goodness and power of the marriage relationship. Both agree that it is God who invented sexuality, and that sexual union is good.

One other great truth asserted by Genesis 1 is that all humans, male and female, are in the "image and likeness of God" (1:26-27). This is a foundation for **ethics**, the branch of philosophy and theology that deals with the principles of **justice**. All human beings share equally in godlike qualities that set us apart from all other living beings. We must not treat humans like animals, or set one gender against the other. The same verse also implicitly denies the Hindu-Buddhist affirmation that we are divine. In the worldview of Genesis, there is no room for the polytheism or pantheism of Eastern religions. We are "like" God, but we are *not God*.[1]

Those Wild and Crazy Gods of Greece

The character of the creator in the Genesis stories (especially the first) is very different from the characters involved in the creation narratives of the polytheistic world. These other traditions are something like long-running soap operas, with a huge cast of characters and bewildering and shocking developments at every turn.

The synopsis of Greek mythology that I give here is cobbled together from various sources, and reflects something of a compromise between disparate traditions. Inventing stories about the escapades of the gods and goddesses was one of the great entertainment industries of the ancient world. Later authors of episodes in the series did not have to make their tales consistent with earlier versions.

The story begins with the Titans, the elder gods. They were all children of *Gaia*. She was the original goddess who, by a virginal conception, gave birth to *Uranus*. She then began to mate with her son, producing the rest of the Titans: Cronus, Rhea, Oceanus, Tethys, Hyperion, Mnemosyne, Themis, Iapetus, Clymene, Coeus, Crius, Phoebe, Thea, Metis, and Dione. At some point, Gaia suggested to their son Cronus that he should castrate his father-brother god, Uranus. This is how Cronus became the top god—for a while.

Knowing how hard a son could be on his father, Cronus ate all of the divine children produced by his union with his sister-wife, Rhea. Rhea saved one of their children, Zeus, by feeding her brother-husband a rock instead of the newborn god. Zeus grew up to become the leader of the Olympians, and just as his father had feared, overthrew Cronus and replaced him as the top god, and replaced the Titans with the Olympians.

In some sources, Prometheus fashioned males out of clay and stole fire from Zeus to give them warmth and light.[2] Zeus then created females as part of his retribution for the theft of fire:

> In Greek mythology, Pandora [Greek, *pan*, "all" + *dora*, "giver" = "giver of all," or "all-endowed"] was the first woman. Each god helped create her by giving her unique gifts. Zeus ordered Hephaestus to mold her out of Earth (Gaîa-Gaia) as part of the punishment of mankind for Prometheus's theft of the secret of fire, and all the gods joined

---

[1] I am thinking here of a whole spirituality of recovery found in the book *Not God: A History of Alcoholics Anonymous* by Ernest Kurtz (Center City: Hazelden, 1979); it is a brilliant title and a hugely important aspect of Western monotheism.

[2] "Prometheus," *Wikipedia*. The article lists six other creation narratives that imagine humankind being made from clay. Genesis 2 is clearly not unique in this regard, and almost certainly was inspired by preexisting creation narratives.

in offering these "beautiful evil" seductive gifts. Her other name, inscribed against her figure on a white-ground kylix in the British Museum, is *Anesidora*, "she who sends up gifts." According to the myth, Pandora opened a jar (*pithos*), in modern accounts referred to as "Pandora's box", releasing all the evils of mankind—greed, vanity, slander, envy, pining—leaving only Hope inside once she had closed it again.[3]

"From [Pandora] is the race of women and female kind," Hesiod writes; "of her is the deadly race and tribe of women who live amongst mortal men to their great trouble, no helpmeets in hateful poverty, but only in wealth."[4]

Zeus was a very sexually active god:

As the sky god, Zeus had easy access to the women of the world and took full advantage of it. Also, his power as a supreme god made him difficult to resist. Prior to his marriage to Hera he was married first to Metis, then Themis. He was interested in Demeter but she resisted him. His third wife was Mnemosyne. He was involved with Leto shortly before his marriage to Hera. The list of lovers after his final marriage, to Hera, is considerable: Europa, Io, Semele, Ganymede (a boy), Callisto, Maia, Metis, Dione, Danae.[5]

Zeus also deceived Almenes, a mortal woman, by disguising himself as her husband, and fathered Hercules on the same night that her husband fathered Hercules' twin, Iphicles.

Roman mythology told essentially the same kind of stories, although they gave different names to the central characters. Cronus became Saturn, Zeus was called Jupiter or Jove, Hera was known as Juno, Ares became Mars, Aphrodite was Venus, Athena was known as Minerva, etc.

The Jewish creation stories, in contrast to Greco-Roman mythology, present a God who creates purposefully, and with complete sovereignty. The God described in the Genesis myths does not engage in sex, marriage, adultery, rape, incest, murder, warfare, or jealous retribution against opposing gods and goddesses. He acts freely and without opposition from any other divine or quasi-divine beings. Borrowing the word **"demythologization"** from Rudolph Bultmann (1884-1976), a Lutheran theologian (and giving it a spin that he undoubtedly would have disliked), we might say that the Genesis myths *demythologize* the world around us. Gods, goddesses, and indwelling spirits are implicitly denied by the way the story is told in Genesis 1 and Genesis 2.

---

[3] "Pandora," *Wikipedia*.

[4] "The Theogony of Hesiod," translated by Hugh G. Evelyn-White (1914), line 590.

[5] John M. Hunt, "Zeus Lovers," *http://edweb.sdsu.edu/people/bdodge/scaffold/GG/zeusLover.html*

Besides emptying the divine realm of other gods and goddesses, the Genesis myths also silently banish spirits from the world. Things that are gods or goddesses in other traditions (the sun, the moon, the stars), the home of gods and goddesses (mountains, rivers, seas), or the particular possessions of a deity (thunder, lightning, rain, fire, wind) become creatures fashioned by the one God. Both polytheism and animism are ruled out by this worldview. Events in nature are no longer interpreted as the results of warfare, lust, jealousy, vengeance, or stupidity among the gods and goddesses. Everything we see around us in the universe becomes just a "thing"—a form of matter that possesses its own nature. Rodney Stark, a contemporary American sociologist, argues that this de-sacralization of the natural order paved the way for the development of science in Western civilization.[6]

If events around us are not caused by the caprice of gods, goddesses, and indwelling spirits, then the cause must be sought in the natural order. That is the focus of scientific investigation. Science is methodologically atheist. "God" is not a proper scientific answer to the question, "Why did this happen?" Science seeks *physical*—not metaphysical—answers to its questions. When scientists become involved in debates about whether or not God exists, they cease to act as physical scientists, and start to act as philosophers, specifically as metaphysicians.

Besides understanding the things and events in the world as creatures and natural events, and not as the effects of invisible conflicts between gods and goddesses or inhabiting spirits, Judaism also affirmed that nature has its own Torah. We still use this concept whenever we talk about the "laws of science."

For some in our day, the treatment of the universe as mere matter following the laws of nature is a desecration; they are reviving ancient cults based on a renewed belief in lesser spirits (see, for example, those who think of themselves as Druids and who organize regular worship services at Stonehenge). We might say that such people are *remythologizing* the world. When Christianity became the official religion of the Roman Empire (381 AD), someone associated the term "**pagan**" with those who refused to give up the polytheistic worldview. Christian missionaries then extended the term to include all the religions of the world that they encountered outside the Western Abrahamic tradition. When I was a boy, we took up collections in Catholic schools during Lent to "save pagan babies." The Latin word *paganus* meant something like "country folk," those who lived outside the city. Some of those who are reviving forms of ancient polytheistic animism accept the term "pagan"; others do not.

---

[6] Stark, *For the Glory of God: How Monotheism Led to Reformations, Science, Witch-Hunts, and the End of Slavery* (Princeton: Princeton University Press, 2003), 147-148.

Demythologizing Genesis

Both biblical literalists and atheist philosophers of science argue that the Genesis accounts of creation must be treated as history. The literalists think that this is the only way to read the Scriptures, even though there is no verse in the Scriptures that requires this approach; the thought that we should deny the chronology of Genesis but affirm its religious meaning is appalling to them. Those who interpret science from the atheistic standpoint want to require a literal reading of Genesis, because it is so easy to show that the stories are scientifically absurd. There is no sky-dome keeping us from being drowned by the waters above it (1:6); the earth and vegetation (1:9-12) cannot be older than the sun, the moon, and the stars (1:16); the sun, the moon, and the stars are not inside the sky-dome (1:14); dinosaurs and humans did not come to exist in the same 24-hour day (1:24-28), or co-exist in the same epoch. Demythologization—grasping the *religious meanings* of the story and denying the historical meaning—is appalling to the atheists, because it robs them of their favorite straw man.

Not to put too fine a point on it, reading Genesis stupidly is stupid, whether the interpreter's motivation is religious or irreligious. If it is true that one God created everything, then it follows that science studies what God created. If science shows that one form of life descends from previous forms of life, then it follows that we must believe that God created an evolving universe.

Sin Enters the Picture

The great question of **theodicy** (Greek, *theos*, "god" + *dike*, "justice" = "judging or justifying God") is "If God is good, how can there be so much evil in the world?" Another version of the question is "Why do bad things happen to good people?" The first two chapters of Genesis point only to the good things that came from God when the world was new. We shouldn't forget the truths those chapters teach—everything that is, is good, because "God does not make junk"; life is good; sexuality is a blessing from God—He invented orgasm and made the marriage bond more powerful than the birth bond (Gen 2:24); there is no god of evil opposed to the one and only God who made all things *ex nihilo* (out of nothing). But something went wrong: sin happened.

The **Original Sin** in Genesis 3 is an act of disobedience: Adam and Eve chose to do what God had told them not to do (2:16-17, 3:2, 3:11). The myth employs the image of a "tree of the knowledge of good and evil" (2:17), as if there were a magical fruit that could produce spiritual effects. The power of gaining knowledge was not in the tree or its fruit; it was in the decision to obey or disobey God. If Adam and Eve had resisted the temptation, they would have *gained knowledge of good by doing good*. Instead, they chose to gain knowledge of evil by doing evil.

This is the moment of their transition from notional apprehension to real apprehension. Up until they made a personal choice, they could only "know" about good and evil by hearing what God or the serpent *said* about such realities. Only after making a choice (an act of real assent) could they have *personal experience* (real apprehension) that it is good to be good and evil to be evil. Because God Himself is determined that humans should be godlike in their freedom to choose their own destiny, He cannot force us to choose good. Nor can He give us the kind of personal experience that comes from choosing by just *talking* with them about the difference between good and evil (notional apprehension). Only when we make the choice for ourselves are our eyes opened to the meaning of the words. Then we *know* in an entirely different way from before.

Parents go through this crisis thousands of times with their children. They say, "Don't touch the stove. It's hot!" If they're lucky, the child will learn the meaning of the word "hot" without suffering third-degree burns—but children won't *know* what the word really means until they actually touch something hot enough to make them wish they hadn't touched it. *After* the child has "eaten from the tree of knowledge," then it understands exactly what others mean when they say "Hot!"

Elements of the Hindu understanding of karma can be integrated with the story of the Original Sin. There is a real difference between good and evil. Those who do good *become good*, and good things will come to them; those who do evil *become evil*, and evil things will befall them. There is no way around this spiritual law. We benefit or suffer from the choices we make in life—we may choose between good and evil, but we may not choose to have good come from evil choices.

The three religions derived from Abraham give different weight to the story of the Fall. It takes on a greater significance in Christianity than in Judaism or Islam. The Hebrew word for **sin**, *het*, and its Greek translation, *amartia*, both come from archery practice. They mean "to miss the mark." An archer who misses the mark should take another arrow and try again. They do not have the theological overload given in the Christian tradition, where sin is understood as breaking our relationship with God in such a way that we ourselves are unable to heal the breach. The Jewish worldview is relatively calm about the reality of "missing the mark." "The just man sins seven times a day and rises again" (Prov. 24:16). Sin happens. So? It's not the end of the world. Try again. See if you can aim better next time.

Sin and evil are not "things." They are not creatures of God on a par with the sun, the moon, the stars, the dry land, the seas, and all living things. God allows sin and evil to happen in the world, because He loves freedom. St. Augustine (354-430 AD) taught that sin and evil are not created things, but come from the absence of goodness, just as darkness is not a thing, but the absence of light. A recent Hindu author echoes this view: "Evil is like a shadow—it has no real substance of its own, it is simply a lack of light. You cannot cause a shadow to disappear by trying to fight it, stamp on it, by railing against it, or any other form of emotional or physical resistance. In order to cause a shadow to disappear, you must shine light on it."[7]

---

[7] Shakti Gawain, teacher and author (b. 1948) http://www.shaktigawain.com/ Gawain does not identify herself with any classical religion; she seems to have been most influenced by Hinduism and Buddhism.

Abraham's Bargain with God

We have no exact dates for Abraham, or for many of the events recounted by his descendants. People in the ancient world did not share our passion or talent for locating events within the framework of a global calendar system. There is no scientific reason from archaeology to assert that Abraham was a real person, nor is there any scientific reason to deny his existence. The solemn voice of the TV narrator announces "Archaeologists have no proof that Abraham existed," as if that were a hugely important observation. All of us—including the archaeologists and the baritones they hire to narrate their shows on TV—had an ancestor alive 1,700 years before Jesus was born—otherwise, we would not be here today; other than our own existence, we have no other record of our ancestors from back then. Locating Abraham somewhere around the 17th century BC and accepting the name given him by his descendants is good enough for our purposes.

A story doesn't have to be true to be true. There is no way to establish the historical accuracy of the details in the narrative that follows; in some cases, we have very good reasons to doubt some of the assertions made in the sacred text. The religious *meaning* of the stories is that God chose to develop a committed personal relationship with one man and his descendants. As a consequence, some of us Westerners call them the **Chosen People**.

The family of Abraham claims that God made a **covenant** (bargain, agreement, deal, testament) with him: if he would follow God, God would bless him with land and children (Gen 12:1-4). **Canaan** came to be known as the "**Promised Land**," because it was the territory God promised to give to Abraham and his descendants.

The second blessing promised in God's covenant with Abraham was a multitude of children. In our day, this would be bad news, not good, because children are a liability, not an asset. They divide the wealth of the family and diminish the net disposable income. In our world, the wealthiest families are DINKs, couples with "Double Income, No Kids."

To Abraham, having many children was a promise of abundant wealth. For the poor, children are an asset. They begin to work with their parents at a very early age, and increase the earning power of the family as they reach maturity. They help to manage and protect the family's interests. There was no such thing in those days as Medicare, Medicaid, or Social Security. When their parents became old and infirm, the children provided them with all they needed. The more children in a family, the more land the family could control; the more land the family could control, the more children they could support.

Beyond the wealth God promised Abraham, there was another blessing: life after life. As we saw just a few pages ago (page 59), the early Israelites had no vision of a heaven or hell. All of the dead went to Sheol (Gen 37:35), a spiritual wasteland. Real life was here on earth. To live on after death, one needed to have children. This was taken so seriously that in later times, the brother of a man who died childless was obliged to take the dead man's widow as his own wife, and raise up an heir for his dead brother (Gen 38:7-10; Dt 25:5-10). This belief also, lamentably, provided **a rationale for genocide** (Latin, *gens*, "tribe, nation" + *caedere*, "to cut, kill" = "kill the whole group"), because a man was not truly dead and gone if any of his family was still alive. If Abraham agreed to the terms God offered him, that would mean that Abraham would essentially live on forever in his descendants, who would be as numberless as the stars in the sky (Gen 15:5).

Abraham signed the agreement twice, once by killing some animals (Gen 15:0), and later by circumcising himself and the males in his family (17:9-14). **Circumcision** means "cutting around" the head of the penis, so as to remove the foreskin. The results of the surgery are very dramatic; one can tell at a glance whether or not a man belongs to the covenant community.

The Miracle Baby

There was a serious problem with fulfillment of the contract. Sarah had reached menopause (18:11), and knew that she was biologically incapable of having children. She suggested that Abraham have sexual intercourse with her maidservant, **Hagar**, so that he could begin to collect on the promises made in the covenant (Gen 16:1-3). Hagar gave birth to **Ishmael**, Abraham's firstborn son.

God had other plans. He wanted Sarah to be the mother of the heirs to the covenant promises. Sarah laughed when she heard God declare that she would have a boy (Gen 18:9-15); she must have thought that God did not understand the relationship between menstruation and fertility. But God had the last laugh. Sarah did have a son after all, and Abraham named him Isaac, which is based on the verb "to laugh." It's not clear whether it is God who laughs, or his mother, or Isaac himself—but there is no doubt that his name is full of laughter.

Abraham later had another five sons with another concubine (Gen 25:1-5), but apart from noticing that **polygamy** (Greek, *poly*, "many" + *gamos*, "wife" = "many wives") was taken for granted in the early Semitic tradition, we will not concern ourselves about the other sons. The problem that confronted Sarah was that in the ancient world, the elder son inherited *everything* and became the head of the family on the death of the **patriarch** (Greek, *pater* "father" + *archein* "to rule" = "father ruler"). Sarah could not stand the thought of her miracle baby having to serve under the son of a slave, so she persuaded Abraham to drive Hagar and Ishmael out of the tribe (Gen 21:9-13) so that her boy would be the heir of all of Abraham's possessions. Hagar and her son would have died if God had not sent an angel to rescue them (Gen 21:27). God promised that He would make a "great nation" of Ishmael, just as He had promised that He would make a "great nation" of Abraham (Gen 21:18); as things turned out, the Hebrew Scriptures portray Ishmael as the patriarch of the **Arabs**.

The **Quran**, the basic scripture of Islam, tells exactly the same story up to this point, and agrees that Abraham is the father of the Arabs through his firstborn son, Ishmael. This means that from the standpoint of both scriptural traditions, the current conflict between Arabs and Jews is a *family feud*. They have the same father, Abraham, and are blood relatives of each other;

they both worship the God of Abraham as the one and only God who exists (radical monotheism). In this chapter, we will follow the rest of Isaac's story; what happened to the Ishmaelites will concern us in the chapter on Islam (see page 156 and page 160).

Would You Murder Your Child if God Asked You?

"Some time after these events, God put Abraham to the test" (Gen 22:1). We don't know how long afterward. Later storytellers, like nature, abhor a vacuum. We start to fill in details not specified by the sacred text. When I think about this story, I imagine Isaac as old enough for his **Bar Mitzvah** (Hebrew, *bar*, "son" + *mitzvah*, "commandment" = a person now capable of obeying the commandments on his own), which is around age 13 in most Jewish traditions. But this is an **anachronism**—the error of taking material from a much later date and inserting it into an earlier story. The Bar Mitzvah ceremony as we know it today didn't develop until more than two thousand years after God put Abraham to the test. Nevertheless, if I were making a movie about Abraham's life, I would cast a young teen for the role of Isaac in this part of his story.

The test that God gave Abraham was to offer Isaac as a **holocaust** (Greek, *holo*, "whole" + *caustos*, "burnt" = killing an animal and burning it completely). In the fully developed tradition, there were other kinds of **sacrifice**, in which the best parts of the animal were given to God by being burned, and the remainder distributed among the priests and people. In either case, the animal was to be killed by having its throat slit with a sharp knife in one stroke, so that the jugular veins were severed completely. The blood was sacred to God, because it was the very life of the animal; by giving the blood to God alone, the priest was returning the life of the animal to the source of all life.

By the time Abraham and Isaac went up the mountain, Isaac had probably seen his father offer holocausts many times. He knew the ritual. "Father! … Here are the fire and the wood, but where is the sheep for the holocaust?" (Gen 22:7). When his father tied him up and laid him on the wood, he had his answer.

This is an ugly story. It wouldn't make it into our Bible today, given our modern tastes. What kind of man was Abraham to think that God would ask him to murder his son? What kind of God would demand that his covenant partner be willing to murder an innocent victim? What did this do to Isaac's relationship with his father? The Scriptures as they stand do not answer these questions. The story is told simply, without filling in these blanks.[8] At the very least, staying

---

[8] For Christians, the story of an only son being offered in sacrifice **prefigures** (foreshadows) the story of Jesus dying on the wood of the Cross. When Isaac is spared death, it must have been something like a resurrection for him. Jesus' resurrection took place after dying as a sacrificial victim. In the eyes of Christians, Isaac is a **type** (in the sense of *prototype*, early model) of Jesus. See p. 85 for more remarks on the **typological interpretation** of the Jewish Scriptures by Christians.

within the bounds of this perplexing story, we may say that Abraham proved that he valued obedience to God's commands more than he valued the life of his son. We might guess (or argue) that the moral of the story is that we, too, should obey God, even when we don't understand His commands, but the Scriptures as they stand do not make that idea explicit.

Child sacrifice may not have been uncommon in the ancient world. Archaeologists have found the mummified bodies of Inca children high in the Andes. The king of Moab apparently offered his son and heir in sacrifice (2 Kings 3:27). Jepthah seems to have offered his daughter as a thanksgiving sacrifice for victory in battle (Judges 11). Later Scriptures expressly forbade God's people from sacrificing their children (Lv 20:1-4). The Romans claimed that the Carthaginians engaged in child sacrifice; the archaeological evidence seems inconclusive at present. It may be that Abraham did not find it surprising that God would ask him to prove his loyalty to the covenant by murdering Isaac; but such a concept of God is far removed from the understanding of God later on in the tradition.

Sibling Rivalries

Isaac became the father of two sons, **Esau** and **Jacob** (Gen 25:19-26). Esau was a manly man who hunted game. Jacob stayed at home and tended the sheep. One day, Esau came home from a fruitless hunt and found Jacob cooking some lamb stew. He rashly promised to give his younger brother the right of inheritance in exchange for a bowl of stew (Gen 25:27-34). Esau may not have thought anything about the deal he struck with his brother. It was an absurd dialogue, and not the kind of thing that would ever stand up in a court of law. But years later, Jacob's mother conspired with him to trick poor old Isaac, who had gone blind and was on his deathbed, to pass the inheritance on to the younger son, instead of the rightful heir (Gen 27:1-29). Once Isaac had done so, he could not take back his word of blessing (Gen 27:37). From the standpoint of the authors of our scripture, Esau got what his foolish words deserved, and Jacob became God's covenant partner, instead of the firstborn son.

Many years later, Jacob engaged in some kind of wrestling match with a supernatural figure all night long (Gen 32:23-27). He was injured in the fight, and walked with a limp for the rest of his life (Gen 32:32-33). The mysterious stranger gave him a new name, **Israel** (Hebrew, *isra*, "he fought" + *El*, "god" = "he fought God"), "because you have contended with divine and human beings and have prevailed" (Gen 32:29). Israel had 12 sons from four wives, who in turn became the patriarchs of the **Twelve Tribes of Israel**: Reuben, Simeon, Levi, Judah, Issachar, Zebulun, Joseph, Benjamin, Dan, Naphtali, Gad, and Asher (Gen 35:22-25).

"Jacob loved Joseph best of all his sons, for he was the child of his old age" (Gen 37:3). The story of the trouble caused by Jacob's favoritism is recounted in the play and the movie, *Joseph and the Amazing Technicolor Dreamcoat* (1968, 1999). It wasn't at all hard for the older boys to figure out who was their father's favorite son. They knew that Jacob had played fast and loose with his older brother, Esau, and reasoned that Joseph's dreams of being king over them were very likely to come true (Gen 37:6-11). They toyed with the idea of murdering him, but decided instead to sell him into slavery in Egypt (Gen 37:26-28).

Joseph made a great slave. He was handsome, educated, hard-working, and trustworthy (Gen 39:1-6). Although he was imprisoned on a charge of attempted rape (vv. 7-20), his jailer let him run the jail (v. 22). During the two years of his imprisonment, he gained a reputation for interpreting dreams (Gen 40), and gained his release by explaining that Pharaoh's dreams foretold seven years of good harvests and seven years of famine (Gen 41:25-32). Pharaoh was so impressed that he put Joseph in charge of the whole Egyptian economy, so that the surplus from the good years could be used to carry the nation through the bad years (Gen 41:41-43).

God Brings Good Out of Evil

Instead of preventing Joseph from suffering at the hands of his brothers and Potiphar's wife, God allowed the evildoers to prevail for a time. "God writes straight with crooked lines."[9] If He had merely protected Jacob's favorite boy and made him the next patriarch of the clan, the headlines might have read (as they should have read when Jacob himself stole the inheritance from his older brother), "Mommy's Boy Makes Good." Going from favored child to head of the clan wouldn't have given Joseph the chance to exhibit the sterling qualities of character that make him truly admirable and lovable.

God let Joseph go from bad to worse, from slavery into imprisonment. He gave Joseph what he needed to thrive in adversity, and allowed him to earn promotion in Egyptian society through his own merits. Early Christian sages called this **God's Providence**, because God *provides* for the needs of His children; the term is not as popular nowadays as it once was, though many people do still believe that God cares for his children in all circumstances.

When famine came, just as Joseph had predicted, his own brothers had to come to Egypt and negotiate with him for the food they needed to save their lives (Gen 42-44). They were saved from death by Joseph's decision to forgive them: "I am your brother Joseph, whom you once sold into Egypt. But now do not be distressed, and do not reproach yourselves for having sold me here. It was really for the sake of saving lives that God sent me here ahead of you. ... So it was not really you but God who had me come here; and he has made of me a father to Pharaoh, lord of all his household, and ruler over the whole land of Egypt" (Gen 45:4-8).[10]

---

[9] Actually, so do we. There's scarcely a straight line in the word "straight." The source of the proverb is disputed. It is not in the Scriptures per se, but it is a theme that is consistent with many events in the scriptural tradition.

[10] As with the story of Isaac, Christian commentators see many parallels between the story of Joseph and that of Jesus: Both are sold into slavery by their brothers, suffer as a consequence, and save the very persons who injured them by an act of forgiveness that the wrongdoers do *not* deserve in the least.

In fairy tales, the traditional last line is: "… and they all lived happily ever after." But God allowed evil to come to the **Israelites** (the members of the 12 tribes descended from Jacob). Over the course of four hundred years (Ex 12:40), they came to suffer "the whole cruel fate of slaves" (Ex 1:11-14). This gave God a whole new batch of crooked lines to play with. This brings us down to somewhere around 1200 to 1300 BC, depending on what kind of assumptions one makes about the lifetimes of Abraham, Isaac, and Jacob.

Moses Rides to the Rescue …

Pharaoh decided that it was time to force the Israelites to become part of the Egyptian melting pot. He ordered the murder of all newborn Israelite boys (Ex 1:15-22). He was foolish to do so, because—for the Israelites—their tribal identity was carried through the mother, not the father. All children born of Israelite mothers were Israelites, regardless of who fathered the child; all children born of non-Israelite mothers were not Israelites, regardless of who fathered the child. Pharaoh was targeting the wrong gender.

Pharaoh's daughter saved one baby boy from the slaughter (2:1-9). She "adopted him as her son and called him **Moses** [Hebrew, *moshe*]; for she said, 'I drew him out [Hebrew, *meshitihu*] of the water'" (2:10).[11] When Moses was a young man, he murdered an Egyptian who was "striking a Hebrew, one of his own kinsmen" (2:12). He skipped town, and eked out a living as a shepherd in the desert (2:15-22). One day, he was attracted by a burning bush that was not consumed by the flames (3:3). Things got stranger still when a voice began to talk to him from the bush.

God told Moses that he wanted him to "lead my people, the Israelites, out of Egypt" (3:10). When Moses asked whom he should say sent him, the voice answered, "This is what you shall tell the Israelites: **I AM** sent me to you. … The **Lord** the God of your fathers, the God of Abraham, the God of Isaac, the God of Jacob, has sent me to you."

… after this brief message from our Sponsor …

The **Name of God** revealed to Moses in Exodus 3:14 consists of four consonants:

---

[11] Many people argue that "Moses" may be derived from an Egyptian root, rather than from the Hebrew verb. I don't see a simple way to decide the issue one way or the other.

Reading *from right to left*, the four consonants are **transliterated** ("translated letter-for-letter") into English as "**yhwh**." When Greek became the common language of the Mediterranean world after **Alexander the Great** (died 323 BC), some people referred to the Divine Name as "the **Tetragrammaton**," which in Greek literally means "the Four Letters."

All of the ancient Hebrew texts were written solely in consonants. Vowels (a, e, i, o, u; sometimes y) were invented in other, later languages, such as Greek and Latin. People who knew Hebrew could figure out what vowels were needed to pronounce the words.

- Y cn d th sm thng wth nglsh, srt f, lthgh t s prtty dffclt t wrt nd rd.
- NdthHbrwsrgnllywrtwthnspcsbtwnwrds. Thtmdtvnmrdffclttrd!
- ndthyddnthvcptllttrsrpncttnswd[12]

The **Torah** (Hebrew, "law") forbids taking "the Name of the Lord" in vain (Ex 20:7). As a way of "building a fence around the Law," the Jews ceased to pronounce the original word. They substituted "Adonai," meaning "The Mighty One," instead. Some pious Jews won't even spell out the word "God"—instead they write "G-d." In modern editions of the Bible and in this book, when you see "L ORD" (notice that the small letters in the word are small capitals) in a verse, that means that the original Hebrew text contains the four sacred consonants of the divine name.

The Masoretic Text of the Hebrew Bible, which may date to as early as 600 AD, used "vowel points" sprinkled around the consonants to show readers how to pronounce the words correctly; the Jewish scribes did not feel authorized to separate the sacred consonants, which came from God, by inserting full-size vowels, which came from humans. When the Masoretes came to the Divine Name, they did not put in the correct vowels for "**yhwh**." Instead, they put in the vowels for **Adonai** (somewhat modified to match proper rules of spelling and pronunciation): e + o + a. In the 15th and 16th centuries, European Christian translators misunderstood this custom. They transliterated the consonants and vowel points as if they were from the same word:

(y + h + w + h) + (e + o + a) ==> ye + ho + wah

---

[12] I'm not going to put the translation down where you can read it out of the corner of your eye. Wrestle with the lines a bit, then turn to page 210 to see how well you did.

71

In one more quirk of linguistics, the "y" became "j" and the "w" became "v" in English, giving us the final monstrosity: **Jehovah**.

"Jehovah" is neither fish nor fowl. No sense can be given to it in Hebrew. The consonants are from one word, and the vowels from another. If I do the same with "Martin" and "Catherine", we get a nonsense word:

$$(m + r + t + n) + (a + e + i + e) \longrightarrow \text{Maretine}$$

Scholars suggest that the proper vocalization (insertion of vowels into the consonants) of the Divine Name is "**Yahweh.**" In deference to the customs of the Jews, I do not say this word aloud in class, nor do I encourage my students to do so. When the Jews are forced to write the Divine Name on temporary materials (say, for the celebration of Passover), the pages are marked with the warning, **"This page contains the Name of the Lord. It must be treated with the greatest reverence."** I am very unhappy with those Christian songwriters who have used the Divine Name in their compositions; to me, it seems disrespectful of the Jewish tradition of not saying the Name aloud. On June 29, 2008, the Vatican's Congregation for Divine Worship and the Discipline of the Sacraments ruled that the name of the Lord should not be pronounced in Catholic hymns or services.

"Yahweh" is the first person singular of the causative form of the verb "to be." It may be translated as **"I am the one who causes to be."** When the Jewish rabbis translated "yhwh" from Hebrew into Greek around three centuries BC (see p. 183), they chose "**ego eimi**" ("I am") as the best translation of the Divine Name. In the New Testament, then, when Jesus says of Himself, "I am," *He is identifying Himself as God* (Jn 8:28, 58); the fact that His audience wanted to execute him for committing the sin of blasphemy shows that they understood what He was saying about Himself. Another translation of the Divine Name favored by medieval philosophers like Thomas Aquinas is **"I am Who am."**

Christians have transferred all of the Jewish thinking about the Name of the Lord to the Name of Jesus:

> Therefore God has highly exalted Him and bestowed on Him *the Name which is above every name*, so that at the Name of Jesus every knee should bow, in heaven and on earth and under the earth, and every tongue confess to the glory of God the Father that Jesus Christ is Lord (Phil 2:9-11).

Many Christians apply the commandment about "the Name of the Lord" to "Jesus." The nuns taught me to bow my head when I say "Jesus." Like the Jews of old, many older Catholics are fearful of saying "Jesus" and instead call Him "Christ" or "the Lord" or "Our Savior," or some other respectful and loving title.

... by Calling on the Name of the Lord

When God revealed His personal name to Moses, it was a gift that allowed Moses to get in touch with God more deeply and personally than before. The same thing happens when one of us learns the name of a person we find attractive. Up until then, the two are strangers to each other. After exchanging names, the possibility of a deeper friendship comes into view. In more formal cultures than ours, introductions have to be made by third parties, and one would never presume to use familiar names until the courtship was well advanced.

In our culture, the exchange of personal information goes beyond just the name. We also need to know the person's telephone numbers, e-mail address, ICQ handle, and Facebook URL. For Moses, the Divine Name was all of these things—and more—rolled into one. God was inviting Moses to rely on Him when he returned to a country where he was wanted for murder, in order to help his people escape from the slave-masters. Moses could call on God directly and personally, because he was on a first-name basis with the Lord.

Acting in God's Name, Moses brought ten plagues upon Pharaoh and the Egyptians: Water turned into blood; frogs; gnats; flies; pestilence; boils; hail; locusts; darkness; and the death of the firstborn male (human and animal), of those who did not hear or heed Moses's instructions to mark their homes with the blood of a lamb (Ex 7-11). When the Angel of Death came to kill the firstborn males in the homes of Egyptians and of those Israelites who refused to obey Moses, it "passed over" the homes whose doors were properly marked. The night that the firstborn were saved by the blood of the lamb is celebrated every spring as Passover (Ex 12:1-20).

The Scriptures claim that *600,000* slaves followed Moses out of Egypt into the desert, along with "their livestock, very numerous flocks, and herds" (Ex 12:37). This is the kind of claim that modern archaeology is perfectly equipped to test, because that many people and animals would leave a huge swath of destruction and waste as they journeyed from Egypt eastward toward Canaan, the Promised Land. That many people would trample the earth with their feet, uproot whole forests for their campfires, and leave sewer pits that would still be detectable thousands of years later. Moreover, if Pharaoh had really lost that many slaves, one would expect some note to have been made in Egyptian records; it seems that it would be too large an event to leave unrecorded.

The absence of such archaeological and historical evidence suggests that the number given in the passage is **hyperbole** (a gross exaggeration). Biblical literalists have to imagine God sending angels following in the wake of His People, restoring the desert to a pristine state. All of the big parades have got folks like that who come along and clean up after the horses and elephants. Maybe God was equally interested in having nothing left behind to mark the path His people followed through the Wilderness. If you believe in a miracle-working God (and I do), then, in the abstract, there is no reason why God and his angelic hosts couldn't hide all evidence of the **Exodus** (Greek, *ex*, "out of" + *hodos*, "road" = "the road out," the escape). I prefer to think that God did not dictate historical details to the authors whom He inspired to tell the story of His love affair with His People. As far as I can tell, God allowed them to exaggerate the details of their history.

This is just our first encounter with the problem of **exegesis** (Greek, *ex*, "out of" + *hegeisthai*, "to lead out of" = "getting a meaning out of a text"); we will stumble over this problem many times before trying to come up with an adequate account of how to decide what ancient texts mean for us today (see page 147). For the moment, I merely note that my preference is to accept the difficulties that come from imagining a kind of inspiration that leaves human authors free to write in a human fashion, rather than the difficulties that come from imagining God sending pooper-scoopers behind His People on their **40-year journey** (Ex 16:35) toward the Promised Land.

Some **exegetes** (people who do exegesis, i.e., provide interpretations of the Scriptures) consider the story of the Great Escape from Egypt (Exodus) to be as fictional as the number 600,000 seems to be. My own bias is to think that there is nothing intrinsically absurd about the thought that a tribe might have entered Egypt, become enslaved, and then escaped from slavery long afterward. For me, the overwhelming evidence of the existence of Moses and some kind of heroic and inspired leadership of God's People on a lifelong pilgrimage is the existence of the Israelite religion and its descendants, Judaism, Christianity, and Islam. I am convinced that Moses existed, and is the person who inspired the Israelites' love of God's law (Torah). In my view, his role as the law-giver makes him the most important figure in the development of the Israelite religion—greater than any of the patriarchs (Abraham, Isaac, Jacob [Israel], the patriarchs of the 12 tribes), greater than any of the kings (David, Solomon, and their descendants), and greater than any of the other Israelite prophets (see page 96). The Book of Deuteronomy, which is traditionally attributed to Moses, also ranks him higher than any other prophets: "Since then no prophet has arisen in Israel like Moses, whom the LORD knew face to face. He had no equal in all the signs and wonders the LORD sent him to perform in the land of Egypt against Pharaoh and all his servants and against all his land, and for the might and the terrifying power that Moses exhibited in the sight of all Israel" (34:10-12).

The Covenant at Mount Sinai: Obey Torah!

The first meaning of the Hebrew word, **Torah**, is "teaching, instruction, law," but it can also be used to refer to the first five books of the Bible (Genesis, Exodus, Leviticus, Numbers, Deuteronomy), which are also known as **the Books of Moses** and the **Pentateuch** (Greek, *pente*, "five" + *teuchos*, "container" = "five books"). In this latter sense, Torah is one of the three divisions of the **Hebrew Scriptures**. The other two are Kethubim, "writings," and Nebi'im, "prophets." The acronym for the three parts of the Hebrew Scriptures is **TNK**; in time, this came to be vocalized (given vowels) as "Tanakh." That acronym was a lot easier to say than "tau nun kaph."

At the core of the Pentateuch is the story of Moses receiving the Torah directly from God on Mount Sinai; some rabbis in the Orthodox tradition calculate the year of this event as 1280 BC. In time, the material given to Moses in that theophany came to be known as the Ten Words (Hebrew; the Greek translation of the Hebrew phrase was **Decalogue**) or the **Ten Commandments** (Ex 34:28; Dt 10:4). A close examination of the two versions of what God told Moses to tell the People shows that some interpretation has to be done to get ten—and only ten—commandments out of the scriptural passages (Ex 20:1-17; Dt 5:6-21). Jews, most Protestants, and the Eastern Orthodox Christians have two commandments about the sovereignty of God, but only one commandment about coveting:

1. I am the Lord, your God (you shall not have *false gods before me*).
2. You shall make no graven images.
3. You shall not take the Name of the Lord, your God, in vain.
4. Keep holy the Lord's Day.
5. Honor your father and mother.
6. You shall not [*murder*].[13]
7. You shall not commit adultery.
8. You shall not steal.
9. You shall not bear false witness against your neighbor.
10. You shall not covet your neighbor's [spouse] or your neighbor's goods.

Lutherans and Catholics see a difference in two different kinds of coveting (lust vs. greed), and have just one commandment that expresses our commitment to **radical monotheism**—the belief that there is one, and only one, God in existence, and that no other being deserves to be called "god":

1. I am the Lord, your God; you shall not have false gods before me.
2. You shall not take the Name of the Lord, your God, in vain.
3. Keep holy the Lord's Day.
4. Honor your father and mother.
5. You shall not [*murder*].
6. You shall not commit adultery.

---

[13] The early translators of the Bible into English chose "kill" instead of the more accurate "murder." Murder is the deliberate and intentional taking of an innocent life; that is what the commandment prohibits. It cannot be taken to mean that capital punishment is outlawed, because the penalty for violating the commandment was death: "Whoever strikes a man a mortal blow must be put to death" (Ex 21:12). Objections to capital punishment must be based on other grounds than the faulty translation of this commandment as "You shall not kill."

7. You shall not steal.
8. You shall not bear false witness against your neighbor.
9. You shall not covet your neighbor's [spouse].
10. You shall not covet your neighbor's goods.

In *Civilization and Its Discontents*, Freud argued that **sublimation** is the foundation of civilization: "Sublimation of instinct is an especially conspicuous feature of cultural development; it is what makes it possible for higher psychological activities, scientific, artistic, or ideological, to play such an important part in civilized life."[14] We must resist our impulses to murder, rape, steal, and lie for the sake of society. The ethical core of the Ten Commandments (no murder, adultery, theft, or lying) is found in all of the civilizations of the world, because societies that tolerate such behavior quickly disintegrate. In *The Abolition of Man*, C. S. Lewis calls this common core of all religious traditions the Tao:

> The Chinese also speak of a great thing (the greatest thing) called the *Tao*. It is the reality beyond all predicates, the abyss that was before the Creator Himself. It is Nature, it is the Way, the Road. It is the Way in which the universe goes on, the Way in which things everlastingly emerge, stilly and tranquilly, into space and time. It is also the Way in which every man should tread in imitation of that cosmic and supercosmic progression, conforming all activities to that great exemplar.[15]

In the appendix of the book, Lewis gives examples from a variety of religions to show how all affirm "The Law of General Beneficence" (97), "The Law of Special Beneficence" (101), "Duties to Parents, Elders, Ancestors" (104), "Duties to Children and Posterity" (107), "The Law of Justice" (109), "The Law of Good Faith and Veracity" (112), "The Law of Mercy" (115), and "The Law of Magnanimity" (117).

The Ten Commandments (however they were counted) were only the beginning of God's instruction to His People through Moses. When the **rabbis** (Aramaic, "teachers") of a later age began a systematic study of the Books of Moses, they counted **613 commandments** ("mitzvot"). Taken together with the oral tradition that helped to define and explain them, the instructions define a complete way of life. Some of the principles include:

---

[14] Translated by James Strachey (New York: Norton, 1961), 84.

[15] *The Abolition of Man: Or Reflections on Education with Special Reference to the Teaching of English in the Upper Forms of Schools* (New York: Macmillan, 1955), 28; Lewis provides a reference to *The Encyclopedia of Religion and Ethics*, vol. ii, p. 454 B; iv. 12 B; 1x. 87 A.

- Circumcision of males as a sign of belonging to the Covenant. The ceremony is called "berith milah," the covenant of circumcision; you may hear it referred to as "brit" or "bris."
- Avoidance of non-**kosher** food (*kosher* means "according to the law," legal, acceptable). Most people know that pork is not kosher, but there are many other **unclean** foods as well.
- Separation of meat meals from dairy meals. This developed into the tradition of having a completely separate set of dishes and two different sinks for washing them.
- An annual cycle of holy days:
- **Sabbath** observance. Saturday is the "day of rest," the "Lord's Day" mentioned in the Ten Commandments. In TNK, one day ends and another begins after sundown, when three stars are visible in a clear sky. Expressed in our pagan terminology, the Sabbath begins on Friday evening and concludes on Saturday evening.
  - **Rosh Hashanah**: "head of the year" = New Year's Day (autumn)
  - **Sukkot**: Feast of Booths (autumn harvest festival)
  - **Yom Kippur**: "Day of Atonement" (10 days after Rosh Hashanah)
  - **Hanukkah**: Festival of Lights (winter)
  - **Passover**: spring celebration of the Exodus from Egypt
  - **Pentecost**: 50 days after Passover; celebrates the giving of the Torah to Moses on Mount Sinai.

Note that only one of these holy days involves fasting and penitence (Yom Kippur). There is a time of "unleavened bread" after Passover, but most of the liturgical year is concerned with remembrance of and thanksgiving for God's kindnesses.

Pious legend, both in Judaism and Christianity, holds that Moses was the author of the whole Torah, including those parts of the Pentateuch that recount his death and that deal with ritual observances in the Temple in Jerusalem, which was not constructed until two or three centuries after the Exodus. What seems more likely is that many people contributed to the growth and development of the Torah after Moses set the process in motion. The Israelites felt privileged to know the Torah, and celebrated it in the feast of Pentecost and in many passages in TNK, especially in Ps 19 and Ps 119: "The law of the LORD is perfect, refreshing the soul; the decree of the LORD is trustworthy, giving wisdom to the simple" (Ps 19:8).

With so many mitzvot to observe, many rabbis asked what was the most important of them all. The consensus was that this was the greatest of the commandments:

Hear, O Israel! The LORD is our God, the LORD alone!
Therefore, you shall love the LORD, your God, with all your heart, and with all your soul, and with all your strength. Take to heart these words which I enjoin on you today. Drill them into your children. Speak of them at home and abroad, whether you are busy or

at rest. Bind them at your wrist as a sign and let them be as a pendant on your forehead. Write them on the doorposts of your houses and on your gates. (Dt 6:4-9)

The name of the first verse above is the **Shema**. It is the first word in Hebrew in the verse and means "hear, listen": *Shema Yisrael: Yhwh Elohenu, Yhwh ehad!*[16] There is some evidence from TNK itself that the original meaning of this fundamental slogan or creed may not have been truly **monotheistic.** To say that the Lord is "our God … alone" leaves open the question of whether the gods and goddesses worshipped by other nations exist. When I say that the Buffalo Bills are "my team, my team alone," I am not denying the existence of other NFL teams. Far from it. For me to root for my team, there must be other teams for them to compete against.

The four Hebrew words in the Shema are compatible with a polytheistic interpretation: "The Lord is *our* God; *we* don't associate with any of the other gods and goddesses." This may be how the original Israelites understood the verse. It may have taken as many as eight centuries from the time of Moses for the Chosen People to understand and accept that their covenant partner was not just one God among many, but the one—and *only*—God. The later interpretation is **radical monotheism,** which is held in common by the three descendants of the Israelite tradition: Judaism, Christianity, and Islam. This is to be distinguished, both from the kind of attachment to one god out of many (known as *henotheism*), or from the kind of "monotheism" found in Nirguna Hinduism (*pantheistic monotheism*: there is only one divine reality, and everything else is part of that same reality).

The Covenant on Mount Sinai is not a replacement of God's Covenant with Abraham, but a development within the covenant tradition.

> If you hearken to my voice and keep my covenant, you shall be my special possession, dearer to me than all other people, though all the earth is mine. You shall be to me a kingdom of priests, a holy nation. This is what you must tell the Israelites.
> So Moses went and summoned the elders of the people. When he set before them all that the Lord had ordered him to tell them, the people all answered together, "Everything that the Lord has said, we will do." (Ex 19:5-8)

Keeping all of the injunctions of the Torah is an inward continuation of the same journey that began when Abraham agreed to leave his homeland and follow God.

---

[16] If you ever hear a pious Jew say this verse, he or she will substitute "Adonai," the Mighty One, for the sacred Name of God. In the pronunciation influenced by Yiddish, the word may come out sounding more like "Adenoi."

The Judges: Charismatic Superheroes (~1200–1047 BC)

Moses, the great friend of God, the one who knew Him on a first-name basis and met with Him face to face (Ex 33:11, Dt 34:10), the one through whom God gave his People the Torah, offended God in the desert, was not allowed to enter the Promised Land himself: "Because you were not faithful to me in showing forth my sanctity before the Israelites, you shall not lead the community into the land I will give them" (Num 20:12). Moses was only allowed to look at Canaan from the mountain, on which he died (Dt 32:48-52). The leadership of God's People passed to Joshua through the laying on of hands (Dt 34:9); he was the first of the charismatic (Greek, *charisma*, "gift" = "gifted") leaders raised up by God over the next two centuries who helped to conquer the tribes living in Canaan.

Joshua is famous for the Battle of Jericho (Josh 6), because of the folk song that tells how "the walls come a-tumblin' down" (6:20). All that the Israelites did to win the battle was march around the city for six days; then they raised a mighty shout on the seventh (6:15-16). The song does not go into the subsequent details. "They observed the ban by putting to the sword all living creatures in the city: men and women, young and old, as well as oxen, sheep, and asses" (6:21). Such complete massacres of defeated populations are typical of the stories in the Hebrew Scriptures. We can't rescue these stories by saying that "a story doesn't have to be true to be true." In all likelihood, the stories of genocide *are* factual. This was the ideal of conquest for the People of God at that time in their history—an ideal most probably shared by other tribes and nations of that day. The need to destroy every member of a man's family was rooted in the conviction that the life of the man was in his children; he was not dead until they, too, were dead.

This is horrible.

It is bad enough that the Scriptures describe such murderous hostility with enthusiasm; it is worse that they portray God as *demanding* the annihilation of their enemies and punishing His People when they fail to carry out His orders to kill every living being (Josh 7:1). I wish that stories like this were not in the Scriptures that I call "sacred." Apart from the evil done to the victims, this is the kind of thing that gives religion a bad name.

In our day, we do not think that racism, genocide, and ethnic cleansing could ever be positively willed by God. So far as I can tell, there is no dogma in the Catholic tradition about how to interpret these events. I see two broad kinds of defense that might be made of these passages in the Scriptures.

1. We might argue, as Krishna does in the *Bhagavad-Gita*, that it is in God's power to end the lives of whomever He wishes. If God says, "Kill them all," it is our job to kill them all. We are simply returning the lives of our enemies to the One who created them; after that, they're His problem, not ours. I don't like imagining that God could be so savage, but this is the natural and straightforward reading of the passages. God said to do it, so they did.

2. We might imagine that the People of God attributed their own bloodthirstiness to God, and wrongly claimed divine permission for their murderous impulses. This gets God off the hook at the expense of introducing a whole series of questions about the right way of reading the Scriptures. I much prefer this set of difficulties to those inherent in the first approach.

I read the book of Jonah as the beginning of a scriptural condemnation of racism. The book is, in my view, not about God's miracle-working power. I don't believe the story ever happened—I don't think Jonah existed, and therefore, I don't think he ever spent three days in the belly of a big fish (2:1). In my view, the whole point of the Parable of the Apoplectic Prophet is to show that Jonah's hatred of his foes is ridiculous. God *cares* for those whom He has created (4:10-11), even if they are the enemies of His Chosen People. Something was going on in the development of the scriptural tradition in the writing of the book of Jonah; it is in the same *collection of Scriptures* as Joshua, Judges, and Kings, but it is not in the same *worldview*. From the Christian standpoint, recognizing that God cares for all of His children, even if they are our enemies, is a big step forward, heading in the direction of Jesus' command to "love your enemies and pray for those who persecute you" (Mt 5:44).

The **judges** in the book of Judges are: Othniel (3:7-11), Ehud (3:12-30), Shamgar (3:31), Deborah and Barak (4:1-5:31), Gideon (6:1-8:32), Tola and Jair (8:33-10:5), Jephthah (10:6-12:7), Ibzan, Elon, and Abdon (12:8-15), and Samson (13:1-16:31). Some also count Ruth as one of the judges, because her story takes place "in the time of the judges" (Ruth 1:1), although her story does not fit the pattern of Heaven-sent wonder workers who come to the aid of God's people when they are in need; instead, it is a love story that tells how Ruth came to be one of King David's great-grandmothers.

Samson is probably the best-known of the 13 judges. He, like Isaac, was a miracle baby, an answer to prayer. In gratitude for conceiving him, his mother agreed to an angel's request that "no razor shall touch his head, for this boy is to be consecrated to God from the womb. It is he who will begin the deliverance of Israel from the power of the **Philistines**" (13:5).[17] Samson's uncut hair was a symbol of his relationship to God. When Samson revealed this secret to Delilah (16:17), which led to his first haircut (16:19), it was a symbol of him breaking his relationship with God. After his eyes were gouged out, his hair began to grow again (16:21-23). With his relationship to God restored, he then had the strength to topple a temple full of Philistines, killing them and himself (16:28-30).

---

[17] As noted in the discussion of the Divine Name (see page 71), it is the consonants that are the foundations of words and the chief carriers of meaning in the Semitic languages. The consonants in "Philistine" (PLSTN) took on a different set of vowels over time, and became "**Palestine**," which, in turn gives us "**Palestinian**" as the word for those who live in that territory. Modern Palestinians are ethnically Arab, so they are not genetically related to the Philistines—but they bear the same name as Israel's historic enemies.

As a general rule, people like to hear stories about heroes who overcome great odds and pay back their enemies in full. This is the plot line of dozens—if not hundreds—of plays, novels, movies, and songs (*Rambo, Die Hard, Lethal Weapon, Mad Max, Star Wars*, etc., etc.). The Samson story is full of memorable details, and as far as I can tell, is still a best seller among a certain segment of our population; I have seen Samson dolls that are sold as action figures for little boys. It wasn't until after 9/11 that I realized that he is a suicide murderer and a model for all terrorists who use this tactic. For me, it is another blemish in the ancient Scriptures for them to praise him so highly: "Those he killed at his death were more than those he had killed during his lifetime" (16:30).

King Saul: The Mad Messiah or the Crazy Christ (1050-1010 BC)[18]

Samuel—the third miracle baby so far in our story, for those keeping score at home (1 Sam 1:9-18)—like Samson, was dedicated to the LORD by his mother while he was still in her womb (1 Sam 1:22). Samson's gift was prowess as a warrior; Samuel was a **prophet**, a person called by God to speak and act on His behalf (see page 96). This gift of understanding and speaking for the LORD was interwoven with his role as a judge: "Samuel judged Israel as long as he lived" (7:15). He appointed his sons to be judges after him, but they lacked his integrity (8:1-3). "Therefore all the elders of Israel came in a body to Samuel at Ramah and said to him, 'Now that you are old, and your sons do not follow your example, appoint a king over us, as other nations have, to judge us'" (8:4-5).

The Israelites were tired of the chaos they had experienced during the time of the judges. They were vulnerable to the great nations that surrounded them: Egypt, Assyria (Syria), Lebanon, Babylon (Iraq), Persia (Iran). They wanted a leader who could raise an army and make their nation strong enough to defend its wealth from foreign invaders and to keep peace in the land.

Up to this point, God had been the only King of Israel:

> The LORD is king, in splendor robed;
> robed is the LORD and girt about with strength;
> And he has made the world firm, not to be moved.
> Your throne stands firm from of old;
> from everlasting you are, O LORD. (Ps 93:1-2)

---

[18] With the history of the kings of Israel and Judea, we are passing from the misty past where events can only be very loosely dated to the beginning of the kind of chronology obtainable in modern history. The dates for Saul, David, and Solomon are disputed, but all of the suggested dates are within four or five years of each other. The dates that I give here and elsewhere are sufficiently accurate for our purposes; arguing about the evidence for and against alternative dates is a topic for advanced students to pursue in their later research.

God gave Samuel permission to appoint a king, but told him to warn the people about all of the evils that would come as a consequence:

> The rights of the king who will rule you will be as follows: He will take your sons and assign them to his chariots and horses, and they will run before his chariot. He will also appoint from among them his commanders of groups of a thousand and of a hundred soldiers. He will set them to do his plowing and his harvesting, and to make his implements of war and the equipment of his chariots. He will use your daughters as ointment-makers, as cooks, and as bakers. He will take the best of your fields, vineyards, and olive groves, and give them to his officials. He will tithe your crops and your vineyards, and give the revenue to his eunuchs and his slaves. He will take your male and female servants, as well as your best oxen and your asses, and use them to do his work. He will tithe your flocks and you yourselves will become his slaves. When this takes place, you will complain against the king whom you have chosen, but on that day the Lord will not answer you."
>
> The people, however, refused to listen to Samuel's warning and said, "Not so! There must be a king over us. We too must be like other nations, with a king to rule us and to lead us in warfare and fight our battles." When Samuel had listened to all the people had to say, he repeated it to the Lord, who then said to him, "Grant their request and appoint a king to rule them." (1 Sam 8:11-18)

We will need to reconsider this passage in the next section about the War between the Messiahs (page 8383). For the moment, let us merely observe that we have a story very much like that of *The Monkey's Paw*. The Lord granted His People what they have asked for, but they did not get what they expected.

Anointing: The Great Symbol of Kingship

The prophet took a flask of oil and poured it over the head of Saul, saying: "The Lord anoints you commander over his heritage. You are to govern the Lord's people Israel, and to save them from the grasp of their enemies roundabout" (1 Sam 10:1). The Hebrew word for "the person who has been anointed" is transliterated as **Messiah**. When the rabbis translated TNK into Greek, they used the word *Christos*, which is based on *chrismos*, "oil." This, of course, has become **Christ** in English. Please note well: *what the Israelites meant by "Messiah" or "Christ" was "a person who was anointed" or "anointed one."* Christians have overloaded the term with a multitude of other meanings that have nothing to do with the original Hebrew word or its Greek equivalent (see p. 115). For the 12 tribes of Israel and the sole remaining tribe, the Jews, an "anointed one" was a human being who served as king or high priest; the Messiah (Christ) would get married, have children, serve the people in office, and then die, making room for one of his descendants to become the Messiah (the Christ).

Because he was *anointed* by God to be King, Saul was *the Messiah* or, if we are speaking Greek, *the Christ*. This anointing was the dominant image or symbol of kingship for the Israelites. In our culture, our chief symbol for kingship is the crown. People sometimes speak about "the crowned heads of Europe" (i.e., the kings and queens) or the actions of "the crown." We call the installation of a king or queen their "coronation," from the Latin word, *corona*, "crown": A coronation is the ceremony in which a king or queen is crowned. Crowns were also used by the kings of Israel and of Judah, among many other symbols of royalty (the best clothes, the best chair, the best house, a big stick, royal processions, jewels, fine feasts, etc.), but being anointed was more important than any of these other signs of power and prestige.

Hebrew has a separate word for king, *melech*, as does Greek—*basileus* (from which we get "basilica," a king's house). Not all Messiahs in Israel were kings. The high priest in the Temple (a much later development) was also anointed, and therefore, could be called a Messiah or a Christ. Although the term was not restricted to monarchs, when dealing with the story of the kings of Israel and of Judah, we need to remember that they were *all* Messiahs (Christs). This will help us later on to understand why most Jews have judged that Jesus is *not* "the Christ" (see page 107).

War between the Messiahs: Christ Saul vs. Christ David (~1010 BC)

Saul offended God by failing to kill all living beings in the city of Amalek. "He took Agag, king of Amalek, alive, but on the rest of the people he put into effect the ban of destruction by the sword. He and his troops spared Agag and the best of the fat sheep and oxen, and the lambs. They refused to carry out the doom on anything that was worthwhile, dooming only what was worthless and of no account" (15:8-9). Saul argued with Samuel that he and his men were only moving the plunder elsewhere to offer to "sacrifice to the LORD their God in Gilgal" (15:21). But God was offended by Saul's disobedience. "The LORD regretted having made him king of Israel" (15:34). First he sent Samuel to anoint David, making him a Messiah or Christ (16:13). Then "The spirit of the LORD ... departed from Saul, and he was tormented by an evil spirit sent by the LORD" (16:14).

Some cynics say, "history is written by the victors." Whether or not that is a good guide to historiography (the theory of how history is written and read), it is undoubtedly true that many of the Israelite Scriptures (as we have them now) were produced in the court of King David and his successors. They *had* to tell the story of the war between David the Christ, and Saul the Christ, in such a way that David's victory over Saul was understood to be perfectly fair and authorized by God. At the same time, they needed to guard David and his heirs from other families who might think that *they* had been chosen to do unto David what he had done unto Saul.

We have already seen one passage above where the author(s) of the first book of Samuel laid the theological groundwork for the repudiation of Saul (8:11-18)—the people offended the Lord by asking for a human king to take His place. Our Scriptures add many other considerations to the case against Christ Saul: disobedience of God (15:10, 28:18), jealousy of David (18:8), murderous rage (18:10, 19:1-2, 22:18), admission of unworthiness to be king (24:17-22, 26:17-25), cowardice (28:5), necromancy (consulting the spirits of the dead; 28:8-19), and suicide (31:5). David, by contrast, is portrayed as handsome (16:12), favored by God (16:13), talented musically (16:21-23), successful in battle (especially against the giant Philistine, Goliath, 17:32-51; 18:7—everybody knows the story of David and Goliath!), a faithful friend (18:1, 20:17, 20:42; 2 Sam 1:26), compassionate to the Lord's anointed (Messiah, Christ; 24:11, 26:8-12), generous (30:26), and righteously angry at those who would dare to harm the anointed king of Israel (2 Sam 1:14-16).

There is no scientific reason why these stories can't be true. Perhaps Saul was as bad and David was as good as all that. But the suspicion remains that the scribes employed in the court of the king may have been inspired by something other than the Holy Spirit to spin the tale of the two Christs to the advantage of *their* employer, Christ David.

God's Covenant with David, the Christ, the King (1010–970 BC)

Once the old Christ was safely dead and gone, along with his son and heir, Jonathan (2 Sam 1:17-27), David was able to consolidate his reign over his tribe, Judah, and eventually over the other 11 tribes of Israel. Somewhere along the line, God decided that having a human king wasn't such a bad idea after all, and decided to endorse David's reign. He takes credit for David's successes: "I myself have set up my king on **Zion**, my holy mountain" (Ps 2:6).[19] He speaks of the king as His own son, and promises to fight on the behalf of the king in battle:

I will proclaim the decree of the Lord:
The Lord said to me, "You are my son;
this day I have begotten you.
Ask of me and I will give you the nations for an inheritance
and the ends of the earth for your possession.
You shall rule them with an iron rod;
you shall shatter them like an earthen dish. (Ps 2:6-9)

---

[19] Zion was a hilltop within Jerusalem; that part of the city came to stand for the whole city, and the city came to stand for the whole of the Holy Land. In 1898, Theodor Herzl chose to use the term "Zionism" to designate his dream of restoring the People of God to the Holy Land. The present hilltop, which has been called "Mount Zion" since the first century AD, is almost certainly not the original high place denoted in the Old Testament.

If God said to the king, "You are my son," then it is logical to call the king the "son of God." That the king is the son of God is asserted in Psalm 89:27 as well: "He shall say of me, 'You are my father, my God, the Rock, my savior.'" Since God plans to fight on the side of the king of Israel, that means that the king will eventually conquer all the kingdoms of the earth: "I will make him firstborn, highest of the kings of the earth" (Ps 89:28). The Hebrew method of expressing superlatives is to say, "_____ of _____." The greatest football team would be the "team *of* teams." The greatest song would be the "song *of* songs." The "highest of the kings of the earth" is the "King *of* Kings." If you have ever heard Handel's "Messiah" sung around Christmastime, you know what a resounding tone of victory can be given to this phrase. "King of Kings! Hallelujah! Hallelujah! And Lord of Lords! Hallelujah! Hallelujah!"

God apparently was so enchanted with his anointed son, David, that He decided to extend his contract. And it was no dinky little six- or ten-year extension, or even a lifetime arrangement. God promised that His Covenant with David would last *forever* (Ps 89:2-5, 29-30, 37-38): "I will make your dynasty stand forever and establish your throne through all ages" (v. 5). This promise was independent of the behavior of David's descendants:

If his descendants forsake my law, do not follow my decrees,
If they fail to observe my statutes, do not keep my commandments,
I will punish their crime with a rod and their guilt with lashes.
But I will not take my love from him, nor will I betray my bond of loyalty.
I will not violate my covenant; the promise of my lips I will not alter.
By my holiness I swore once for all: I will never be false to David.
His dynasty will continue forever, his throne, like the sun before me.
Like the moon it will stand eternal, forever firm like the sky! (Ps 89:31-38)

We know now that neither the sun nor the moon are eternal. Science tells us that they came into being, and are doomed to die in another four or five billion years or so. But even if we pass over that scientifically false assertion in the psalm, we're still left with a more difficult problem: the sun and the moon are still in the heavens, just as they were in David's day three thousand years ago—as we shall see on page 89 *there is no longer a king in Israel and there hasn't been a king in Israel for about 2,600 years!*

Christ David: the Murderous Messiah (1010-970 BC)

Despite God's extravagant love for him, David was not a thoroughly admirable man. He stayed home one war season, hanging around the palace he'd built for himself, while his troops "ravaged the Ammonites and besieged Rabbah" (2 Sam 11:1-2). These were the days before air conditioning was perfected, and David went out on the roof of the palace to get some fresh air. They were also the days before indoor plumbing was developed, and he happened to see a beautiful woman taking a bath on the roof of her house. David liked what he saw. He sent for her. They did what comes naturally. And, as often happens, she became pregnant as a result (11:2-5).

Bathsheba knew that she was as good as dead. Her husband, Uriah the Hittite, was a hired gun fighting for David at Rabbah. She knew that he would figure out that he wasn't the father of the baby. David brought Uriah home from the front lines and tried to trick him into spending some quality time with his wife, but the plan failed (11:6-13). Although Uriah was not Jewish, he nevertheless was keeping the Torah, which prohibits Jewish soldiers from having sex on the eve of a battle. *Uriah the Hittite kept the Torah better than David the Messiah!* As Bathsheba's husband and as a foreigner, he was not obliged to obey the Torah; it would have been perfectly acceptable for him to have intercourse with his wife. David had a solemn commitment with God to obey the Torah, however; he had no right at all to sleep with another man's wife—especially while that man was risking his life on behalf of David in battle!

When David realized that he could not trick Uriah into thinking he was the father of Bathsheba's baby, he sent Uriah back to the regiment with sealed orders that read, "Place Uriah up front where the fighting is fierce. Then pull back and leave him to be struck down dead" (11:15). Uriah faithfully delivered his death warrant to his commander, and was soon lying dead on the battle field as planned (11:17). Bathsheba moved into the palace, became part of David's harem, and bore him a son (11:27).

God allegedly got rid of Christ Saul because he failed to kill all of the people and animals that God told him to kill. One might think that God would be angry at David for not keeping the Torah. The penalty for adultery and murder was death. When Nathan the prophet confronted David with his evildoing (12:1-8), David repented of his sins, and was spared execution (12:13-14). Instead of killing David, as the Torah demanded, God made his little baby suffer for a week before he finally killed him on the seventh day (12:15-18). Afterward, David and Bathsheba did more of what comes naturally, leading to the birth of Solomon, who, as we have already noted, became the Christ, the king, after David.

Some of the lines God writes straight with are more crooked than others.

Christ Solomon's Wisdom, Temple, Harem, and Sins (970-930 BC)

Solomon was not David's firstborn son. Far from it! David's first son raped his half sister, Tamar (2 Sam 13:14). David failed to punish his son (13:21). Absalom, the full brother of Tamar, murdered his brother (13:28-29), and then waged war against his father (15:1-19:15). Adonijah, Absalom and Tamar's brother, was next in line. He was so sure that he would be made king that he started acting like a king (1 Kings 1:5-10). Bathsheba persuaded David to have Solomon anointed (christened) as king (1:45). One of Christ Solomon's first acts was to have his half brother, Adonijah, murdered (2:25), along with Joab, who had been David's chief henchman (it was Joab who arranged Uriah's death) and who had backed Adonijah's campaign to become king (2:34). Solomon put another coconspirator of theirs under house arrest, and completed the trifecta a few years later when the man left the grounds of his house to chase two runaway slaves, thus giving Solomon the opportunity to have him killed, too (2:42-46).

The authors of the Scriptures say that "Solomon loved the Lord." There was no official place of worship for Israel, so he would go to the mountaintops that were natural "temples," so to speak. On one such pilgrimage, he offered a thousand animals as holocausts to the Lord (2 Kings 3:4). The Lord was pleased with the offering, and gave Solomon one wish: "Ask something of me and I will give it to you" (3:5). Solomon asked for wisdom, the gift that gives all other gifts: "Give your servant … an understanding heart to judge your people and to distinguish right from wrong" (3:9). God was pleased with Solomon's request, and added wealth, power, and length of days to go along with the gift: "I give you what you have not asked for, such riches and glory that amongst kings there is not your like. And if you follow me by keeping my statutes and commandments, as your father David did, I will give you a long life" (3:13-14).

Solomon now decided to build a temple in Jerusalem for the Lord (2 Kings 5:17-20).

> I intend to build a house for the honor of the LORD, my God, and to consecrate it to him, for the burning of fragrant incense in his presence, for the perpetual display of the showbread, for holocausts morning and evening, and for the sabbaths, new moons, and festivals of the LORD, our God: such is Israel's perpetual obligation. And the house I intend to build must be large, for *our God is greater than all other gods*. (2 Chron 2:3-4; emphasis added)

Notice that Solomon was not a thoroughgoing monotheist; his infidelity to the God of Israel was to be the downfall of his kingdom. "Our God is greater than all other gods"—but in Solomon's worldview, other gods and goddesses also existed.

Solomon's Temple was constructed on Mount Moriah, a rocky crest in Jerusalem. The innermost part of the Temple was the holy of holies (or, to translate the Hebrew expression fully into English, "the holiest place") where the Ark ("carrying case") of the Covenant was kept; inside the Ark were "the two stone tablets which Moses had put there at Horeb, when the Lord made a covenant with the Israelites at their departure [*exodus*] from the land of Egypt" (2 Kings 8:9). According to Genesis, the rock at the peak of Mount Moriah was where Abraham bound Isaac and prepared to slay him in sacrifice (Gen 22:2).

The primary function of the Temple was to provide a central location for killing and burning animals in sacrifice to the Lord. On opening day, "King Solomon and the entire community of Israel present for the occasion sacrificed before the ark sheep and oxen too many to number or count" (2 Kings 8:5). Solomon reminded the LORD of the terms of the contract He had made with Solomon's father, linking the covenant made on Mount Sinai to the covenant with David:

> "And now the LORD has fulfilled the promise that he made: I have succeeded my father David and sit on the throne of Israel, as the LORD foretold, and I have built this temple to honor the LORD, the God of Israel. I have provided in it a place for the ark in which is the covenant of the LORD, which he made with our fathers when he brought them out of the land of Egypt." Solomon stood before the altar of the LORD in the presence of the whole community of Israel, and stretching forth his hands toward heaven, he said, "LORD, God of Israel, there is no God like you in heaven above or on earth below; you keep your covenant of kindness with your servants who are faithful to you with their whole heart. You have kept the promise you made to my father David, your servant. You who spoke that promise, have this day, by your own power, brought it to fulfillment. Now, therefore, LORD, God of Israel, keep the further promise you made to my father David, your servant, saying, 'You shall always have someone from your line to sit before me on the throne of Israel, provided only that your descendants look to their conduct so that they live in my presence, as you have lived in my presence.' Now, LORD, God of Israel, may this promise which you made to my father David, your servant, be confirmed." (8:20-26)

Although Solomon knew perfectly well that the descendants of David were supposed to "look to their conduct" as their part in the covenant, he slowly drifted away from the principle that the Israelites were wedded to one and only one God. He was something of a ladies' man, and his tastes in wives and sex-slaves were highly diverse. "King Solomon loved many foreign women besides the daughter of Pharaoh (Moabites, Ammonites, Edomites, Sidonians, and Hittites), from nations with which the LORD had forbidden the Israelites to intermarry, 'because,' he said, 'they will turn your hearts to their gods.' But Solomon fell in love with them. He had seven hundred wives of royal rank and three hundred concubines, and his wives turned his heart. ... By adoring Astarte, the goddess of the Sidonians, and Milcom, the idol of the Ammonites, Solomon did evil in the sight of the LORD" (1 Kings 11:1-3). He started building places of worship on other mountains for the gods and goddesses worshipped by the members of his harem (11:7-10).

It was not wise for Solomon to offend the LORD this way. The authors of this account do not seem to have the clarity of later texts in the Scriptures, that the gods and goddess of other nations were nonexistent. Their criticism of Solomon was that he should have kept his part of the bargain that God made with David and his heirs, which meant that he should have worshipped the LORD alone. God was angry with Solomon, but not angry enough to have him killed straightaway. The punishment for his sin was the breakup of the kingdom.

The Death of the Kingdom and the Kingship (1010–586 BC)

The united kingdom consisting of all 12 tribes of Israel only lasted until the death of **Solomon**, who became the Christ, the king, after David's death, and reigned for 40 years (970-930 BC). The kingdom was then split into two kingdoms: **Israel** consisted of ten tribes in the north, and **Judah** was the kingdom of the two tribes in the south.

Israel was obliterated by the Assyrians in 721 BC. The Scriptures written, collected, and edited by members of the court of the southern kingdom, Judah, contain many prophetic denunciations of the northern kingdom. There may even be a certain *schadenfreude*, a German word meaning "taking pleasure in the suffering of others," because, in the view of the southern kingdom, the northern kingdom got exactly what it deserved. And then **the Babylonians came along in 586 BC and destroyed Judah!** Since then, there have been no more Messiahs on the throne of David ruling over the house of Israel. So much for God's promises! It seems that they weren't worth the parchment that they were written on.

From one standpoint, a contract that lasts four hundred years is a pretty good contract. The Magna Carta (1215 AD, amended 1297 AD) is still on the books eight centuries later. Our U.S. Constitution has continued in force for over two centuries. But there is a huge difference between four centuries and *forever*. It is not a problem with the Hebrew translation. It is a theological issue: *Did God lie to David?*

The Case of the Missing Messiah (586 BC)

The author of Psalm 89 knew that God's contract with David was unfulfilled. After laying out all of the terms of the covenant (89:1-38), the psalmist sums up his frustration and bewilderment about what had happened to the Chosen People in the **Babylonian Captivity**, which is also known as the **Exile** (586 BC).

> But now *you* have rejected and spurned, been enraged *at your anointed*.
> *You* renounced the covenant with your servant, defiled his crown in the dust.
> *You* broke down all his defenses, left his strongholds in ruins.
> All who pass through seize plunder; his neighbors deride him.
> *You* have exalted the right hand of his foes, have gladdened all his enemies.
> *You* turned back his sharp sword, did not support him in battle.
> *You* brought to an end his splendor, hurled his throne to the ground.
> *You* cut short the days of his youth, covered him with shame. (89:39-46; emphasis added)

The psalmist is talking to the LORD; it is *He* who has broken His Covenant with His Messiah (the Christ, the anointed one). The LORD had promised not to let anything interrupt the line of

Kings descended from David: "Once, by my holiness, I have sworn; I will not be false to David. His posterity shall continue forever" (89:37). The psalmist knew perfectly well that after 420 years, the line of Messiahs (Christs) that began with David had come to a shameful, ignominious end. He seems to have had an intuition that God would not allow His promises to remain unfulfilled: "How long, O LORD? Will you hide yourself forever?" (89:47).

The claim that Jesus is *the* Messiah, *the* Christ promised by Psalm 89 is so central to the religion that grew up around Him that it became the root of the name of that religion—Christianity. We will return to this observation in the chapter on Christianity (see p. 81). For those Jews who do not think that Jesus is *the* Christ, *the* King, the problem remains: Is God going to fulfill His contract or not?

Ever since the Babylonian Captivity, Jews have wrestled with this question. They have given different answers. In the **post-exilic** Passover ritual, a place is traditionally left empty at the table for Elijah. This wild prophet had been taken up into Heaven in a burning, fiery chariot (2 Kings 2:11), so the Jews reasoned that God could send him back to earth to anoint the king who would restore the house of David. This is the most natural and straightforward approach to the broken contract. God promised that a descendant of David would always be seated on the throne of Israel; God is not a liar; God will therefore fulfill His promise in due time. Messiah will come, the kingdom and the Temple will be rebuilt, and the king of Israel will be the King of Kings, the ruler over all rulers of the world.

Opinions differ among those who expect that Messiah will return; some think that the king will live and die as Christ David and Christ Solomon did, passing on the kingship to one of his sons, while others think that the return of the Messiah will coincide with the end of the world. Jewish **apocalyptic literature** is one of the latest developments in their tradition, inspired in large measure by being conquered by the Greeks, and then the Romans. Some of the apocalyptic material was taken into TNK and LXX (e.g., Daniel 7-12); the Dead Sea Scrolls found at Qumran (1947-1979 AD) show how popular this literary **genre** (French, "kind of writing") was among the Jews during the last few centuries BC and the first century AD.

As a general rule, Religious Studies scholars classify predictions about what will happen at the end of time as **apocalyptic**. The Greek word *apokalypsis* meant "the lifting of the veil" or "revelation." By telling us what the future holds in store, God provides **revelation** of future events that are ordinarily hidden from view. In the Abrahamic religions (Judaism, Christianity, and Islam) apocalyptic literature forecasts the destruction of God's enemies and the triumph of His people.

Not all Jews share these **messianic expectations**. Some have said that the image of the all-conquering Messiah is merely a symbol of the hope that God will triumph over His enemies at the end of time. On this view, there is no need to be watchful for the return of Elijah to anoint some human being to rule as king in Israel. Some, perhaps, may interpret the reestablishment of a nation of Israel in 1948 (see page 172) as the fulfillment of the psalmist's hopes; the kingdom itself, in this view, would take the place of the king. Some react to Christians harping on this question by saying that they really don't much care about the broken Covenant or the missing Messiah; for them, there are more important things about their religion and history that concern them.

"Remember Jerusalem": The Spirituality of the Exile (586–537 BC)

One might argue that the Chosen People would have been perfectly justified in thinking that their God wasn't faithful to them, and that therefore, they needn't be faithful to Him. Some of the people taken into exile in Babylon may well have lost faith in the LORD for not honoring His contracts with Abraham and David. Not all did. Psalm 137 records the deep grief that the Jews experienced in their time of slavery in Babylon (137:1-4). They could not obey the Torah without the Temple in Jerusalem. All that they could do was to remember the good times that they had enjoyed in the past, and hope for better times ahead. The psalmist asked God to make his right hand wither and his tongue stick to the roof of his mouth if he should ever forget Jerusalem (137:5-6). The slaves dreamed of paying the Babylonians back for all of their suffering; they hoped and prayed for the destruction of the whole of Babylon, down to the last Babylonian baby (137:8-9).

The fidelity of the captive people to their God is praiseworthy. Their genocidal hatred of their masters, though understandable, is not praiseworthy.

Restoration of the Temple (537–515 BC)

In 537 BC, King Cyrus of Persia (now Iran) conquered Babylon (present-day Iraq). To rub salt in the wounds of his enemies and to weaken them, Cyrus granted permission for the slaves of the Babylonians to return to their native lands (Ez 1:1-4). This was such a remarkable and unexpected turn of events that Isaiah calls Cyrus a Messiah of the LORD (45:1)![20] Construction of a new Temple was begun in 535 BC, and eventually completed after several interruptions in 515 BC.

Not everyone in Judah was taken into exile. The Babylonians only wanted the cream of the crop to return home with them: those who were rich, powerful, handsome, beautiful, educated, or talented. Many were left behind. There were many conflicts between those left behind and those who returned from the Exile. The returned exiles had been exposed to many cultures and

---

[20] Cyrus is, in fact, the last Messiah (Christ) mentioned in TNK. In 1985 Vernon Wayne Howell changed his name to "David Koresh." *Koresh* is an alternative way of transliterating and vocalizing the Hebrew spelling of *Cyrus*. For those who have eyes to see, Howell was taking the name of God's favorite Israelite Messiah, David, and the name of the last Messiah, Cyrus (Koresh); in other words, he was implicitly claiming to be the Messiah himself. Koresh and many of his followers died on April 19, 1993, in a violent confrontation with federal agents. The Oklahoma City bombing took place on that date two years later, apparently as retaliation for the Waco deaths.

worldviews in Babylon; they seem to have picked up some of the philosophy of Babylon, which in turn contributed to the development of Wisdom literature, the last stage of the development of TNK.

Some of those who remained in the land (just like some of the exiles) mixed devotion to other gods and goddesses with their traditional devotion to the God of Israel. Ezra denounced marriages between Jews and other ethnic groups, as well as the polytheism that often resulted from such unions (Ez 9:1-2). "Do not, then, give your daughters to their sons in marriage, and do not take their daughters for your sons. Never promote their peace and prosperity; thus you will grow strong, enjoy the produce of the land, and leave it as an inheritance to your children forever" (9:12). The exiles organized an investigation of such improper marriages, and forced the culprits to send away their wives and children (10:16-44).

Nehemiah labored to win the people back to observance the of Torah:

> The rest of the people, priests, Levites, gatekeepers, singers, temple slaves, and all others who have separated themselves from the peoples of the lands in favor of the law of God, with their wives, their sons, their daughters, all who are of the age of discretion, join with their brethren who are their princes, and with the sanction of a curse take this oath to follow the law of God which was given through Moses, the servant of God, and to observe carefully all the commandments of the LORD, our LORD, his ordinances and his statutes. (Neh 10:29-30)

Nehemiah was pretty fierce in his devotion to the way of the LORD:

> I took them to task and cursed them; I had some of them beaten and their hair pulled out: and I adjured them by God: "You shall not marry your daughters to their sons nor take any of their daughters for your sons or for yourselves. Did not Solomon, the king of Israel, sin because of them? Though among the nations there was no king like him, and though he was beloved of his God and God had made him king over all Israel, yet even he was made to sin by foreign women. Must it also be heard of you that you have done this same very great evil, betraying our God by marrying foreign women?" (13:25-27)

By this time in Jewish history (the period of **Second Temple Judaism**, 535 BC-70 AD), the concept of radical monotheism had displaced the earlier polytheistic worldview, in which the God of Israel was just one divinity among many: "Thus says the LORD, Israel's King and redeemer, the LORD of hosts: I am the first and I am the last; there is no God but me" (Is 44:6). For Nehemiah, marrying those who worshipped other deities was, for all practical purposes, a sin against the first commandment.

Although the Temple and the Torah were restored after the Exile, the monarchy was not, despite many prophecies that David's dynasty would be revived. When the monarchy died, so, too, did the Israelite/Jewish tradition of **polygamy**. As with the development of radical monotheism, there are tensions in TNK left over from the transition from polygamy to **monogamy**. The Torah provides rules for the care of a second wife (Ex 21:10) and for the preservation of the privileges of the children of the first wife (Deut. xxi. 15). The stories of the patriarchs and kings, as we have seen, take polygamy (multiple wives) and concubinage (sexual relations with slaves) for granted. In contrast to this traditional material, the idea that husband and wife become a single living being (Gen 2:24) and the prophetic comparison of God's Covenant of fidelity toward Israel to the covenant between husband and wife (Hos 2:21-22) created a dynamic that led to the establishment in fact—if not in the written words of TNK—of monogamy as the ideal. This line of development reached its climax when Jesus claimed that the proper interpretation of the Genesis story prohibits divorce:

> Have you not read that from the beginning the Creator "made them male and female" and said, "For this reason a man shall leave his father and mother and be joined to his wife, and the two shall become one flesh"? So they are no longer two, but one flesh. Therefore, what God has joined together, no human being must separate. (Mt 19:4-6)

Jesus and Christianity were born in the last stages of Second Temple Judaism. Jesus' form of Judaism is deeply indebted to the scriptural, theological, and practical developments in the preceding five centuries.

Rise of the Greek Empire (470–323 BC)

While the Jews were rebuilding their Temple and renewing and purifying their Covenant relationship with the Lord, important developments were taking place in Greece, just a short sail away across the eastern end of the Mediterranean Sea. Wandering philosophers (*peripatetics*) began to raise questions and make guesses about the nature of the world. **Socrates** (470-399 BC) gathered a group of disciples around him. One of his students, **Plato** (427-347 BC), founded a school at Akademia, a shrine to Athena, the goddess of wisdom, and wrote a number of dialogues starring his teacher, Socrates. Scholars disagree about how faithfully Plato recorded Socrates' thought—like most of the peripatetics, Socrates did not put his philosophy into writing himself.

Aristotle (384-322 BC) was one of Plato's students in the Academy. He was an equally prolific writer and successful teacher, although his philosophy was quite different from that of Plato. His most famous student was Alexander III of Macedon, better known to us as **Alexander the Great (356-323 BC)**. His conquest of the Persian empire, and all of the territory around the eastern Mediterranean in 12 short years, was an astonishing accomplishment. Though he did not conquer the western Mediterranean, the power, wealth, and culture of Greece dominated the lands that were not directly under Greek control. The word for Greek culture is **Hellenism**, from *Hellas*, the Greek word for "Greek." Alexander's success *hellenized* the whole of the Mediterranean world. Anyone who wanted to prosper had to learn Greek. It was the language of business and politics.

The Bible has no concept of culture. (Of course, the Bible has no concept of "concept" or "Bible," either.) Some interpreters complain about the fact that Jews and Christians soaked up the culture of their day, wrote in a language that their audience would understand, and used the tools of thought provided by Hellenism. "They should have stayed Hebrew. They shouldn't have interacted with the surrounding culture. They shouldn't have developed their ideas. Primitive (wild, unruly, untouched, pure, isolated, romantic) is better than cultivated (orderly, neat, precise, logical, cut and dried)." I see no reason for this preference for racial and cultural isolation. We are all members of the human race, first and last. Humans learn from other humans, even from those who come from a different tribe. The twin (and conflicting) claims of Judaism and Christianity to be God's true Covenant partner do not imply a monopoly on truth and goodness. Jews and Christians intuitively took what was worthwhile from the nations around them, while rejecting what was contrary to the Torah and the gospel.

After the return from the Exile (the Babylonian Captivity), Judea had been a vassal state of the Persian empire. With Alexander's conquest of Persia, Judea now came under Greek control. When the Hellenic overlords tried to impose Greek religious practices on the Jews, the Maccabees led a successful revolt that gained Jewish independence (167 BC) from the Greek Empire. When the Romans conquered the Greek empire (146 BC), they continued to speak Greek, because it was already established as the language of world affairs. Judea was conquered by the Romans in 63 BC, and remained under Roman domination for the next five centuries.

The **Greco-Roman** culture of the six centuries BC is known as the **"Classical Era."** The Classical Era continued for another five centuries in western Europe, and for a thousand years in the East. The Classical Era was a time of great sophistication in politics, trade, warfare, poetry, drama, philosophy, geometry, mathematics, architecture, and, in a rudimentary fashion, history. The thinkers, writers, and orators of this period were no dummies, although they lacked our communications technology. We still use *their* language and concepts when we talk about democracy, monarchy, republics, politics, economics, government, senators, representatives, justice, and law. The kinds of questions they asked planted seeds that germinated a thousand years later and gave birth to our modern civilization. We would not be who we are without them.

TNK to LXX (3rd century BC)

Some time during the third century BC, the Jews began to translate their Scriptures from Hebrew into Greek. In part, their motivation was to serve those Jewish families living outside of Judea, whose first language was Greek rather than Aramaic (the spoken language that had developed from Hebrew). Legend has it that 70 or 72 **rabbis** (Aramaic, "teachers") spent 30 days translating the whole of TNK into Greek in Alexandria, on behalf of the king of Egypt; when they compared their translations, according to the story, they were allegedly all identical to each other in every respect. The name of the Greek edition is the **Septuagint** (Greek, "seventy"), which is abbreviated as **LXX** (the Roman numerals for "70").

A story doesn't have to be true to be true. The likelihood of any of the Jewish scholars finishing a complete translation in 30 days is nil. That 70 scholars would agree on every letter of a translation without consulting each other is inconceivable. The *meaning* of the legend is that Jews could feel confident that the LXX was just as reliable as TNK, since only God could produce the miracle of such a perfect translation. Jews who could not read Hebrew were assured by the story that they were reading the Word of the LORD. The Jewish confidence that the Word of God can be translated became part of the Christian scriptural tradition, too; by contrast, the Muslim tradition holds that the Quran ought to be read in the original Arabic.

The LXX contained many more books than TNK, most composed in Greek. In the last few centuries of Second Temple Judaism (see page 92), the inconsistencies between the two **canons** (from Greek, "measuring rod" or "standard"; the word came to mean "a list of things that measured up to a standard") were left unresolved. In Jesus' day, LXX was the standard version that He and His disciples quoted in their discussions of the Scriptures. Long after Jesus' disciples began preaching that He was *the* Christ, using passages from the LXX, Jewish rabbis in Jamnia decided that only TNK was really inspired by the LORD (70-90 AD). Fifteen centuries later, Luther decided to follow the rabbinic tradition, and removed the added Greek books from his canon—his *official list* of books that were to be treated as inspired by God.

Of the books added in LXX, the Catholic Church recognizes seven as inspired by God: 1 and 2 Maccabees, Ecclesiasticus (Sirach), Wisdom, Baruch, Tobit, and Judith. Protestants, following Martin Luther's lead, call these **deuterocanonical** (Greek, *deuteros*, "second" = "books of the second canon") or the **apocrypha** (Greek, "hidden, obscure things" = "unreliable books"). Protestant study bibles or ecumenical editions usually place the deuteroncanonicals between the books of the **Old Testament** and the books of the **New Testament**.

Calling the Jewish Scriptures (either TNK or LXX) the "Old Testament" is common to all Christians who believe that Jesus has inaugurated a "New Testament." "Testament" is an archaic word for "covenant." In the gospel of Luke, Jesus says, "This cup is the new covenant in my blood, which will be shed for you" (22:20). St. Paul, who was a devout Jewish rabbi, thoroughly trained in the spirituality of the Temple and Torah, speaks of himself and the other apostles as "ministers of a new covenant" (2 Cor 3:6). But for the Jews, their Scriptures are *not* the "Old Testament."

They are the Scriptures of the one and only Testament (Covenant) that God made with Abraham and renewed through Moses and David.

The Jews in the last few centuries before the birth of Jesus had a perfectly complete religion, even if some elements of God's promises in His Covenants were temporarily missing in action. Second Temple Judaism was a complete way of life. The Jews had God's law (Torah), and therefore, knew what they had to do to please God; they had the Temple and the priesthood in Jerusalem, where they could offer sacrifice and make reparation for their sins. All that they needed or wanted was the restoration of the Davidic dynasty, so that they could raise an army, go to war, get free from the control of the Roman Empire, and see the fulfillment of God's promise that the King of Israel would rule over all other kings of the earth (Ps 2:8-9).

Speaking (and Writing) in the Name of the Lord

Our English word, "prophet," comes from Greek, *pro-* "for" + *phanai* "to speak," which means to speak on behalf of another. The Israelite tradition is prophetic from beginning to end. Abraham claimed to be God's Covenant partner. Moses laid down the Law (Torah) in the name of the Lord. The writings (*kethubim*) in TNK are filled with stories of inspired wonder-working prophets like Elijah, Elisha, and Samuel. The development of the prophetic books (*nebi'im*) began with Amos (circa 750 BC) and continued down to the last apocalyptic passages included in the Septuagint (LXX) in Second Temple Judaism.

Although our ordinary usage of the word "prophecy" suggests foretelling future events, the Israelite prophets spoke about God's entire plan of salvation, past, present, and future. Like the president's Press Secretary in the United States, they would act as spokesmen for the one whom they represented, interpreting the past, offering guidance for the present, and foretelling the consequences of obeying or disobeying the divine ordinances.

The organization of the prophetic books in the Jewish and Christian Scriptures is by length, rather than by chronology, with longest books appearing first and the shortest books last. The Christian reorganization of the Jewish Scriptures treats Isaiah, Jeremiah, Lamentations, Baruch (in LXX, not TNK), Ezekiel, and Daniel as "major prophets," and Hosea, Joel, Amos, Obadiah, Jonah, Micah, Nahum, Habakkuk, Zephaniah, Haggai, Zechariah, and Malachi as "minor prophets." In the Jewish Scriptures, Lamentations and Daniel are classified among the writings (*kethubim*), rather than among the prophets.

When Muhammad portrayed himself as the **"Seal of the Prophets"** (see page 158), he was appealing to the whole of the Israelite prophetic tradition that began with Abraham, not just to the prophets whose sayings came to be recorded in the prophetic books. In the Christian Scriptures of the New Testament, Jesus clearly acts as a prophet in the Israelite tradition, especially in the gospels of Matthew and John. At Vatican II, the Catholic Church emphasized Jesus' prophetic character: "Christ, the great Prophet, who proclaimed the Kingdom of His Father both by the testimony of His life and the power of His words, continually fulfills His prophetic office until the complete manifestation of glory" ("Lumen Gentium," 35).

Subsequent Developments in Judaism

There is much more to be said about the worldview and religious practices of the Jews after the time of the Second Temple (535 BC-70 AD). We will learn much more about them in the next two chapters. Both Christianity and Islam may be thought of as developments *from* Judaism that had a huge influence on further developments *in* Judaism.

CHRISTIANITY
(JUDIASM CONTINUED)

• • • • • •

Jesus was born into two highly sophisticated cultures. The **Greco-Roman world** was in its glory days. Julius Caesar (100-44 BC) expanded the Roman republic, and turned it into an empire under his dictatorship. He was succeeded by his nephew, Augustus (63 BC-14 AD), who took the name "Caesar" after Julius was assassinated. The family name then became associated with the next ten Roman emperors, the German *kaisers*, and the Russian *czars*.

The religious culture of Second Temple Judaism was also highly sophisticated. For more than a thousand years, the Chosen People had accumulated materials that filled their lives with a sense of purpose and meaning: cosmic mythology; family lore; the history of the kings and the kingdoms; the twin mysteries of the Exodus from Egypt and the return from Exile in Babylon; the body of prophetic words and deeds that assured them of God's fidelity and called them to respond in kind; the poetry of the Psalms; the insights of Wisdom literature; many kinds of entertaining and edifying stories (e.g., Jonah and Job); the intricate structure of Torah and tradition that shaped every day of their lives, and gave deeper meanings to the seasons of the year; and the one Temple of the Lord in Jerusalem, the city of David. The Jews, like their Greek and Roman counterparts, were sophisticated readers, writers, and thinkers. They were highly skilled in applying general principles to particular cases, and in generalizing from particular cases to general rules.

The date and place of Jesus' birth are uncertain. The gospels of Mark and John seem to accept that Jesus was born in Nazareth, which was in the province of Galilee (Mk 1:9, 6:1-6; Jn 1:46, 7:26-29, 40-52). Galilee and Samaria were in the historic territory of the northern kingdom, Israel. Matthew and Luke each affirm that Jesus was born in Bethlehem, a small town just six miles away from Jerusalem in the province of Judea (Mt 1-2; Luke 1-2), but then grew up in Nazareth in the province of Galilee. All four gospels agree that He was known as "Jesus of Nazareth," and that he was crucified while Pontius Pilate was prefect of Judea (26-36 AD).

Luke's gospel says that Jesus was born during the reign of Herod the Great (1:5). Because Dionysius Exiguus (see page x) made a miscalculation of the dates of Herod's kingship in Judea, we now know that *if* Luke is right about Jesus being born before Herod died, he had to have been born in or before 4 BC, not 1 AD. Christian tradition takes Luke's statement that Jesus was about 30 years old when He began to preach and gather disciples (3:23), and adds three years to that because of the three Passovers in the gospel of John (2:13, 6:4, 12:1), arriving at the conclusion that Jesus was 33 years old when He died. For the lack of any better way of calculating the dates of Jesus' birth and death, I will use 4 BC to 30 AD; but I recognize that there is a great deal of uncertainty in these dates, and that others may reasonably disagree with them.

Geography of the Holy Land in the Time of Jesus

In the first century AD, there were three regions in the territory of ancient Israel: Galilee in the North, Samaria in the middle, and Judea in the South. The Infancy Narratives are concerned with Bethlehem in Judea, which is about six miles from Jerusalem, and Nazareth in Galilee, which is 70 miles as the crow flies to the North. The Jordan River runs from the Sea of Galilee in the North to the Dead Sea in the South. This is where John the Baptist was preaching repentance and baptizing people to confirm their willingness to be cleansed from sin.

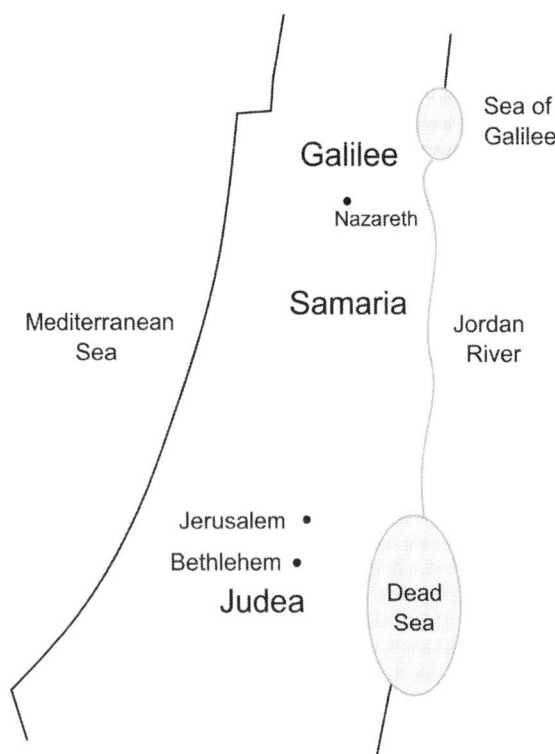

Nature and Storytellers Abhor a Vacuum

Most of Jesus' disciples met Him during his **public ministry**, the last year or years of His life when He was actively and energetically "proclaiming the **gospel**[1] of God: 'This is the time of fulfillment. The kingdom of God is at hand. Repent, and believe in the gospel'" (Mk 1:14-15). Jesus apparently did not talk much, if at all, about His early life. What seems to have mattered most to Him and to His followers was what God was doing in the present moment: changing the whole nature of God's relationship to the world, doing something new and entirely unexpected. The last and strangest book of the New Testament, the book of Revelation, portrays Jesus as saying, "Behold, I make all things new" (Rev 21:5). The people who followed Jesus were not interested in His biography. They were in love with the man whom they knew as an adult. Their days were filled with plenty of other things to think about besides the question of how Jesus spent the years of His life before He became their rabbi and Lord.

In the subsequent centuries, Christians have had plenty of time to wonder about those early days. Mark and John ignore them entirely. The gospels of Matthew and Luke have two contradictory methods to explain how the baby born in Bethlehem of Judea grew up in Nazareth of Galilee. Matthew's explanation is that after Jesus was born in Bethlehem, the visit of the magi and the murder of the baby boys in Bethlehem (2:1-16) caused the family to flee to Egypt and eventually resettle up North, in Nazareth. Luke says that the original hometown of Joseph and Mary was Nazareth, and that they traveled to Bethlehem just to register in a census (2:1-39), then returned home in peace.

Of the next few years, Luke says that Jesus "grew and became strong, filled with wisdom; and the favor of God was upon him." He tells one story about Jesus at 12 years of age. Jesus must have been young enough to have spent the day with the women, but old enough to have traveled with the men, since Mary and Joseph both assumed that He was with the other parent (2:44). After that brief story, Luke summarizes the rest of Jesus' life in Nazareth by saying that He "advanced in wisdom and age and favor before God and man" (2:52).

Inquiring minds want to *know* what it was like for Jesus to live in Nazareth. We have far more questions than answers. Did He know who He was? Did He work miracles as a boy? Did Mary and Joseph worship Him as God? Did his family and friends recognize that He was different? Did He fall in love? Did he have friends? Did He stay in Nazareth, or did He travel to Egypt or India or Persia to study the secrets of magic? Over the centuries, people have written many imaginative stories about the hidden life of Jesus. The Church rejected all of these alleged childhood "gospels," and refused to include them in the **canon of the New Testament** (the *official list*

---

[1] **"Gospel"** is derived from the Greek, *euangelion* (*eu-*, "good" + *angelion*, "message, news"). The Germanic words, *gut*, "good," and *spiel*, "story," led to "good spel" and "godspel" in Old English; over the course of time, the "d" dropped out, giving us the modern form of the word. Meanwhile, we coined other English words from the original Greek root: evangel ("gospel"), evangelism ("preaching the gospel"), and evangelist ("one who preaches the gospel").

of books that are considered to have been inspired by God; see page 123). For some in our day, it seems inexplicable that the Church would throw away stories about Jesus' childhood, because *to us* these are ancient manuscripts and *to us* everything that is ancient is fascinating. But in the time when the childhood gospels were written (second century AD), they were *novelties* that did not correspond to the sober silence of the four gospels. They were rejected, because they did not bear the marks of having come from the people who knew Jesus personally. Perhaps one of the joys of Heaven will be having all of our questions about Jesus answered in full, but for now, it seems to me that God is saying that the history of Jesus' early life is none of our business.

The Coming of the Kingdom and the King

In all four gospels, the story of Jesus' public ministry begins with the preaching of John the Baptist. "People of the whole Judean countryside and all the inhabitants of Jerusalem were going out to him and were being baptized [Greek, "immersed"] by him in the Jordan River as they acknowledged their sins" (Mk 1:5). Only Luke claims that John was a blood relative of Jesus, and was another miracle baby born to a childless couple (1:36). Matthew, Mark, and Luke, are known collectively as the **synoptic gospels**, because they see with the same eye (Greek, *syn-*, "with" + *optos*, "eye"), that is to say, they have the same view of Jesus' life. The three synoptic gospels say that Jesus was baptized by John at the Jordan river (Mt 3:13-17; Mk 1:9-11; Lk 3:21-22). This probably was an embarrassment to the Christian community, because John was washing sinners clean from their sins. The synoptic gospels agree that, for Jesus, this was not a sinner's bath, but the moment when God *anointed Him as the Christ*, with John playing a prophetic role in identifying Jesus that was similar to the role the prophet Samuel had played in identifying the first Messiahs of Israel.

There is not a perfect parallel between the anointing of the Israelite kings and the anointing of Jesus as the Christ, because John did not pour oil over Jesus' head as Samuel did with Saul and David. Instead, "heaven was opened and the Holy Spirit descended upon him in bodily form like a dove. And a voice came from heaven, 'Thou art my beloved Son; with you I am well pleased'" (Lk 4:21-22). In this interpretation of the Baptism of Jesus, He was anointed—not with a symbol of God's favor—but with the reality that had been represented by the oil all along: "the power of the Spirit" (Lk 4:14). The anointing with the Holy Spirit was understood to fulfill the prophecy of Isaiah: "The Spirit of the Lord is upon me, because he has *anointed* me to bring glad tidings to the poor" (Lk 4:18; emphasis added).

For those who believe in Jesus, He is *the* Messiah (Hebrew), *the* Christ (Greek), *the* Anointed One, above all others. This claim was so central in the early proclamation of the gospel that it became the name of this form of Judaism (Acts 11:26). Jesus Himself did not say in so many words, "I am the Messiah, the Christ, the son of David promised in God's Covenant with David." This proposition was deduced by His followers from Jesus' *actions*. He named 12 disciples as His apostles (Lk 3:13-19). For those who had eyes to see, this meant that He was claiming to be the new Israel (Jacob), with 12 symbolic sons who would be the new patriarchs of a new kingdom of David. Jesus drove out demons (Mk 1:34), healed the sick (Lk 7:21), and even raised the dead to life (the widow's son, Lk 7:11; Jairus's daughter, Mk 5:41-42; Lazarus, Jn 11:1-44). When John asked Jesus through messengers whether He was "the one who is to come" (that is, the descendant of David who would restore David's dynasty), Jesus replied, "Go and tell John what you have seen and heard: the blind regain their sight, the lame walk, lepers are cleansed, the deaf hear, the dead are raised, the poor have the good news proclaimed to them. And blessed is the one who takes no offense at me" (Lk 7:22-23).

The disciples who witnessed all these mighty deeds had no doubt that Jesus was *the* Messiah, *the* Christ, whom the Chosen People had been waiting for ever since the Babylonian Captivity in 586 BC.

> Now Jesus and his disciples set out for the villages of Caesarea Philippi. Along the way he asked his disciples, "Who do people say that I am?" They said in reply, "John the Baptist, others Elijah, still others one of the prophets." And he asked them, "But who do you say that I am?" Peter said to him in reply, "You are the Messiah." (Mk 8:27-29)

Jesus then "strictly ordered his disciples to tell no one that he was the Messiah" (Mt 16:20). Scholars call this theme in the synoptics the *Messianic Secret*.[2] None of the gospels explains why Jesus did not want to be called the Messiah, the Christ, during His lifetime. There is no dogma from the Church about this aspect of the gospels.

To be a *Christ*-ian is to believe that Jesus is *the* Christ, the fulfillment of God's Covenant with David. Since this was such a dominant part of the gospel message *after* Jesus vanished from the face of the earth, it is hard for us to see why it had to be kept secret while He was with His disciples. In our political campaigns, we are accustomed to having the candidates come out into the open and declare what job they want. Their staffers print posters, place ads in the media, and beat the streets for their nominee. To our taste, starting a campaign for the kingship in secret is bizarre and inappropriate.

Some scholars argued that the messianic secret was an invention of the synoptic authors to explain why Jesus was not hailed as the Christ before His death (e.g., William Wrede[3]). Some

---

[2] *Das Messiasgeheimnis in den Evangelien* (Göttingen: 1901), translated as *The Messianic Secret* (London: 1971).

[3] Matthew's version of the story is more explicit than Mark's. Mark says, "Then he warned them not to tell anyone about him" (8:30).

say that He thought that He was *not* the Christ and that He was speaking of another who would come after Him (e.g., Albert Schweitzer[4]).

He Shoulda Been a Superman

In my view, Jesus knew who He was and knew what His mission in life was. I am not willing to suppose, as some do in our day (see, for example, *Being There, Life of Brian, Forrest Gump*), that Jesus was a simpleton manipulated and/or misinterpreted by His disciples, who are the true (evil) geniuses behind the religion of Christianity (see page 117). I can see two excellent reasons why the real Jesus would have wanted his disciples to keep quiet about their belief that He was *the* Messiah, *the* Christ, *the* long-awaited King who would restore the house of David.

The first reason to keep quiet about Jesus' kingship was that the disciples had no idea *what kind of king Jesus would turn out to be*. At the time that Jesus challenged them to think about why they were following Him, they had no reason whatsoever to think that He was anything else but Superman. All that they had seen from Him was miracles, signs, and wonders. He drove out demons and controlled their behavior. He made the deaf hear, the blind see, the lame walk, and the dead rise to new life. As good Jews (all of Jesus' original disciples were Jewish), they knew God's promises to His Anointed One, that God Himself would annihilate the enemies of the King in battle: "I will crush his foes before him and those who hate him I will smite" (Ps 89:24; see also Ps 2:8-9). The 12 apostles had every reason to believe, both from their personal experience of Jesus and from the Jewish tradition, that He would very shortly become the King of Kings, "the highest of the kings of the earth" (Ps 89:28), and that they would become the patriarchs of 12 new tribes of Israel. All that they could see ahead was victory, glory, wealth, and power. They were undoubtedly eager to start raising an army to follow King Jesus, overthrow the Romans, and conquer the world.

Jesus had other plans. He intended to exercise His Kingship, not by taking the lives of the enemies of God's people, but by laying down His life for the flock.

> Then he warned them not to tell anyone about him. He began to teach them that the Son of Man must suffer greatly and be rejected by the elders, the chief priests, and the scribes, and be killed, and rise after three days. He spoke this openly. Then Peter took him aside and began to rebuke him. At this he turned around and, looking at his disciples, rebuked Peter and said, "Get behind me, Satan. *You are thinking not as God does, but as human beings do.*" He summoned the crowd with his disciples and said to them, "Whoever wishes to come after me must deny himself, take up his cross, and

---

[4] *The Quest of the Historical Jesus; A Critical Study of Its Progress from Reimarus to Wrede*, translated by William Montgomery (A. & C. Black, London 1910, 1911).

follow me. For whoever wishes to save his life will lose it, but whoever loses his life for my sake and that of the gospel will save it. What profit is there for one to gain the whole world and forfeit his life? What could one give in exchange for his life? Whoever is ashamed of me and of my words in this faithless and sinful generation, the Son of Man will be ashamed of when he comes in his Father's glory with the holy angels." (Mk 8:30-38; emphasis added)

Jesus almost certainly did not want His disciples to start preaching about Him as *the* Christ, because at this point in their relationship, His disciples didn't understand Him or His mission. They were not "thinking as God does, but as human beings do." Jesus didn't blame them, nor should we, for not understanding God's plan of salvation. They did not have all of the pieces of the puzzle until *after* Jesus had died and risen from the dead. Then—and only then—were they in a position to tell all the world that "God has made him both Lord and Messiah, this Jesus whom you crucified" (Acts 2:36). Furthermore, the disciples knew all about God's promises in the Jewish Scriptures, that the descendants of David were supposed to be victorious in battle and come to reign over the whole world. It is not surprising that Peter tried to set Jesus straight about the job of the King, which (he thought) was to go to war against the enemies of the Jews and conquer them in battle, just as David and Solomon had done.

Apart from the fact that the disciples had practically no clue about God's plan for His Messiah, the other excellent reason for keeping quiet about their conviction that Jesus was *the* Christ was that large public demonstrations of enthusiasm for Jesus' Kingship would lead directly to war with the Romans. For the Jews of Jesus' day, including His Jewish disciples, being *the* Messiah, *the* Christ, meant being *the* King of the Jews, and therefore, (like David) *the* King of Israel. This was not some pie-in-the-sky, pious, "spiritual" calling. The Jews expected their King to put on armor, collect an army, and shed the blood of their enemies. The Romans understood as well as the Jews that "Everyone who makes himself a king opposes Caesar" (Jn 19:12). When push came to shove, the Romans crucified Jesus because they recognized that he was claiming to be *the* Messiah, *the* Christ, *the* King of the Jews—and therefore a public enemy of the empire. Pilate had Jesus' name and the charge against him placed on the cross: "Jesus of Nazareth, the King of the Jews" (Jn 19:19).[5]

In my view, Jesus knew that when the Romans realized that He was claiming to be *the* Christ, He would die. By keeping quiet about this claim Himself, and by requiring His disciples to keep quiet about it, He bought time to live and work with His disciples, until they were as ready as they could be to witness His suffering, death, and resurrection.

---

[5] The gospel of John says that the sign was written in three languages, Hebrew, Latin, and Greek (19:20). Catholic crucifixes usually reproduce the four letters from the Latin inscription, *Iesus Nazarenus Rex Judaeorum*: INRI.

Jewish Interpretation of *Their* Scriptures	Christian Reinterpretation of the Jewish Scriptures
The Sacred Scriptures (**TNK/LXX**) are from the *only* Covenant (Testament).	The Jewish Scriptures are part of the **Old Covenant** (Old Testament). Jesus has created a **New Covenant** with new Scriptures (New Testament).
The Messiah was supposed to be a **human** like David.	Jesus is **both human and divine.**
The Messiah was supposed to defeat **human enemies.** The Romans killed Jesus—He lost.	Jesus, our King, has defeated **sin and death.** Jesus rose from the dead—He won.
The Messiah was supposed to restore the **kingdom of Israel** (kingdom of David) on earth.	The Messiah rules a **Kingdom** *not* **of this world.** Anyone who wants to join the Kingdom is welcome.
The Messiah was supposed to marry, have children, and die, just like David and Solomon, and all the other Messiahs in Jewish history.	After His death and resurrection, Jesus lives forever. He causes God's children to be **"born again"** in Baptism.
All the prophecies in the Scriptures can be given **non-Christian** meanings.	All the prophecies are ultimately about **Jesus**, the Christ.
God is **unitarian**—one person in one being.	God is **Trinitarian**—three persons in one being.
No human could ever *be* God. *Note well: Christians do NOT think that Jesus was a human who became God, but that God the Son became human.*	Christians **worship Jesus** as *God Incarnate* (Jn 1:1-18)—God has chosen to *become human* so that humans may become divine.

For those Jews who accepted Jesus as *the* Christ, *the* King, it was necessary to redefine the nature of the Kingdom, the identity of its enemies, and the manner in which victory was to be won. *After* Jesus was raised from the dead, His Jewish disciples understood that Jesus' Kingdom "does not belong to this world" (Jn 18:36). The Kingdom of God is not a geographic district inhabited by an ethnic group that wars against other such entities. Jesus' enemies were not the geopolitical enemies of the Jews, the Romans, but sin and death. His victory was accomplished, not by killing people, but by allowing Himself to be killed. He did not continue the dynasty of David by collecting a harem, fathering a multitude of children, and leaving an heir to be the Christ after Him; He fulfills God's Covenant with David *forever*. because through His resurrection and ascension into glory, He now possesses a Kingship that cannot be taken away. We now know that the sun and the moon will pass away in a few billion years, but if the good news announced by His disciples is true, Jesus will be King *forever*.

The Jews who reject the idea that Jesus is their King have a perfectly logical and straightforward argument from the natural reading of their own Scriptures. Their test of whether someone fulfills the contract with David is whether the purported Messiah-King won victories in battle. Like Jonah, they wanted to see God destroy their enemies. Jesus' life and death made precisely zero impact on the geopolitical situation of the Jews of His day. The Roman Empire continued to oppress them, collecting *their* money to pay for the soldiers occupying *their* country, and sending the surplus back home to Rome to make the Roman elite rich and powerful. From this standpoint, a "king" who dies and vanishes from the scene is no king at all and anyone who preaches that he is *the* Christ, *the* King, is a fool.

In the Jewish Scriptures (TNK/LXX), Messiah/Christ meant "the man anointed to be the King of Israel/King of the Jews." It *never* meant "God," and only indirectly suggested "savior"—the job of the King was to defeat enemies and make the nation safe for its citizens (Ps 2, Ps 89). The general population of the Jews *never* expected their King to save the whole world from sin and death; his job was to save *them* from the hands of their military and political enemies.

To be a Christian is to believe that Jesus is *the* Christ. To say that He is *the* Christ is to say that He is "King of the Jews" and "King of Israel." The Jews, understandably, don't like people who aren't Jewish telling them who *their* king is or how *their* Scriptures are supposed to be interpreted.

The Christian doctrine that the Jewish Scriptures foretell worldwide salvation from sin and death is based on the resurrection of Jesus and the descent of the Holy Spirit on the day of **Pentecost**, the Jewish festival 50 days after Passover that celebrated the giving of the Torah on Mount Sinai (Acts 2). Only after accepting the fact that Jesus is risen from the dead can His death be seen as victory rather than defeat, and only then can one reread the Jewish Scriptures and—by a ***radical reinterpretation*** of them—recognize that they "prove" that the Messiah "first had to suffer before entering into His glory" (Lk 24:26-27).

Second Temple Judaism (515 BC to 70 AD; see page 92) was a very complete religious worldview with a very religiously satisfying way of life. All that the Jews were looking for was the fulfillment of God's Covenants with Abraham, Moses, and David; they were *not* expecting anything like what the Jews who followed Jesus preached: that God, Himself, had come in the Person of God the Son to set all things right, not just for the Jews, the last remnant of Israel, but for the whole human race; that the Old Covenant was fulfilled and ended by the New Covenant; and that the Kingdom of God is open to welcome all who wish to dwell in it.

It was the Jews who preached Jesus as the Christ, the King, who saw the incarnation, life, death, resurrection, ascension, and enthronement of Jesus as *the key to reinterpret the whole of the Jewish Scriptures*. From the standpoint of these Jewish believers in Jesus, everything in the Scriptures of the Old Testament (Old Covenant) was radically reinterpreted as foreshadowing God's saving action in Jesus. Christians saw Jesus as the fulfillment of every Old Testament *type* (or *prototype, antetype, archetype*). In this **typological interpretation of the Jewish Scriptures**, Jesus was seen as the new Adam, the new Melchisedech, the new Noah, the new Abraham, the new Isaac, the new Jacob (Israel), the new Joseph, the new Moses, the new Paschal Lamb, the new David, the new Messiah (Christ) the new High Priest, and the new Prophet.

This **typological interpretation** of Judaism is nonliteral—and even surrealistic. The parallels between the stories of the Old Testament and Jesus are not a perfect match; it takes a sympathetic act of the imagination to see how Jesus fulfills and transcends salvation history. The similarities are suggestive and poetic, not deductive. To accept the standpoint of the New Testament (New Covenant) is to adopt a whole new way of interpreting the Scriptures of the Old Testament. A Jewish professor once said to one of my professors, "You Christians! You think that you understand our Scriptures better than we do!" Although it seems arrogant and may offend modern sensibilities, the only reply Christians can make is, "Yes, that is exactly the claim that the Jewish preachers of Jesus as the Christ make in the Scriptures of the New Testament: we think we know the real meaning of the history and Scriptures of the Jews better than the Jews do themselves." These are fighting words. Both Christians and Jews believe in the God of Abraham, the one and only God of all creation, and honor His words and works in the history of Israel, but their interpretations of Who God is and what He asks of us are diametrically opposed to each other.

In the Jewish Scriptures, the king of Israel was supposed to become King of Kings and Lord of Lords by military conquest (Ps 2:9; Ps 89:21-28). Christians see Jesus enthroned now in Heaven as King of Kings and Lord of Lords by "accepting death, death on a cross" (Phil 2:8). Those who stand outside of the Jewish and Christian traditions do not find either view of the Christ, the King, a pleasing prospect. Modern men and women don't mind a few ornamental royal houses here and there—the marriage of a prince or princess makes such good television!—but we would rather, as a general rule, elect our own leaders in such a way that we can also depose them when their reign becomes offensive to us.

The Witnesses Disagree with Each Other: John vs. the Synoptics

As noted above (page 102), Matthew, Mark and Luke are grouped together as the synoptic gospels, because they have the same outlook on Jesus' life when compared with the gospel of John. The synoptic gospels all indicate that Jesus spent just one year (at most) with His disciples after He was baptized by John at the Jordan River. They made only one trip to Jerusalem and one Passover. On that single visit to Jerusalem, Jesus "cleansed the Temple" (that is, drove out the animal sellers and the money changers; Mk 11:15-18) and then was arrested, tried, and executed (Mk 14-15). The three gospels agree that the Last Supper was a Passover meal (Mk 14:12-17), and that Jesus died the day *after* Passover.

The gospel of John tells a very different story. It says nothing about Jesus being baptized by John. The Baptist does point to Jesus as the Lamb of God, and testifies (as in the synoptic accounts of Jesus' Baptism) that he saw the Holy Spirit "descend as a dove from Heaven" upon Jesus (Jn 1:29-34). Jesus and the disciples visit Jerusalem many times (2:13, 5:1, 7:10, 10:22, 11:55). Three Passovers are mentioned (2:13, 23; 6:4; 11:55). The Cleansing of the Temple takes place on the first trip to Jerusalem at the time of the first Passover (2:13-17). Jesus is not arrested and executed until the third Passover, which is two years later. In John's telling, the Last Supper is unquestionably *not* the Passover meal (Jn 13-17)—a direct contradiction of the synoptic assertion—but takes place the night before Preparation Day, the day when lambs were slaughtered so that they could be consumed at that evening's Passover meal (Jn 19:31, 42).

The differences between the synoptics and John are contradictions at the literal level. It is not possible to have Jesus killed on the same trip on which He cleansed the Temple (the synoptic version), and at the same time to assert that there were two years between the two events (John's version). Jesus could not die both the day *after* Passover (the synoptic account) and the day *before* Passover (Preparation day, John's account). The difference between the day on which Passover fell implies a difference in the year in which Jesus was crucified. The date of Passover is fixed in relation to lunar cycles, and like our birthdays or like Christmas, can fall on any day of the week. All four gospels agree that Jesus died on a Friday, so a disagreement about whether Passover was on Thursday (the synoptic date) or on Saturday (John's date) means a disagreement about the year in which Jesus died.

As I noted in my analysis of the two stories of creation in Genesis, I am convinced that some differences make no difference. The contradictions in the chronologies of the gospels do not lead to contradictions in theology.

The beauty of the synoptic account of the Last Supper is that the most sacred Christian meal (the Eucharist) is instituted within the framework of the most sacred Jewish meal (Passover). The Christian communion is intimately linked to the Jewish tradition. The bread and wine needed for the Passover celebration are taken up by Jesus and given to His disciples as the pledge of a new Covenant (Lk 22:20). The old Covenant (the Old Testament) is fulfilled, and surpassed by the new Covenant (the New Testament) in the same meal.

I have no doubt that the Eucharist is the Christian Passover meal. Just as the Passover meal celebrates God leading His People out of slavery, so every Mass celebrates Jesus freeing us from slavery to sin and death. It is a beautiful connection, and a deep theological truth.

John points to a different connection between the Passover and the Eucharist. In his account, Jesus dies at the very hour that lambs are being killed on Preparation Day. Just as the Jews were saved from death in Egypt on Passover night by the blood of the lamb smeared on the lintels of their homes, so Christians are saved from death by the blood of the Lamb of God shed on the Cross for us. In John's view, Jesus Himself is our Passover lamb. Like the synoptics, John's account also grounds the New Testament in the Old Testament, but it makes the connection evident by using a different set of symbols.

Speaking from the standpoint of history, we can't have it both ways. Either the Last Supper was a Passover meal (the synoptic claim), or it was not (John's claim). From a theological standpoint, the *meanings* of the two different and conflicting stories are perfectly coherent. The Christian Eucharist is descended from the Jewish Passover celebration, whether or not the Last Supper was a Passover meal, and Jesus is our Passover Lamb, whether or not He died at the same hour as the Passover lambs.

The Witnesses Agree: He Rose from the Dead

For Christians, the *evidence* (as distinguished from a strict logical proof) that Jesus is, in fact, *the* Christ, *the* King of the Jews, and therefore, King of Israel, is His resurrection from the dead. The five major accounts of the resurrection (Mt 28, Mk 16, Lk 24, Jn 20-21, 1 Cor 15:1-11) disagree in a multitude of details, but they all affirm the fundamental belief that Jesus did, in fact, rise from the dead. The classical apologists for (defenders of) Christianity see Jesus' life, death, and resurrection as real historical events. Many, perhaps even most academic exegetes (interpreters of the Scriptures) have persuaded themselves that the bodily resurrection of Jesus from the dead is a myth invented by His disciples or by the authors of the New Testament. They claim that finding the bones of Jesus would not shake their faith in the symbol of the resurrection as a sign of hope; for them, calling the resurrection a convenient fiction, a figment of the Church's imagination, an act of fond memory, wish fulfillment, or self-delusion wouldn't change their faith in Jesus by one iota. They might even quote one of my favorite sayings: "*A story doesn't have to be true to be true.* The resurrection of Jesus belongs in the same category as the lies we tell children about the tooth fairy, Santa Claus, and the Easter bunny. It is nothing but a comforting and pleasant piece of fiction."

There have been several scandals in recent years about fictionalized memoirs. Herman Rosenblat has acknowledged that his claim in *Angel at the Fence* that he met his wife-to-be, Roma Radzicky, at the fence of a Nazi concentration camp was pure fiction. "I wanted to bring happiness to people. I brought hope to a lot of people. My motivation was to make good in this world."[6] Oprah Winfrey canceled her order for James Frey's story of recovering from drug addiction, *A Million Little Pieces* (2003), when it was proved that he had grossly exaggerated his prison experiences. I was very disappointed when I learned that James Herriot's books about his

---

[6] Associated Press, December 28, 2008.

Christianity (Judiasm Continued)

Text of the Gloria	Source or Comment
Glory to God in the highest and on earth peace to people of good will.	The angel's greeting to the shepherds in Lk 2:14.
We praise you, we bless you, we adore you, we glorify you, we give you thanks for your great glory, Lord God, heavenly King, O God, almighty Father.	**The Father is God.**
Lord	Greek: *kyrios* = Hebrew: Adonai (Mighty One)
Jesus	Name given by the angel (Lk 1:31); form of Joshua, Hebrew for "Yhwh is salvation."
Christ,	Hebrew, *Messiah* = **"Anointed One"** = person marked out as *King of Israel/Jews*
Only Begotten Son,	Jn 1:18
Lord God,	**Jesus is both God and man.**
Lamb of God,	Reminder of the lambs slaughtered at Passover (Jn 1:29).
Son of the Father,	
you take away the sins of the world, have mercy on us; you take away the sins of the world, receive our prayer;	Atonement for sin by Death and Resurrection (Jn 1:29).
you are seated at the right hand of the Father:	By His Ascension into Heaven.
Have mercy on us. For you *alone* are the Holy One,	Another Hebrew title for God—Jesus is God.
you *alone* are the Lord,	Jesus is Lord.
you *alone* are the Most High,	Another Hebrew title for God.
Jesus Christ,	Jesus is the King of Israel, King of the Jews, King of Kings (Ps 2, Ps 89).
with the Holy Spirit, in the glory of God the Father.	The Holy Spirit is also God.
Amen.	A Hebrew word meaning "It is so."

life as a veterinarian were novels, not autobiographies.[7] I like good fiction and believe that even cartoons can tell us things about ourselves, but, like Oprah, I want modern authors to tell the truth about whether they are telling the truth in their autobiographies.

For me, Christianity stands or falls with the **historical reality of the bodily resurrection of Jesus from the dead**. This is the central and essential miracle on which Christianity is based. *If this miracle is true, then all of the other miracle stories told about Jesus are plausible in principle; if this miracle did not happen, then none of the other miracles that Jesus might have worked make any difference.* If the Romans killed Him and He stayed dead, then the Jews who rejected the statement that Jesus is *the* Christ are correct. He is a loser, and everyone who believes in Him is a loser, too. Without the resurrection, there is no reason to redefine kingship, kingdom, enmity, or victory in other than the common-sense definitions used in TNK. "If Christ has not been raised, then empty (too) is our preaching; empty, too, your faith. Then we are also false witnesses to God, because we testified against God that he raised Christ, whom he did not raise if in fact the dead are not raised" (1 Cor 15:14-15).

It is bad enough that Christians claim that Jesus is *the* Christ, *the* King of the Jews. From the Jewish standpoint, it is worse that Christians *worship Jesus as God*. From the Jewish standpoint, calling some vagrant who got himself crucified "King" shows astonishingly poor judgment; calling him "God" is blasphemy.

Jesus the Blasphemer

According to all four gospels, the Romans executed Jesus because of a crime against the state. To call someone "the Messiah" or "the Christ" was to identify that person as the King of Israel, the King of the Jews; Caesar did not allow his subjects to claim kingship without his consent—to call Jesus "the Christ" was to rebel against the authority of the Roman Empire.

The Jews who judged Jesus worthy of death wanted to see Him dead, because of His claim that He was equal to God in glory. In the synoptic gospels, this claim was made in Jesus' trial before the Sanhedrin, the Jewish religious court:

> The high priest asked him and said to him, "Are you the Messiah, the son of the Blessed One?" Then Jesus answered, "I am; and 'you will see the Son of Man seated at the right hand of the Power and coming with the clouds of heaven.'" At that the high priest tore his garments and said, "What further need have we of witnesses? You have heard the blasphemy. What do you think?" They all condemned him as deserving to die. (Mk 14:60-64)

---

[7] *All Creatures Great and Small* (1972); *All Things Bright and Beautiful* (1974); *All Things Wise and Wonderful* (1977).

People in our day have difficulty understanding this passage. Just as we would prefer Jesus to travel around saying, "I am the Christ" in no uncertain terms, we would like Him to say, "I'm God." *We* don't see any problem with what Jesus said to the high priest. There is nothing in *our* linguistic and symbolic systems that would give his Jewish opponents grounds to ask for His execution. It is not the claim to be the Messiah that is blasphemous. It is Jesus' further statement that He would be "seated at the right hand of the Power and coming with the clouds of heaven" that the Jews in the courtroom understood to be blasphemous. In *their* symbolic system, Jesus was saying that He was God's equal, and that He would come in glory. For a human being to claim equality with God in glory was unthinkable for the Jewish court. They did not need any further witnesses to condemn Him, because He had committed the crime of blasphemy in their presence. To understand the violent reaction of the court to what Jesus said, we have to understand the language and symbols of Second Temple Judaism.

John's gospel is far more explicit about the Christian belief in the divinity of Jesus than the synoptics:

> In the beginning was the Word [Greek, *logos*], and the Word was with God, and the Word was God. He was in the beginning with God. All things came to be through him, and without him nothing came to be. What came to be through him was life, and this life was the light of the human race; the light shines in the darkness, and the darkness has not overcome it. (1:1-5)

This prologue is essentially a concise retelling of the story in Genesis 1. John's gospel begins with the same words as Genesis: "In the beginning." In the six-day story of creation, God creates by *speaking*: "And God *said*, 'Let there be light' and there was light" (Gen 1:3; emphasis added). John sees that God created through His *logos* (the Greek word for "word, speech, reason, logic, principle"); it is natural to think that the *logos* was "with God." He goes far beyond Genesis in claiming that the *logos* "was God." That is an entirely different kettle of fish!

> The Word became flesh [*incarnated*] and pitched His tent among us and we saw His glory, the glory as of the Father's only Son, full of grace and truth. ... While the law was given through Moses, grace and truth came through Jesus Christ. No one has ever seen God. The only Son, God, [Greek: *monogenes theos*] who is at the Father's side, has revealed Him. (Jn 1:14, 17-18)

In John's narrative of Jesus' public ministry, Jesus appropriates the Divine Name to Himself (John 8:21-59; arguably also in John 18:5-8). The rabbis who translated their Hebrew Scriptures (TNK, "Tanakh") into Greek (the Septuagint, LXX) had used *ego eimi* as the translation of *yhwh*.[8] John's gospel was written in Greek. When Jesus says "I AM" (Greek: *ego eimi*) in these passages, He is using the Divine Name of Himself—He is claiming to be God. We can tell that this is what "I AM" meant to Jesus' audience in the gospel, because they picked up stones to execute Him for blasphemy in one case (John 8:59) and fell on the ground in the other (John 18:6—either by a miraculous reaction to Jesus' self-revelation as God, or as an indication of how much they despised Him for blaspheming).

John's gospel ends as it began, with a clear affirmation that Jesus is God. When Jesus invited Thomas, the doubter, to put his fingers into the wounds in Jesus' hand and to put his hand into the wound in Jesus' side, Thomas replied, "My Lord and my God" (John 20:27-28).

The idea that God the Son became human is the doctrine of the **Incarnation** (Latin, *in-* + *carnis*, "flesh, meat"). Please note well that this is a very different idea from that of a human being becoming God. Greek mythology had that concept, as, of course, does Hinduism. The Greek word for a human achieving divine status is **apotheosis** (*apo-*, "up to" + *theos* = "being elevated to the status of a god"). The doctrine of the Incarnation does not teach that a human being became God; it teaches that God the Son took on a human nature. Paul, the earliest author of material that came to be included in the canon of the New Testament, expressed his belief in the Incarnation: "Though he was in the form of God, he did not regard equality with God something to be grasped; rather, he emptied himself, taking the form of a slave, coming in human likeness" (Phil 2:6-7). Paul is probably quoting an early Christian hymn, which suggests that faith in Jesus' divinity was well established in the earliest Christian communities.

In that same hymn, the name of Jesus takes the place of the Divine Name revealed to Moses: "Because of this, God greatly exalted him and bestowed on Him the name that is above every other name, so that at the name of Jesus every knee should bend, of those in heaven and on earth and under the earth, and every tongue confess that Jesus Christ is Lord, to the glory of God the Father" (Phil 2:9-11). The confession of faith probably should be typeset with small capitals—"Jesus Christ is Lord"—in order to bring out the full flavor of the hymn's argument, but the Greek is somewhat ambiguous; we cannot say that everywhere the Greek word for Lord (*kyrios*) appears that it is a substitution for the Divine Name.

There are many elements of the gospels that do not prove Jesus' divinity. There were miracle-workers in the Scriptures as great as He. Every kind of miracle attributed to Jesus was worked in the Old Testament by the prophets, or in the New Testament by the disciples of Jesus, none of whom is thought to be God. The stories about the **Virginal Conception of Jesus** (Mt 1-2 and Lk 1-2) do *not* directly prove His divinity. Muslims tell the very same story of the miraculous, virginal birth of Jesus in the Quran, but explicitly deny that Jesus is God. Calling Jesus *the* Christ definitely does not assert His divinity. As we have seen, for the Jews, Christs (Messiahs) were

---

[8] On the spelling and meaning of the Divine Name, see p. 57. For the story of the translation of TNK to LXX, see p. 76.

human beings like David and Solomon, who were *anointed* (christened) to serve as the king of the Jews and as the king of Israel.

Calling Jesus "**Son of God**" does *not* directly prove His divinity. "Son of God" was a Jewish term applied to the king of Israel (Ps 2:7; Ps 89:27) and to the angels, including the Adversary (Hebrew, *hasatan*; Job 1:6). Luke calls Adam "Son of God" (Lk 3:38). "Son of God," therefore, *may* be interpreted as a synonym for the Messiah (Hebrew), the Christ (Greek), the person anointed to be the king of Israel (king of the Jews). *If*, on other grounds, one is persuaded that Jesus is God the Son *then*, of course, the phrase "Son of God" takes on a whole new meaning different from the original Old Testament meaning. This may well be the case in the Centurion's confession at the moment of Jesus' death: "Truly this man was the Son of God" (Mk 16:39). It is impossible for me to decide what the demons meant (or what the gospel writers thought the demons meant) when they called Jesus "Son of God" (e.g. Mk 5:7).

The *tone* of Jesus when He revises the Torah suggests His **personal authority as the lawgiver** (Mt 5:17-48), "for he taught them as one who had authority, and not as their scribes" (Mt 7:28). This is not a direct proof of divinity, but it is *consistent* with the claim that Jesus acted as if He were God. In many passages, Jesus does reason like a well-trained rabbi from the Pharisaic tradition, using interpretations of Old Testament passages to make things clear to His disciples; some of those interpretations do not correspond to the way I would read them myself.

Jesus does claim a **unique relationship with the Father**, something not possessed by other human beings: "All things have been delivered to me by my Father; and no one knows the Son except the Father, and no one knows the father except the Son and any one to whom the Son wishes to reveal Him" (Mt 11:27; Luke 10:22). This is *not* a direct claim to divinity, but is consistent with it. "The Son of Man is **Lord of the Sabbath**" (Mt 12:8; Mk 2:27; Lk 6:5). For the Jews, the Sabbath was the "day of the Lord." The *tone* of this saying suggests that Jesus is *the Lord*. When Jesus **forgave the sins of the paralytic** (Mt 9:2; Mk 2:5; Lk 5:20), his opponents (scribes in Mt and Mk, scribes and Pharisees in Lk) accuse Him of blasphemy: "Who can forgive sins but God alone?" (Mk 2:7; Lk 5:21). This is powerful evidence that the synoptic evangelists believed Jesus is God the Son but it is not as clear as the affirmations in John's gospel.

For me, Jesus' resurrection from the dead is the strongest evidence we have that Jesus is Who He claimed to be. It is not a strict proof by any means. All humans are to rise from the dead, and our resurrection will not prove that we are God—just that we are loved by God. Matthew claims that "many saints" were raised from the dead when Jesus rose from the dead and appeared "to many" in Jerusalem (27:52-53), so just being raised from the dead does not logically entail that one is God. Nevertheless, like Thomas the doubter, the resurrection of Jesus from the dead causes me to say to Jesus, "My Lord and my God!" (Jn 20:28).

The Catholic Church worships Jesus as God the Son. Here is the text of the Gloria which is said at Sunday Masses (except during most of Lent):

For the Jews and for their other descendant religion, Islam, worshipping Jesus is a violation of the first commandment. Neither Jews nor Muslims see how Jesus could be both God and human, so worshipping Him *must* be idolatry. Christian **apologists**[9] argue that if Jesus claimed to be God, he had to be:

- mentally ill (a madman);
- deliberately lying (a criminal, a blasphemer);
- badly mistaken (stupid); or
- telling the truth (He really was God).

For those who accept that Jesus was not crazy, lying, or stupid, the only reasonable conclusion is that He really was God; and that, therefore, we have to change our ideas about what is and is not possible for God to do.

We will come back to the question of how God the Son took on a human nature in the Incarnation (see page 139). Before considering the **dogmas** (unchangeable Church teachings) based on what Jesus revealed to His apostles, we need to deal with some doubts about what we can—and cannot—know about His teaching.

Did Jesus Really Say That?

The gospels are not transcripts. The Gospel of Mark can be (and often has been) recited from beginning to end—from memory!—in under two hours.[10] Whether Jesus spent one, two, or three years with His disciples, He would have said a *lot* more than that to them. The gospels are highly selective, and each one has its own peculiar approach to recording what Jesus said, did, and meant. In my view, there are many contradictions between the gospels that cannot be harmonized at the literal level. I am well aware of the differences, but I judge that *some differences make no difference* in the basic gospel message: "For God so loved the world that he gave his only Son, so that everyone who believes in him might not perish but might have eternal life" (Jn 3:16).

---

[9] **Apologetics** is the branch of theology that explains why the act of faith is a *reasonable choice*. The word comes from the Greek, *apo-* "to, up to" + *logos*, "word, speech, reason, principle" and means that we address or "speak to" questions that people have about the faith. The first letter of Peter says that we should "always be ready to give an explanation [Greek: *apologos*] to anyone who asks you for a reason [Greek: *logos*] for your hope" (3:15). C. S. Lewis and Peter Kreeft both use the classic argument presented here, that we really have only two choices when confronted with Jesus' claim to divinity: to discredit Him entirely or take Him at His word.

[10] Mark Corso performs "St. Mark's Gospel: The Message Comes Alive!" Robert Brock has a DVD of his recitation of the gospel, *The Gospel of Mark*. Bruce Kuhn does the gospel of Luke in a one-man show, inspired by Alec McCowan's off-Broadway presentation of Mark—and both use the New King James Version!

• CHRISTIANITY (JUDIASM CONTINUED) •

This was the judgment of the Church as well, in its earliest years. Marcion (circa 110-160 AD) wrote his own gospel based on Luke, rejecting the other three, and denied that the God of the New Testament had inspired the Old Testament. Tatian, a contemporary of Marcion, wove the four gospels into the *Diatessaron* (c. 150-160 AD), a single harmonized account. The Church rejected both approaches to the problem of conflicts between the four gospels. All four gospels came from communities known to have been associated with the work of the apostles, and all four had been in use continually from the time of their composition (which we do not know with any precision). In a sense, what we have are four portraits of the same Person by four different artists, who used different literary techniques under the inspiration of the Holy Spirit to tell what they knew about Jesus.

Protestants, as a general rule,[11] tend to think that the earliest form of Christianity is best, and that subsequent developments are corruptions. Protestant scholars have relentlessly pressed to figure out what parts of the New Testament are from Jesus Himself. They want to separate His own words (Latin, *ipsissima verba*) from those composed by later authors. The result of cutting away everything that is attributed to later theology is a gospel in which Jesus never claimed to be divine, did not accept death on purpose for the sake of sinful humanity, and did not rise from the dead. On this view, all of the supernatural material in the New Testament came from the unruly imagination of the Church, not from Jesus, and therefore is a distortion of His simple rabbinic message of religious and social reform.

This is the end result of Rudolph Bultmann's original program of **demythologization**, which was intended to remove all traces of the supernatural from the Scriptures. If God cannot become human and if God does not act within human history, then it makes perfect sense to sift all of those elements out of the Scriptures, and see what is left over afterward. On this view, all of the assertions about Jesus' eternal relationship to the Father, foreknowledge of His destiny, acceptance of His role as the suffering Savior, predictions of His resurrection, and Ascension into Heaven must be set aside as inventions by a later generation; all stories of exorcism and miracle working, including the miracle of the resurrection, also have to be cut out of the Scriptures, because it is inconceivable to the modern mind that God could or would work such marvels—if there is a God at all, of course.

The apology (explanation, defense) for belief in Jesus' divinity now shifts to the apostles. Modern culture claims that Jesus was ***betrayed by all of His disciples***, who promoted Him to

---

[11] The word "Protestant" is based on the verb "to protest." There is no pope, council, or catechism for Protestants; they disagree, not only with the Catholic Church, but with each other. That is why there is no one statement about Protestantism that fits all Protestants, other than to say that they are "not Catholic." There are at least two new movements among Christians that object to being identified as Protestants: nondenominational Christians, who aspire to be completely isolated from all other forms of historic Christianity, and contemporary schismatics, who want to be called Catholic. in spite of their rejection of the teaching and discipline of the Roman Catholic Church.

divine status in order to become rich and famous by creating a religious racket. Many novels, movies, and scholarly treatises present the theory that Jesus was just a good man who was turned into a god by his followers (e.g., *The Passover Plot*, *The Last Temptation of Christ*, *Life of Brian*, *The Da Vinci Code*).

Again, there are only a few possibilities. When the apostles told others about what Jesus said, did, and meant, they were:

- mentally ill (madmen);
- deliberately lying (criminals, blasphemers);
- badly mistaken (stupid); or
- telling the truth.

The judgment of the people converted by the apostles was that they were not insane, criminal, or mistaken. They watched the apostles lay down their lives to testify to the truth of the gospel. Ten of the original 12 were **martyred** (killed because of their testimony about Jesus); John is said to have lived to old age (a legend that corresponds to the implication of Jn 21:23), and Judas committed suicide (Mt 27:3-10).

Note that the apostles did not convert every person to whom they told the story of Jesus' resurrection from the dead. That shows that first-century converts made a choice that others of their generation did not. That, in turn, shows that the credentials of the apostles were being examined. People didn't just buy the story uncritically! They scrutinized the apostles themselves, and asked whether these men were sick, stupid, criminal, or trustworthy. Some decided that the story they were being told was true; others rejected the story and the storytellers. That is the same kind of choice we face today.

We have been *culturally conditioned* by the success of science in the last five centuries to desire impersonal observations that can be verified by anyone, anywhere, at any time, using repeatable experimental methods. By "cultural conditioning," I mean that our culture will reward those who buy into the theory that science is the sole form of real knowledge and punish those who deny that proposition; the result of such operant conditioning is a knee-jerk reaction of hostility to the Christian claim that the knowledge we have about Jesus from the apostles is reliable. We do not have a time machine to take us back to the time of Jesus so that we can *see Jesus for ourselves*. We do not have a resurrection laboratory, where we can murder Jesus at our leisure and watch Him come back to life. There is no way to get the Church out of the way. *Either the apostles were honest and reliable witnesses to Jesus, or else we have no knowledge of Jesus whatsoever.*

It isn't just the Jesus story that can't be converted into scientific knowledge. All claims about historical figures (that they existed, that they said, thought, or did thus and such) are based on exactly the same kinds of considerations as belief in the apostolic tradition. The only way we can know anything about historical characters and events is to trust the testimony of human witnesses. In the absence of a time machine or a replay lab, we have no other access to knowledge of history than through the testimony of witnesses.

Henry Ford, founder of the Ford Motor Company, is said to have said that "history is bunk." The original quotation seems to be: "History is more or less bunk. It's tradition. We don't want tradition. We want to live in the present, and the only history that is worth a tinker's damn is the history that we make today."[12] Although this corresponds perfectly with our cultural conditioning, and, perhaps, with our aspirations to be done with vexing questions about past truth and historical meanings, it is utterly unscientific. Science *makes* history and depends on history in order to continue to make progress. Scientists do not start from scratch, and ignore everything that other scientists have learned in the past. Instead, they *rely on the scientific tradition* to identify what is and is not known.[13] This is essential, so that scientists do not waste their lives reinventing the wheel. A good scientist wants to learn something new. In order to do that, the scientist must know *what has already been discovered by others*. The only way to know that is to do history.

Jesus Left a Body, Not a Book

On the day that Jesus ascended into Heaven, His apostles had no books of the New Testament. All of their knowledge of Jesus was in their hearts and minds. Jesus authorized them to "go into the world and proclaim the gospel to every creature" (Mk 16:15), without Himself authoring *any* written version of the gospel message. From the Protestant point of view, this was the wrong thing for Jesus to do. They would have preferred Him to write down all of His instructions in His own hand, so that there would be one perfect, indubitable book, by which we could determine what to believe and how to act as Christians. (The Muslims claim to have such a divinely authored book, the Quran. If the proper way to preserve a message for all generations is to write a book, then Jesus is clearly inferior to Muhammad!)

We don't have any saying from Jesus or any teaching from the Church about why He chose to entrust His gospel to people, rather than to a book. The fact is that the community came first, and the Scriptures only long afterward. *The Church produced the Scriptures; the Scriptures did not produce the Church*. Since manuscripts were copied by hand, they were rare and valuable. It is highly unlikely that anyone would ever be able to read a part of the material that eventually became identified as inspired by God and included in the New Testament canon without having the owner of the manuscript nearby to answer questions and provide interpretations. In the first century of Christianity, the Scriptures were written in the faith community, read in the faith community, and copied in the faith community. The writings were never approached outside the context of the oral, lived

---

[12] Interview in *Chicago Tribune*, May 25, 1916.

[13] In the works of Michael Polanyi, this is a major theme that he introduced in *Personal Knowledge: Towards a Post-Critical Philosophy*, corrected edition (Chicago: University of Chicago Press, 1962), 195-202.

tradition. When some aspects of the faith were expressed in writing every now and again, the living community did not die out, nor was the written work thought of as a substitute for being educated by the community in the life of the faith.

Scholars theorize that it may have taken as many as 70 or 80 years for the 27 books of the New Testament to be written; the question about which books belonged in the canon was not fully settled until around 420 AD. *No book in the New Testament lists the other books of the New Testament.* When people treat the 27 books as The Word of the LORD, they are relying on the teaching authority of the Catholic Church. During the three centuries of debate about which books to include in the canon, many alleged gospels, acts, epistles, and revelations were rejected as inauthentic. Today, some people find it scandalous that the Church thought itself capable of recognizing which works reflected real apostolic traditions, and which were phony. There is a strange veneration for old manuscripts, as if people who lived 17 or 18 centuries ago did not know how to write hogwash or produce counterfeits. They seem to think that the Church should have mindlessly accepted every manuscript at face value and kept them all intact in the Church's libraries.

Good counterfeits always resemble authentic realities. Excellent counterfeits require expert analysis to distinguish the fake money or work of art from the real thing. No government would agree to keep fake money in circulation, simply because it bore a striking resemblance to real money—because real money would lose its value if the government tolerated the fakes. When the Church refused to lend its authority to things that only superficially resembled the four gospels, the Acts of the Apostles, the epistles, and the book of Revelation, it was acting responsibly, protecting its apostolic heritage from newly invented distortions.

For us, as we look back, we do not feel that there could be a great deal of difference between something written in the second or third century and things written in the first. It's all "a long time ago in a faraway place." We do not feel much difference between 17, 18, or 19 hundred years ago. But for the Church in the second, third, and fourth centuries, something that appeared for the first time in those centuries was one hundred, two hundred, or three hundred years removed from the time of Jesus and the apostles. It was *new and different* in its own day, not something (as we perceive it) almost simultaneous with first-century Christianity. To see how easy the judgment was to make that these novelties were not from God, just ask yourself whether you would try to write something today on your own authority about the American Civil War (1861-1865), and then seek to pass it off as part of the real historical record because we are "so close in time to the events of the war." In 2011, that war is "only" 146 years away from us. The year 175 AD was "only" 146 years after Jesus' death, but the Church of that day knew as well as we do that we don't have any firsthand knowledge of events that far removed from us.

The Canon of the New Testament

Because of the dominance of Greek culture, all 27 books of the New Testament were composed in Greek. Jesus' native language was Aramaic, a Semitic language related to Hebrew and Arabic; we know that this is so from the few Aramaic words and phrases embedded in the New Testament: "Abba" (Mk 14:36), "Ephatha" (Mk 7:34), "Talitha koum" (Mk 5:41), "Kephas" (1 Cor 1:12), "Eloi, Eloi, lema sabacthani" (Mk 15:34). There is a legend that the gospel of Matthew was composed in Aramaic, but no manuscripts have been found of that version, if it ever existed; if the legend is true—or if it contains a grain of truth—the Aramaic version of the gospel ceased to be copied and preserved, while the Greek translation and/or augmentation of it became a best seller.

The following table of the New Testament canon is adapted from *The New Jerome Biblical Commentary* (1990). It represents what was a scholarly consensus back then about the sequence in which the books of the New Testament were written. I'm sure that things have changed since then. There is nothing scholars love so much as overturning the scholarly consensus of their day. There is fame and fortune to be won by figuring out how to date the Scriptures differently and/or attribute them to a different author; there is no payoff for meekly accepting others' conjectures about date and authorship. Be that as it may, I present the table to give *some* sense of how the Scriptures of the New Testament emerged slowly and unsystematically over the course of time. The life of the Church came primarily from oral tradition, not from interpreting the Scriptures. *If oral tradition is untrustworthy, then so are the writings derived from it.*

The first thing to notice about the table is that Paul is the author of the oldest writings in the New Testament canon. This is very bizarre, because Paul was not one of Jesus' 12 apostles. He was converted to the Christian faith some time after Jesus was dead and gone (some time in the 30s AD). The first letter we have from him was written after he had been a member of the community for many years. Even if Paul wrote all 13 letters attributed to him (which some scholars think is doubtful), that is less than one letter every two years over the course of his Christian life. Paul evidently spent most of his time doing something other than writing.

The seven letters of Paul at the top of the table are unquestionably authentic. They circulated as a group in the early Church and were quoted often in other writings that have survived, but that did not become part of the New Testament.

A second observation to make from the table—however much it may need to be revised in order to keep it abreast of the latest and greatest scholarship—is that scholars think the gospel of Mark came first, and that Matthew and Luke were based on it and another common source (called "Q" from the German word for source, *quelle*) that has not survived independently of Matthew and Luke. Scholars generally agree that John was probably the last gospel written; opinions about its date and historicity (reliability as a historical source) vary considerably.

You will notice that after the seven unquestionably authentic letters of Paul, there are lots of question marks about who wrote the rest of the New Testament, and especially the other six letters attributed to Paul. The people of the New Testament era did not have our passion for copyrights or for exact dates and times. There was no need to attach the information about authorship and date to the front of manuscripts (as we do), because the author, audience, and copyists *knew each other personally*, as a general rule. There were practically no libraries or bookstores as we have today, where the texts would be isolated from the originating community (the series of libraries in Alexandria, Egypt, were a notable exception to this general rule). The writings that made their way into the New Testament collection were handed on, person to person; the authentication of the writings came not from what was written *in* the text, but from the person or community from whom the text was obtained.

This web of trust is entirely hidden from us now, because the knowledge of who got what from whom died with the authors and copyists; a few of the paths taken by the texts have been noted in the writings of the **Fathers of the Church** (e.g., the legend that Mark's gospel was written by a disciple of Peter), but we do not have such written accounts for each of the books that the Church judged were inspired by God. There were four touchstones of authenticity that shaped the long debate about which writings were to be treated as "the word of God":

- **Apostolic Origin**—attributed to and based on the preaching/teaching of the first-generation apostles (or their close companions).
- **Universal Acceptance**—acknowledged by all major Christian communities in the ancient world (by the end of the fourth century).
- **Liturgical Use**—read publicly when early Christian communities gathered for the Lord's Supper (their weekly worship services).
- **Consistent Message**—containing a theological outlook similar or complementary to other accepted Christian writings.

With some of the 27 books of the New Testament, it was easy to see that they met all four criteria. The seven letters of Paul, the four gospels, the Acts of the Apostles, and many of the other epistles (letters) gained widespread recognition in the second century. The canon of the Old Testament and New Testament, as used by the Catholic Church today, was affirmed in a series of local councils of the Church: the council of Rome (382 AD) under the authority of Pope Damasus I; the council of Hippo (393 AD); and two councils held in Carthage (397 AD and 419 AD).[14] When the **Council of Trent** (1545-1563 AD) dealt with Martin Luther's subtractions from the canon (seven books removed from the Old Testament and four books removed from the New Testament), it solemnly reaffirmed the same canon that had been agreed upon between 382 AD and 419 AD.

The word "Bible" originated in Greek in the third century AD. In both Greek and in Latin, *biblia* was a plural term meaning "books," and was used in the phrase "the holy books." When this

---

[14] James Akin, "Defending the Deuterocanonicals," *http://www.cin.org/users/james/files/deuteros.htm*

• CHRISTIANITY (JUDIASM CONTINUED) •

Date	Name	Author	NT #	Genre
50-51	1 Thessalonians	**Paul**	13	epistle
54	Galatians	**Paul**	9	epistle
54-8	Philippians	**Paul**	11	epistle
54-7	1 Corinthians	**Paul**	7	epistle
54-55	2 Corinthians	**Paul**	8	epistle
57-8	Romans	**Paul**	6	epistle
56-63	Philemon	**Paul**	18	epistle
60s	**Mark**	disciple of Peter?	2	gospel
65?	1 Peter	disciple of Peter?	21	epistle
before 70?	Hebrews	Jewish Christian?	19	treatise
63	*Peter and Paul martyred in Rome during Nero's reign*			
66-70	*Jewish revolt against Romans—ended with destruction of Temple*			
70s-80s	**Matthew**	Jewish scribe?	1	gospel
70s-80s	**Luke** = Volume I by Luke	Syrian gentile	3	gospel
after Luke	*Acts* = Volume II by Luke	author of Luke	5	"history"
70-80	Colossians	*not Paul?*	12	epistle?
after Col	Ephesians	*not Paul?*	10	epistle?
51-100?	2 Thessalonians	*not Paul?*	14	epistle?
60s-90s?	James	James of Jerusalem	20	epistle
90-100	**John**	Beloved Disciple	4	gospel
95-96 (The Apocalypse) John the Apostle	Revelation	not the B.D. or 27		apocalypse
circa 100 John the Apostle	1-2-3 John	not the B.D. or 23-5		epistles?
circa 100	Titus	*not Paul*	17	pastoral
circa 100	1 Timothy	author of Titus	15	pastoral
circa 100	2 Timothy	author of Titus	16	pastoral
circa 100	Jude	*not Jude*	26	epistle?
after Jude	2 Peter	*not Peter*	22	epistle?

term descended into our modern languages, it was transliterated as a *singular* word instead of plural, so that in our ordinary language people call the Bible "the good *book*." This, unfortunately, may give some people the mistaken impression that there is only one kind (*genre*) of writing in "the Book," and only one way to read "the Book." The Bible is *not* "a book." It is a collection of books, a sacred *library*. The Sacred Scriptures were written:

at different times,
in different places,
by different people,
in different languages (Hebrew, Greek, Aramaic),
using different literary techniques (different *genres* or *forms of writing*),
for different audiences,
addressing different concerns,
expressing the same faith,
under the inspiration of one and the same God.

The different kinds of writing (*genres*) in the collection demand different methods of interpretation (principles of **exegesis**). A joke should not be read as if it were a law, nor should a law be treated as a joke; the revelatory creation stories in Genesis should not be read as if they were modern scientific textbooks, nor should modern scientific textbooks be treated as if they were sacred Scripture.

Despite the multitude of differences in the texts, the claim of Christians is that the sacred Scriptures (Old and New Testament taken together) express **one faith.** There are no self-interpreting sentences (including this one); for a text to make sense, a reader has to make sense out of it. **Exegesis** means *"a method of interpretation"* or *"interpretation."* The goal of exegesis is to "get" (Latin, *agere*) the meanings "out of" (Latin, *ex*) the texts that God intended the texts to have. An "exegete" is someone who interprets a text. In philosophy, exegesis falls under the general heading of **hermeneutics**, which is the study of how people make and interpret meaning.

From the history of the development of the canon, it is very clear that Jesus did not give His disciples a list of books that would be written after He vanished from the earth. The apostles spoke about what they knew when they preached Jesus. They did not rely on "a book" to tell the story of His life, death, and resurrection. The books of the New Testament were written almost at random, from the human point of view, in response to various crises in the Church. Most of the authors of the New Testament show no consciousness that they were writing something for the ages to come. It was only after the writing was completed that the Church realized that the authentic remnants of the apostolic era needed to be certified as authentic, and set apart from other Scriptures and grouped together as "the word of God"—or, as it came to be known, the "New Testament."

If we take "Bible" to mean both the Old and the New Testaments, then it is clear that the Church is older than the Bible. Members of the Church wrote the books of the New Testament; other members collected and preserved them; still others, much later, certified them as inspired by God, and therefore, as a privileged part of tradition.

But People Garble Things

The fact that the Scriptures are the product of a Church that was itself the product of oral tradition raises the hackles of modern men and women: "Everybody knows that oral tradition is unreliable. You can't stake your life on a story that didn't get written down until decades after the fact. You fools! Haven't you ever played the **telephone game?**"

The rules of the telephone game (also known as "operator" or "Chinese whispers") are:

- Pick an unfamiliar sentence.
- Whisper it from person to person.
- Say the message only once.
- Repeat the message immediately to the next person in line.
- Prohibit questions.
- Put nothing in writing.
- Play the game in a sufficiently noisy environment so that only one person hears the message.
- Forbid the listeners to check to make sure that they have received the message correctly.

The whole point of the game is to see how garbled the message will become as it goes from person to person. If you do it when people have been drinking, and if you start with the right sentence, people will hear (or think they hear) sexually suggestive things. With the right crowd and the right amount of intoxication, it can be uproariously funny.

It is clear that there is *some* garbling in the minor details of the Scriptures. It seems to me that **whenever a story is told twice in the Bible, it is told differently**.[15] Some differences can be harmonized, others can't. The telephone game probably *does* explain how some those differences got into the Scriptures.

The Church has used **error-correcting protocols** to maintain the integrity of tradition, and to keep it true to the revelation Jesus made to His disciples. Computer systems use communications

---

[15] For the present time, I am calling this *Moleski's Conjecture*. I am too lazy to do the work necessary to turn it into a theorem. I would have to read the whole of the sacred Scriptures, keep track of all of the doublets, and show that they do, in fact, differ from one another. I have yet to come across such a pair; if I do, I will revise the conjecture to read, "Most of the time when a story is told twice in the Bible, it is told differently." That should be safe from falsification, although less dramatic than the original form of the conjecture.

protocols to make sure that material that is sent is correctly received. **They are authoritarian systems.** If an error is detected in a transmission, the receiver will reject the packet and ask for a retry. Most Internet communications are governed by **TCP/IP** (*Transmission Control Protocol/ Internet Protocol*): "IP is inherently unreliable, so TCP protects against data loss, data corruption, packet reordering and data duplication by adding checksums and sequence numbers to transmitted data and, on the receiving side, sending back packets that acknowledge the receipt of data."[16]

Long before the development of computer science and information theory, the Church adopted strategies that allowed the message of Jesus to be **transmitted intact** from one generation to the next in an extremely noisy (*sinful!*) environment. The Church:

- Developed **creeds**—sets of **dogmatic propositions** that could be defined and memorized.
- Preached the message aloud and in public.
- Repeated its basic message continually (Jesus is always "the same, yesterday, today, and tomorrow": Heb 13:8).
- Allowed itself to be questioned by any honest inquirers, either from within the community or from without. We can't answer all questions; we *can* meet all objections (that's the purpose of *apologetics*).
- Put its basic beliefs in writing (Scripture, the decrees of the councils, papal encyclicals, etc.).
- Created a sacred environment within which to share the message with the faithful.
- Always checked to make sure the message has been received correctly.

Old Covenant (Old *Testament*)	New Covenant (New *Testament*)
First sign of acceptance: **circumcision** (surgery on the males).	First sign of acceptance: **Baptism** (a bath—the same sign for all).
Salvation came through obedience to the **Torah**.	Salvation came as a **grace** (a gift, unearned).
Messiah (Christ) was a **human king** who would marry, father an heir, win battles, and die.	Messiah is the **God-Man** who conquered sin and death and now lives and reigns *forever* (fulfilling Psalm 89).
Life was regulated by **613 commandments** in the Torah.	Life was regulated by the **Holy Spirit**.
The official place of worship was the **Temple** in Jerusalem: one God, one People, one Holy Land, one Holy City, one Temple.	The official place of worship is the **Body of Christ**: "wherever two or three are gathered in My Name, there am I" (Mt 18:20; Acts 9:5, 22:8, 26:15).

---

[16] http://www.faqs.org/faqs/internet/tcp-ip/tcp-ip-faq/part1/

- Prohibited false teachers from teaching in the name of the Church.

The whole point of the authority of the Church is to see that the **Deposit of Faith** (the body of knowledge that Jesus revealed to the apostles) does not become garbled as it goes from person to person. The doctrine of *apostolic succession* teaches that **the bishops are the successors of the apostles**. The authorized teachers of the Church are **ordained men** (bishops, priests, and deacons); no one gets *ordained* (placed in one of these three **Holy Orders**) unless they give good evidence that they know, believe, and can transmit the faith.

The Judas Factor

Jesus Himself, true God and true Man, the Way, the Truth, and the Life, the light of the world that cannot be overcome by darkness, chose 12 apostles. *All* of them abandoned Him when he was arrested (Mk 14:50), and one of them was *directly* responsible for handing him over to His murderers (Mk 14:43). The first Judas was not the last. *Jesus has been betrayed in every age by people who have been chosen to represent Him to the world.*

The **infallibility of the Church and of the pope** is due to the infallible power of **God** to protect what He has revealed. The doctrine that **God will not permit the Church or the pope to officially *teach* what is false about faith and morals** is a doctrine about the goodness and power of God, not about the goodness or power of the members of the Church or of the papacy. The infallibility claimed by the Church is limited to faith (dogma, the creeds) and morals; the Church does not claim to be infallible about science, history, politics, economics, literature, aesthetics, and the like.

The Catholic Church does *not* now teach, and *never has taught* that popes, bishops, priests, or deacons are *sinless*. There are, unfortunately, all too many proofs from the past and the present that the sacrament of Holy Orders does *not* automatically make men holy. Ordained men have committed every form of sin imaginable, including **apostasy** (abandoning the faith entirely), **heresy** (keeping part of the tradition and denying part of the tradition), adultery, rape, incest, pedophilia, pederasty, sodomy, murder, theft, lying, and blasphemy; they have indulged in every form of pride, greed, lust, anger, gluttony, envy, and sloth; they have committed crimes against God and against humanity.

The sins of ordained men have not changed the teachings of Jesus or of the Church. Anyone who can condemn the sins of priests affirms that they know the difference between right and wrong and the difference between fidelity to Jesus and infidelity. *Those who condemn the sins of the ordained prove that they have received the gospel message through the unbroken tradition of the Church.* They can tell—quite easily!—that the ordained have not lived up to their **vocation** (Latin, *vocare*, "to call" = "calling") to "Believe what you read, teach what you believe, and practice what you teach."[17] Even outsiders who reject the teaching authority of the Church can judge that the sinful bishops, priests, and deacons have not served the gospel faithfully. If we *know for sure* that popes, bishops, priests and deacons have sinned, then we affirm that we *know for sure* what the teaching of the Church is.

Tradition is fault-tolerant. I don't mean that we should tolerate sin in our own lives or in the lives of the ordained. "Fault-tolerance" is another concept from the world of computers. It means that a breakdown in one piece of hardware does not cause the whole system to collapse. Neither Judas nor the multitudes who have committed the sin of Judas have destroyed the power of the remainder to transmit the Deposit of Faith *fully and faithfully*. If Tradition were like a chain, breaking one single link would break the whole chain. But it is much more like a rope, in which thousands of strands are woven together; though a few strands may snap, the rest are able to take up the remainder of the load.[18] The message of Jesus' saving death and resurrection is carried now by millions of messengers; great harm can be done *locally* by the sins of messengers who betray the message, but **the truth of the gospel** is still carried to the ends of the earth.

The sins of the ordained discredit the sinners, not the Church. *Not one teaching of the Church is changed by the sad fact that Jesus has been betrayed by His disciples.* The sin of Judas said nothing about Jesus' own goodness and integrity; it does show that those who have freely chosen to follow Jesus may freely choose to cease following Him. The sins of priests prove that priests can sin. The sins of the ordained should come as no surprise to people who know the text of the Mass.[19] In addition to praying with the whole congregation for the forgiveness of sins, there are prayers said quietly by the priest alone, reminding him of his need for repentance and forgiveness:

> **Before the Gospel:** "Lord, cleanse my heart and my lips that I may worthily proclaim Your holy gospel."
> **After the Gospel:** "By the words of this holy gospel may my sins be blotted out."
> **After the Offertory** (while washing his hands): "Lord, wash away my sins and cleanse me of my iniquities."
> **After the Lamb of God:** "Lord Jesus Christ, Son of the living God, by the will of the Father and the work of the Holy Spirit your death brought life to the world. By your holy body and blood free me from all my sins and from every evil. Keep me faithful to your teaching and never let me be parted from you." Alternatively: "Lord Jesus Christ, with faith in your love and mercy I eat your body and drink your blood. Let it not bring me condemnation but health in mind and body."

---

[17] From the Latin rite for the ordination of deacons.
[18] John Henry Newman; see "Reasoning from Wholes to Wholes" in Moleski, *Personal Catholicism*, 126.
[19] I am quoting from the Latin rite. I am confident that other rites in the Catholic tradition have similar prayers that remind the ordained of their need to repent of their own sins.

> **At Communion:** "May the Body of Christ bring me to everlasting life. ... May the Blood of Christ bring me to everlasting life."
> **After Communion**, while purifying the chalice and paten: "Lord, may I receive these gifts in purity of heart. May they bring me healing and strength, now and forever."

Many people in our culture have a strange affection for Judas. They portray his act of betrayal as noble and worthy of praise, as if his treachery toward Jesus is the cause of our salvation, instead of Jesus' willingness to lay down his life to save us. Judas clearly miscalculated what he was doing—otherwise he would not have committed suicide, but would have stayed on earth, happy about and proud of what he had accomplished. That Jesus allowed Judas to make bad choices is not an indication that Judas did what Jesus wanted him to do. **God's knowledge of the choices we make does not diminish our freedom in making those choices.** So, too, with Judas. God, in His mercy, can bring good out of evil; that does not mean that evil is good, or that good is evil.

There is a proverb in Latin that applies here: *corruptio optima pessima*—"corruption of the best is the worst." The ordained *should* be like Jesus. When they are not, all hell breaks loose, and great harm is done to the victims of their sins.

The obligation to be like Jesus does not rest solely upon the ordained. All the members of the Body of Christ are meant to be saints. The sins of Christians through the centuries are a scandal both to believers and unbelievers. The sins of the ***ordained*** (those who have been placed in a Holy Order) are more evident and cause greater distress, because of the role that bishops, priests, and deacons are meant to play in the life of the Body. The sins of priests prove that priests are not perfect—but the Church never claimed that they were. In the same way, the sins of baptized and married Catholics prove that Catholics, in general, are not perfect, even though that is the ideal toward which all Catholics should strive.

The bottom line is this: **Don't leave Jesus because of Judas.** The love of God poured out in the death and resurrection of Jesus is our remedy for all sin, whether it is the sin of believers or unbelievers, or the sin of the ordained or the unordained.

The Origin and Development of the Holy Orders

The letters of St. Paul have two lists of gifts, both headed by the gift of apostleship.

1 Cor 12:28	Eph 4:11
One Body with many gifts:	Gifts for building up the body:
apostles	**apostles**
prophets	**prophets**

teachers	evangelists
workers of miracles	*pastors* (similar to administrators)
healers	**teachers**
helpers	
administrators (similar to pastors)	"… so that we may no longer be infants, tossed by waves and swept along by every wind of teaching arising from human trickery, from their cunning in the interests of deceitful scheming" (Eph 4:14)
speakers in various kinds of tongues	

The Church's understanding of the **office of bishop** is that the bishops are the *heirs and successors* of the apostles. One of the first acts of the original Christian community in Jerusalem was to select a successor to Judas: "May another take his office" (1:20). The apostle was dead; his office lived on. The Greek word for "office" was *episkopen* (*epi-*, "over, upon" + *skopein*, "to look or watch" = "to watch over"); in English, we transliterate it as "episcopacy." *Episkopos*, literally, "overseer," turned into "bishop" in English through the marvels of linguistic evolution. The initial vowel and inflected ending both dropped off, "p" became a "b" and "sk" became "sh." For those who have eyes to see and ears to hear, "bishop" is unquestionably the same word as "episkopos"; everyone else will have to take the linguists' word for it.

The offices of **priests** and **deacons** are developments of the role of the bishop—the bishop's authority is vested in and delegated to the lower orders. The word "priest," like "bishop," has been derived through linguistic evolution from the Greek word, *presbyteros*, "elder." First the ending dropped off, leaving us with "presbyter." People changed that to "prester" and eventually "priest." The apostles often appointed elders to watch over the community (Acts 11:30, 14:23, 15:22, 20:17; Titus 1:5,7; 1 Peter 5:1). "Deacon" is derived from the Greek word *diakonos*, "servant" (Acts 6:1-6; 1 Timothy 3:8-13).

These three **Holy Orders** (*bishop, priest, and deacon*) preserve the gifts of evangelization, teaching, and administration. The miraculous gifts mentioned by St. Paul have never been institutionalized, although the Church does expect miracles as a confirmation of sanctity.

The chain of apostolic succession has been preserved in the Roman Catholic Church. The pastoral gifts are found in every age of her history. The **papacy** is a special development within the office of bishop. The Pope is the **Bishop of Rome**. He is not *ordained* to the papacy the way that bishops, priests, and deacons are *ordained* in the sacrament of Holy Orders. The Bishop of Rome is the successor of Peter, and therefore, inherits the special role of Peter within the "college" (group) of other successors of the apostles (Mt. 16:18-19). Paul also died in Rome during the same persecution in which Peter died, so the pope also inherited some of St. Paul's charisma, even though Paul was not the Bishop of Rome.

The word "pope" and "papacy" derive from the Greek name given to all bishops, *pappas*, which means "father." The more restricted association of this term with the Bishop of Rome seems to have developed in the second or third century. Bishops of Rome claimed authority over other bishops in a number of conflicts, beginning with Clement in 95 AD, who tried to establish a universal date for Good Friday and Easter (there were—and are—different methods for calculating the time of Passover). The first successors to Peter are listed in the first Eucharistic Prayer in the Latin rite: Linus, Cletus, and Clement are the first three; Sixtus, the next person mentioned in the prayer, is the "sixth" successor of Peter. Over the centuries, the Church came to affirm the **primacy** (literally, "firstness") of the Bishop of Rome over all the other bishops of the Church. The doctrine of the primacy of the pope means that he is the chief legislator, executive, and judge in the Church. This was one of the major points of dispute in the schism between Roman Catholicism and the Eastern Orthodox (see p. 129).

Well, That's Your Interpretation

Following the lead of Vatican II,[20] I think of the faith as deriving from a single source, the **Deposit of Faith**, which was given both orally and tacitly by Jesus to the first disciples, and which, in turn, *developed* into what we now call tradition and the New Testament. In my view, the New Testament is best understood as a development of tradition, and not an alternative to it; it is a sacred and privileged *form* of tradition.

The authority of the Old Testament is quite different from that of the New Testament, since those sacred texts precede the decisive revelation given in Jesus to His disciples in the Deposit of Faith. The authority of the Old Testament is not negligible. The first Scriptures created the religious context within which Jesus became human, and Jesus relied on Old Testament Scriptures to define Himself, but the New Testament creates a decisive framework for *reinterpreting* the revelation given in the Old Testament. As we saw previously (page 106), to be a Christian means to reinterpret the meaning of Christ, King, Kingdom, enemy, and victory. In this section, we will consider how the Christian community **de-literalized the Scriptures of the Old Testament**.

The literal contradictions between different versions of the same stories, both in the Old and New Testament, cause me to reject the **dictation model of inspiration**, and the associated theory that the Bible is meant to be read literally. On this model, God is responsible for every syllable of every word and every letter of every syllable. The human authors are thought of as nothing but zombie secretaries, who mindlessly copy down exactly and only what God tells them

---

[20] In Roman Catholic reckoning, **Vatican Council II (1962-1965)** was the 21st *ecumenical* ("worldwide") council of the Church. When all of the bishops of the world gather together in a council with the pope, they are able to define matters of faith and morals. Nicea (325 AD) was the first such council; see p. 107.

to. It is this theory of how God inspires the authors of Scripture that led to the bumper sticker: "God wrote it; I read it; that settles it."

I don't believe that God's truth was dropped into the Scriptures from Heaven back in the past in such a way that it pops straight out of the Bible in our own day, untouched by human interpretations. Unless people have the same *principles of interpretation* (hermeneutics, exegesis), they won't get the same message out of the same texts. I see no evidence that the authors of the New Testament took the Old Testament Scriptures literally. Far from it! My impression is that they almost never do so.[21]

The early Church was disturbed by the question of whether **Gentile** (non-Jewish) converts to Christianity needed to become law-abiding Jews, in order to become members of the Kingdom of *the* Christ, *the* King of the Jews. The **Judaizers** said "yes." They had both Scripture and tradition on their side:

- Jesus was a Jew because his mother was Jewish.
- He was circumcised and worshipped in the Temple.
- His 12 apostles and *all* of the disciples He made were Jews; all of the males were circumcised and kept the Torah.
- He focused His work on Jews living in the territory of ancient Israel (which in His day was divided into Galilee, Samaria, and Judea).
- He said that none of the Law (**Torah**) would be changed: "Amen, I say to you, until heaven and earth pass away, not the smallest letter or the smallest part of a letter will pass from the law, until all things have taken place" (Matt 5:18). Heaven and earth have clearly *not* passed away; therefore, the Torah should still be in effect for Jesus' disciples.

The Judaizers—the biblical literalists of their day—concluded: "Unless you are circumcised according to the Mosaic practice, you cannot be saved" (Acts 15:1). Circumcision was just the first of the **613 principles of the Torah** in the Pentateuch that the converts would have to accept.

Paul strenuously disagreed with the Judaizers. In his letter to a community that he had founded in Galatia, he said that he hoped that the next time the Judaizers were circumcising one of their converts, the "knife would slip" (Gal 5:12) and (by implication) cause the castration of the convert. (This is one of many passages that makes me think that God did not dictate the Scriptures word for word!) Paul and the Judaizers took their argument to Jerusalem to talk with "the apostles and presbyters about this question" (Acts 15:2; Gal 2:1-10).

---

[21] This is my second unproven—but not unprovable—conjecture. All I have to do to test this theory is read the New Testament, and note all the quotations, paraphrases, and allusions to the Old Testament, then decide whether the author is treating the original text literally or figuratively.

At the council in Jerusalem, Peter told how God had spoken to him in a vision. He was up on a roof terrace waiting for the mid-day meal to be prepared. Three times he saw something like a sheet lowered toward him containing "all the earth's four-legged animals and reptiles and birds of the sky" (Acts 10:11). Each time, a voice said to him, "Kill and eat," but Peter replied that he was a good Jew and would not eat non-kosher food (10:13-14). The voice then said, "What God has made clean [*kosher*], you are not to call unclean" (10:15).

While Peter was still trying to figure out the meaning of this weird and unexpected vision, a group of men asked him to come to the house of Cornelius, who was a centurion in the Roman army of occupation (10:1,22). From the point of view of the Jews, such a man was religiously unclean. Soldiers in the Roman army had to *worship Caesar as a god* when they were sworn in. Their presence in the Holy Land was an abomination. They enforced a rapacious tax code that paid for their presence in the region, and produced profits that were sent back to Rome to benefit the ruling classes there.

Peter violated the Torah by accepting the invitation to go into Cornelius's house: "You know that it is unlawful [*not kosher*] for a Jewish man to associate with, or visit, a Gentile, but God has shown me that I should not call any person profane or unclean" (10:28). Notice how Peter is reasoning *symbolically* from the content of his vision, not *literally*. The vision was about *food*, not *people*, but Peter understood that God was using the example of the abolition of the food rules in the Torah to stand for the abolition of the rules against associating with religiously unclean people.

God confirmed Peter's insight into the vision by giving Cornelius and his whole household the very same gift that Peter and the disciples of Jesus had received on the day of Pentecost (Acts 2:4-13): "While Peter was still speaking these things, the holy Spirit fell upon all who were listening to the word. The circumcised believers who had accompanied Peter were astounded that the gift of the holy Spirit should have been poured out on the Gentiles also, for they could hear them speaking in tongues and glorifying God" (Acts 10:44-46).

This event must have been a terrible shock to the "circumcised believers" who accompanied Peter on his law-breaking visit to Cornelius's house. For Jesus' original followers, the gift of the Holy Spirit came *last*, after they had followed Jesus, witnessed His death and resurrection, and watched Him vanish into the heavens (Lk 24:51; Acts 1:6-10).[22] These soldiers, who had worshipped Caesar as a god in order to join the Roman Legion and whose job was to enforce an unjust tax system on captive nations, received the Holy Spirit while they were uncircumcised,

---

[22] Students who plan to be Scripture scholars should note that the story of the disciples seeing Jesus taken up into the heavens appears only in Luke, who admits in his introduction that he is not an eyewitness (1:1-4) of the events in the gospel. Whether the disciples saw the decisive moment or not, all of the NT writings agree that the time of Jesus' appearances to His disciples came to an end. Luke is the only author who tells the story of the day of Pentecost, so I am following his account.

and before they began to keep *any* of the other 612 provisions of the Torah. God's action in pouring out His Spirit on the foreigners seemed to be saying—without words—that the age of Torah was over. Peter summed up the argument:

> God, who knows the heart, bore witness by granting them the holy Spirit just as he did us. He made no distinction between us and them, for by faith he purified their hearts. Why, then, are you now putting God to the test by placing on the shoulders of the disciples a yoke that neither our ancestors nor we have been able to bear? On the contrary, we believe that we are saved through the grace of the Lord Jesus, in the same way as they.
>
> The whole assembly fell silent, and they listened while Paul and Barnabas described the signs and wonders God had worked among the Gentiles through them. (15:8-12)

In view of the argument that the act of faith in "the grace of the Lord Jesus" was all that was necessary to join the Kingdom of the King of the Jews, the council decided to cease treating the rules and regulations of the Old Testament as binding on Christians, except for four principles:

> It is the decision of the holy Spirit and of us not to place on you any burden beyond these necessities, namely, to abstain from meat sacrificed to idols, from blood, from meats of strangled animals, and from unlawful marriage. If you keep free of these, you will be doing what is right. (Acts 15:28-29)

Three of the four commandments imposed on the Gentiles have become a dead letter in subsequent centuries. We no longer have pagan temples trying to support their operations by selling meat left over from sacrifices to false gods (or, if we do, it is not on the same scale as in the first century AD). Our view of biology has changed radically, so that we no longer think of the blood of animals as being a more sacred part of the animal than any of the other organs and systems that keep them alive, so we no longer feel the force of the requirement to leave the blood for God alone.

With this decision to set aside the Torah, the council of Jerusalem *de-literalized* the Scriptures of the Old Testament. Christians have kept the old Scriptures in our collection, because "All scripture is inspired by God and is useful for teaching, for refutation, for correction, and for training in righteousness so that one who belongs to God may be competent, equipped for every good work" (2 Tim 3:16-17), but we do not treat all of the 613 precepts of the Torah as God's law for the Body of Christ.

For me, the decision to cut the Christian community loose from the Torah is one of the most extraordinary events in all of Scripture, because it was a group of Jewish disciples of Jesus who decided that the Jewish Torah tradition was no longer binding. Ceasing to impose the Torah on

Gentile converts helped to create the conditions under which what had been a completely Jewish religious movement could become almost completely non-Jewish. Some of the consequences of the de-literalization of the Old Testament are summarized in the following table.

"Hindsight is 20/20 vision." For those who experienced or accepted the testimony of the eyewitnesses that Jesus rose from the dead, all of these rearrangements and reinterpretations of the Jewish tradition seem perfectly straightforward and logical. As we saw previously in the discussion of why it is logical for Jews to reject the claim that Jesus is the Christ (see page 107), for those who do not believe that Jesus rose from the dead, there is a huge discrepancy between the natural reading of the Jewish Scriptures and the interpretation placed on them by Christians.

Destruction of Jerusalem, the Temple, and Jewish Christianity (66-73 AD)

We can identify four major groups of Jews around the time of Jesus.

- **Sadducees** were priests associated with Temple worship; their religious worldview was conservative, which meant that they tended not to believe in angels and the resurrection of the dead (Mt 22:29-32; Acts 23:8).
- **Pharisees** were devout teachers (rabbis) and students of the Torah; this is the group that bears the most striking resemblances to the group of disciples gathered around Rabbi Jesus. Paul also came from the Pharisee tradition: "Circumcised on the eighth day, of the race of Israel, of the tribe of Benjamin, a Hebrew of Hebrew parentage, in observance of the law a Pharisee, in zeal I persecuted the church, in righteousness based on the law I was blameless" (Phil 3:5-6).
- The **Essenes** founded their own communities in the desert, apart from Jerusalem and the ordinary towns and villages of the Holy Land; we know about them primarily through the discovery of the Dead Sea Scrolls (1947-1979). People like to associate John the Baptist with the Essenes, but there is nothing definite in the Scriptures to confirm or deny that identification, other than the fact that both John and the Essenes withdrew to the desert.
- The **Zealots** were nationalists who wanted to wage war against the Romans and gain independence for Judea.

In 66 AD the Zealots got the war they had been waiting for. The Jews had many notable successes in battle, until the Romans brought their military reserves into Judea from elsewhere in the empire. From then on, things went from bad to worse. Jerusalem was conquered in 70 AD; the city and the Second Temple were demolished; the final pockets of resistance were defeated over the next few years.

The destruction of the Temple and the defeat of the rebels obliterated the Sadducees and Zealots. Some of the Essene communities seem to have survived until the next century; we have no clear record of how their settlements came to be abandoned. The Pharisees survived the calamity—not all, of course, but enough rabbis remained to cope with the catastrophe and figure out how to preserve their faith and way of life, despite the loss of Jerusalem and the Temple. As in the days of the Exile in Babylon, all that they could do in the face of such overwhelming misfortune was to *remember Jerusalem* (Ps 137:5-6) **and keep the Torah** as best they could. Since the destruction of the Second Temple in 70 AD, God's covenant partners can no longer obey the precepts in the Torah about Temple sacrifice, but they can meditate on the law of the Lord, and think about what it *means* to them. Some Jews do call their synagogues "temples," but there is no priesthood and no animal sacrifice in them as there was in the one and only Temple of God in Jerusalem.

In the next few centuries, **rabbinic Judaism** produced two great commentaries on the Torah, the *Mishnah* (circa 200 AD), a collection of oral traditions, and the *Talmud* (also known as the *Gemara*; circa 500 AD), an intricate discussion of the texts in the Pentateuch. The dedication of the rabbis made it possible for Judaism to survive and even flourish in **diaspora**, small communities of Jews scattered throughout the world from 70 AD until the nation of Israel was reestablished in 1948 (see page 172). Their ability to keep their faith in God's covenant and to preserve their distinctive way of life, despite the loss of the Promised Land and the Temple, is a moral miracle.

Up until 70 AD, Jerusalem had been the center for Jewish Christianity, which, of course, was the original form of the new religion. Luke portrays that first community as being "continually in the temple praising God" (24:53). For them, the belief that Jesus was the Christ was a *fulfillment of their Jewish identity*. There was no need to cease being Jewish in order to be Christian, as became the case in later centuries. The destruction of the Temple meant the destruction of the original form of Christianity as well. The loss of the Jewish roots of Christianity paved the way for the Gentiles to dominate the Church, and helped create the strange amnesia among Christians about their debt to God's Chosen People, the descendants of Abraham through Isaac: "salvation comes from the Jews" (Jn 4:22).

Ya Gotta Believe: The Council of Nicaea (325 AD)

The Church sees the time from the Ascension of Jesus until the death of the last of the original 12 apostles as the **apostolic era**. When the last person died who knew Him personally, there could be no further additions to the **Deposit of Faith**, the body of knowledge that Jesus transmitted to His disciples. The next six centuries or so are known in Church history as the **patristic era**, the age of the **Fathers of the Church** (Latin, *pater*, "father," becomes *patri* in the plural, "fathers").

The task of the Church from the time of Jesus' disappearance from the face of the earth was to *hand on what it had received*; this is what the word "tradition" means. Paul uses this expression when writing to the Corinthians about the resurrection from the dead:

> For I *handed on to you* as of first importance *what I also received*: that Christ died for our sins in accordance with the Scriptures; that he was buried; that he was raised on the third day in accordance with the Scriptures; that he appeared to Cephas, then to the Twelve. After that, he appeared to more than five hundred brothers at once, most of whom are still living, though some have fallen asleep. After that he appeared to James, then to all the apostles. Last of all, as to one born abnormally, he appeared to me. (1 Cor 15:3-8; emphasis added)

When we give a package to UPS or FedEx or the U.S. Post Office, we expect them to hand on what was handed on to them without changing the contents of the package. The same is true of the packets we use when transmitting materials across the internet. TCP/IP makes sure that the packet that is received is identical to the packet that was sent.[23] As we saw above (p. 99), the Church instinctively developed error-correcting protocols to protect the gospel message from being changed as it was handed on from one generation to the next.

It is perfectly evident that a *lot* of changes have taken place since Jesus walked and talked with the first generation of believers. While He was with them, there were no New Testament Scriptures at all; no popes, bishops, priests, deacons; no sacraments, other than Baptism and the **Eucharist** (instituted at the Last Supper), no vestments, candles, incense, bells, processions, banners, statues, stained-glass windows, golden vessels, or church buildings; no definitions, dogmas, creeds, or catechisms. The group gathered around Jesus probably didn't even have a distinctive name or any consciousness of being very much different from their fellow Jews. They almost certainly did believe that Jesus was *the* Christ and that great things were about to happen, but it is equally likely that they had no sense of the shape that the faith community would take in the centuries ahead.

John Henry Newman believed that "In another world it may be otherwise, but in this world, to grow is to change, and to be perfect is to have changed often."[24] The Church has changed dramatically from the day when Jesus called His first disciples to follow Him. The claim that the Church makes is that the Deposit of Faith has not changed (and cannot change) since the death of the last apostle, even though the Church itself has undergone countless transformations. In the development of a human body, the genetic code embedded in the DNA of the cells remains the same, even as it causes the original cell to divide into the trillions of differentiated daughter cells that constitute our bones, muscle, sinew, organs, tissues, and blood. In the same way, the

---

[23] Students who are familiar with computer science know that the algorithms that check data integrity are only probabilistic, not deterministic. The checksum used in TCP/IP provides *practical* certitude that the packet has not been corrupted, not perfect certitude. The number of errors that escape detection is negligible.

[24] *Essay on the Development of Doctrine* (New York: Sheed and Ward, 1960 [1845]), 30.

genetic code of the Church (the Deposit of Faith) has remained the same, while causing the Church to develop new aspects and dimensions that are not at all visible in the original group of disciples gathered around Jesus.

This **Organic Model of Revelation** emphasizes the developmental nature of Judeo-Christian faith. God planted the **seeds of revelation** that change as they grow—but they change in a way that is *consistent with their nature*. In each stage of organic growth, the living being preserves the DNA that guides the entire process. This model explains why Christianity looks so different when the images found in the New Testament are compared to the later versions found in history. **If the seed remains unchanged, it is dead; its purpose in life is to *grow***. If the Church had remained in the form it first took in first-century Palestine, it would be *dead*, not authentic Christianity. People who want to "go back to the beginning" don't understand that the purpose of the beginning was to start the process of development that has led to the (relatively) mature Church we know today.

Newman argues that the Church changed in order to "remain the same" (*ibid.*). Our fully developed bodies are the result of countless changes that continue to the day we die. Food is metabolized; wastes eliminated; stresses, injuries, and illness countered; cells replaced. The Church has incorporated hundreds of millions of new members, some (many?) of whom asked questions that were not discussed or that were not recorded in the first century of Christianity. Besides such internal reasons for development of doctrine, the Church has also been forced to adapt continually to new and unexpected pressures arising from external circumstances, just like the living organisms studied in ecology.

In the apostolic era, individual apostles made practical decisions about what to teach and how to guide the life of the Christian community. During the patristic era, apostolic communities were able to compare notes with each other, so that some developments in doctrine and discipline became common to all. The papacy eventually emerged during the age of Roman persecutions (63-305 AD) as a kind of Supreme Court that could resolve conflicts between local bishops. After Constantine granted Christians freedom of worship in the Edict of Milan (313 AD), there was an opportunity for the Church to hold an *ecumenical* (all-inclusive) council to settle some matters of doctrine and discipline.

The great doctrinal issue disturbing the peace of the Church and of the Empire in 325 AD was the **Arian heresy**. Arius taught that the Son who took flesh and dwelt among us (Jn 1:14) was a god compared to us (superior in every respect), but was not God when compared to God the Father; the Arian view was based on their interpretation of the assertion that Jesus was "firstborn of all creatures" (Col 1:15). On this view, the Father first created the Son, then created everything else through the Son. The Son, then, was *homoiousios* (Greek, *homoi*, "like, similar" + *ousios*, "substance, being"), *like* the Father in being but not possessing the *same substance* (Greek, *homo*, "same," + *ousios*).

Notice that there is just one *iota* of difference between *homoiousios* and *homoousios*. In this case, the "one iota of difference" makes a huge difference. Christians were sharply divided between the two theological camps.

Constantine, the Roman emperor, wanted an end to the theological wrangling. He summoned the bishops of the Church to meet near his new imperial capital that was being constructed on the site of Byzantium in eastern Greece. Moving the capital of the Roman Empire out of Rome and into Greek territory shows how Greek culture (Hellenism) still dominated the Mediterranean four centuries after the Romans took possession of the western half of Alexander's empire. As a consequence, the Scriptures of the New Testament were all composed or preserved in Greek. The first eight councils of the Church, beginning with the **Council of Nicaea** in 325 AD, all took place near **Constantinople** (Greek, *Constantinos* + *polis*, "city" = Constantine's city) and were conducted primarily in Greek, the original sacred language of Christianity.

The 21 ecumenical councils of the Catholic Church are the primary source for **dogma**, the official teachings that the Church considers to be essential for all believers. At Nicaea, the council fathers composed a **creed** (Latin, *credo*, "I believe") that is still used every Sunday in most Roman Catholic Masses, Orthodox liturgies, and in many mainline Protestant worship services as well.

Notice how the Nicene Creed **demythologizes** the Scriptures—it leaves out "fairy tale" elements from the original stories, but preserves the **religious truth** embodied in them (see page 58). Catholics are *not* obliged to believe in the six-day story of creation, the male-first story, the Bethlehem stories in Matthew and Luke, or any of the disparate and contradictory details of the Resurrection narratives or other doublets in the Scriptures. The creed tells us how to read (interpret, exegete) the Scriptures. The central dogmas of the faith expressed in the creed are:

- **Trinity**: God is three *persons* in one *being*.
- **Incarnation**: One divine person, the Son, took on the nature of a human being.
- **Atonement**: Jesus' acceptance of death on the cross and His resurrection from the dead conquers sin and death for the whole of humanity.

We do not *see* these realities with our physical eyes. They are inaccessible to scientific instruments, which merely extend the range of our physical senses and are used to observe and measure physical realities. From our own personal experience, we know nothing about what it would be like to be one of the three persons of the Trinity—our healthy experience is *one person per being*. If some human being manifests more than one person within them, we call them demon-possessed, schizophrenic, victims of multiple personality disorder, or Siamese twins.

Similarly, we do not understand from our own personal experience what it was like for one of the divine persons, the Son, to take on a second nature so that, after the Incarnation, He was true God and true man. Our healthy human experience is of one nature per person. There are some

Text of the Nicene Creed (325 AD)	Comments
I believe in one God,	Radical monotheism.
the Father, the Almighty, maker of heaven and earth,	Genesis 1 and 2 *demythologized*.
of all things visible and invisible.	"Visible" = the physical universe; "Invisible" = metaphysical realities.
I believe in one Lord,	"Jesus is Lord."
Jesus	His human name was Jesus of Nazareth.
Christ,	**"Messiah"** = **"Anointed One"** —-> *King of the Jews*.
the *Only Begotten* Son of God,	Contrast angels (hasatan), Adam, King of Israel: "sons of God" who were not God the Son.
born of the Father before all ages.	The Son has always existed and cannot not exist.
God from God, Light from Light, true God from true God,	John 1:1 — "The Word *[logos]* was *with* GOD and the Word *was* GOD."
begotten, not made, consubstantial with the Father.	"Not made" = *uncreated*. "*consubstantial*" = same being with the Father.
Through him all things were made.	John 1:3—A Christian Genesis.
For us men	Males and females constitute *one* Human Being.
and for our salvation	Implicit notion of **Original Sin** (Gen 3).
He came down from heaven and by the Holy Spirit was incarnate of the *virgin* Mary,	**"Incarnation"**—John 1:14. Infancy narratives: Mt and Lk agree on this point. Dogma: **Virginal Conception of Jesus.**
and became man.	God the Son took on a true human nature without ceasing to possess His divine nature.
For our sake	"Our" means *the whole of humanity*.
He was crucified under Pontius Pilate;	A real historical date.
He suffered death and was buried,	GOD the Son suffered and died (vs. *docetism*, the heresy that claims that the Son only pretended to suffer and die).
and rose again on the third day	Resurrection narratives—reduced to their core agreement.
in accordance with the Scriptures;	The Scriptures of the Old Testament *as reinterpreted in the light of Jesus' death and resurrection*.

He ascended into heaven and is seated at the right hand of the Father.	From the synoptic trial scenes, in which Jesus is convicted of blasphemy for claiming equality with God, using this imagery.
He will come again in glory	"**Ad-vent**" (Latin, *ad* + *venire*) = "coming."
to judge the living and the dead,	Judgment is not intrinsically evil. Judgment alone can produce a just resolution of human history.
and his kingdom will have no end.	*Spiritual* fulfillment of Ps 2 and Ps 89.
I believe in **the Holy Spirit**	It is not clear here that the Holy Spirit is also God—clarified in 381 AD.
the Lord, the giver of life, who proceeds from the Father	The "*filioque*" clause: Western innovation.
[***and the Son***],	
who with the Father and the Son is adored and glorified,	Implicit affirmation of the divinity of the Spirit.
who has spoken through the prophets.	Christians must respect TNK/LXX.
I believe in	The four "marks" of the Church.
one	
holy,	
catholic, and	
apostolic	
Church.	
I confess one baptism for the forgiveness of sins	Baptism, like circumcision, can be administered only once.
and I look forward to the resurrection of the dead, and the life of the world to come. Amen.	That is *our* bodily resurrection!

humans who try through surgery, tattoos, implants, and change of behavior to take on other natures (for example, that of a snake, a leopard, a lion, or a bear), but we do not have the power to do more than achieve a very poor imitation of the real thing. The changes we can make are only skin deep, and amount to nothing but permanent Halloween costumes.

    The reason Catholics believe and teach the doctrine of the Trinity, that God is three persons in one being, and the doctrine of the Incarnation, that Jesus is true God and true Man, one person in two natures, is that this is what Jesus revealed to his disciples. We believe on the basis of what we have heard from Jesus through the disciples—"faith comes from hearing" (Rom 10:17). As noted above (p. 88), the gospels attribute the claim to divinity to Jesus Himself. In revealing Himself as God the Son, He also revealed God the Father, and God the Holy Spirit.

St. Athanasius (296-298 AD), a father and doctor of the Church, taught that "God became human so that humans might become divine."[25] This view of the Incarnation is reflected in the prayer said by priests in the Latin rite of the Catholic Church when adding a drop of water to the wine at the Offertory of the Mass: "By the mingling of this water and wine, may we come to share in the divinity of Christ, Who humbled Himself to share in our humanity."

Heaven and Hell (and Purgatory Besides)

The Council of Nicaea was most concerned about getting clarity about Who Jesus really is (true God and true man; one person *in* two natures; *homoousios* with the Father). It did not mention the doctrine of Hell, and only indirectly suggests its understanding of Heaven as "the life of the world to come."

TNK, as we have seen, is ambiguous about the nature of the afterlife (see page 59). The deuterocanonical books added in the Septuagint (LXX) very strongly affirm the idea of resurrection to eternal happiness or eternal sorrow (e.g., 2 Maccabees 7). Hell is a reality *partially* revealed to us by Jesus (e.g., Mt 25:31-46). It is a dogma (irreversible Church teaching) that there is a state of complete alienation from God, from true self (Hinduism: *atman*), and from others.[26] *We do not know everything there is to know about the condition of souls in Hell.* What we do know is that Heaven and Hell are for those who *choose* to be there; no one goes to Hell except by their free choice to do so. Hell is for loners, for those who choose to serve self rather than God (Jn 12:47-48); Heaven is for lovers.

The classical imagery of Hell (demons, fire and brimstone, darkness, misery) are given to help us realize it is not a *state* that we would like to end up in. The *images* must not be confused with the *spiritual reality*; the revealing stories told by Jesus and the authors of the New Testament need to be demythologized to extract the doctrine held by the Church. The same is true of the images given that are meant to show that Heaven is a spiritual state of limitless existence, limitless understanding, and limitless bliss (Hinduism: *sat-chit-ananda*).

I speculate that the same light that causes the joys of Heavens also causes the cleansing in Purgatory and the pains of Hell: total revelation of God's glory to the human soul and total revelation of the human soul to God's light. Those who have accepted God as God will rejoice

---

[25] *De Incarnatione* 54:3, PG 25:192B; also *Catechism of the Catholic Church*, #460.

[26] *Catechism of the Catholic Church*, second ed. (Washington: United States Catholic Conference, 1997), #1033-1037. I will abbreviate this as CCC in other references.

in His light shining upon them; those who have rejected God as God will find God's light an unending torment.

Heaven is a reality *partially* revealed to us by Jesus (e.g., Jn 14:2). It is a dogma of the Church (CCC 1023-1029). *We do not know everything there is to know about the condition of souls in Heaven.* What we do know is that no one goes to Heaven because they *"deserve"* eternal bliss. Heaven is God's **gift** (Latin: *gratia*, **grace**) to us. In the Christian understanding, God loves us because *He* is good, not because *we* are good. "Just as through one transgression [*the sin of Adam and Eve*] condemnation came upon all, so through one righteous act acquittal and life came to all" (Rom 5:18).

Christians do not keep the commandments in order to *make* God love us. That is the heresy of **"works righteousness"** (Martin Luther's term, from after 1517 AD, condemning Pharisaism, Pelagianism, Jansenism, Puritanism, legalism, perfectionism, minimalism, and the like). We strive to keep the commandments *because* God loves us, and because they describe the good life (love, joy, peace, patience, kindness, generosity, gratitude, worship, innocence, justice, integrity, self-control, humility, etc.). **It is good *for us* to be good; it is bad *for us* to be bad**. It is impossible for us to *do evil* and not *become evil* and suffer evil consequences (Hinduism: law of *karma*). It is insane to say, "Since Jesus died so that I can become a truly loving person, I can choose not to become a truly loving person and still enjoy all the benefits of loving God, neighbor and myself; I can use God's remedy for sin as an excuse to continue sinning" (Rom 6:1; 1 Cor 5:1-5).

Purgatory is a reality partially revealed to us by Jesus (e.g., Mt 5:25-26; 1 Cor 3:11-15, 1 Pet 1:7, 2 Macc 12:46). It, too, is a dogma (CCC 1030-1032). The name means "a place of cleansing." *We do not know everything there is to know about the condition of souls in Purgatory.* There is no room in Heaven for any shred of self-centered love. We must become selfless selves (Hinduism: atman is true self; Buddhism: nirvana, extinction of self) in order to endure and enjoy "the weight of glory."[27] Many of us live and die without becoming truly selfless. Many Christians owe amends to others at the time of our death. We have "unfinished business" that would keep us from enjoying Heaven.

Heaven would be Hell if we were not first cleansed (*purged*) of sin. The souls in Purgatory *want* to be cleansed from all of the effects of their personal wrongdoing. They do not want to enter Heaven unprepared for perfect intimacy with God and with other perfected beings (angels and saints). Charles Dickens's classic short story, *A Christmas Carol*, illustrates the dynamics of Purgatory beautifully. When we realize how our own choices have cut us off from life and love, like Scrooge, we are powerfully motivated to undo the evil we have done, and embark on a new way of life.

All souls in Purgatory are guaranteed entrance into Heaven when they have finished making **reparation for sin** (all of their *self-serving* choices). In that sense, Purgatory is part of Heaven. No one in Purgatory goes to Hell; Purgatory does *not* last forever. In the end, there are only two

---

[27] C. S. Lewis, *The Weight of Glory and Other Addresses* (New York: Harper Collins, 1976 [1949]).

choices: either Heaven or Hell, with nothing in between (C. S. Lewis calls the final separation between the two "the great divorce").[28]

Limbo was a *theory* proposed by some theologians in the Middle Ages. The theory has not been adopted by the Church as a dogma. It is based on the fact that there must be some real difference between a baptized and unbaptized baby (CCC 1261). The theory of Limbo suggested that there must be a different kind of *eternal happiness* for baptized and unbaptized babies. Catholics may in good conscience accept, reject, or modify this theory. They may not deny that baptized infants really participate in the life of God as a consequence of their Baptism. Baptism is the first and most fundamental **sacrament** in the life of the Church; to deny that it has proper effects is to deny the whole of sacramental theology, a topic that we take up in the next section.

Heaven, Hell, Purgatory, and Limbo (if it exists) are *states of being* defined by one's relationship with God after death. They are not "places" in our spatiotemporal sense. Those who, by their own choice are in union with God and who love to be loved by Him, are "in" the state of eternal bliss that we call Heaven; those who, by their own choice, have accepted God's judgment of and mercy for their sins, but who are still in the process of making amends for sin, are in the state that we call Purgatory; those who, by their own choice, reject God's judgment of and forgiveness for their sins are in the state of eternal alienation that we call Hell. If Limbo is a spiritual reality, then within Heaven there are two different kinds of perfect happiness, distinguished by the kind of grace of union bestowed by Baptism, in contrast with that which comes from the gift of creation.

From this standpoint, it is not so much that souls are *in* Heaven as that Heaven is *in* the hearts of God's people: "All the way to Heaven is Heaven because He said, 'I am the Way.'"[29] Similarly, it is not so much the case that the damned are *in* Hell as it is that Hell is *in* them; because they are full of self, there is no room in them for love of God and love of neighbor.

Coping with the Wrath of God

Wherever God appears angry in the Scriptures, I suggest that:

- **God's anger is always reasonable.** His wrath is always directed at people who deserve to be rebuked (sinful Israel, the enemies of Israel, sinful Christians, the enemies of Christians). God is perfectly just.

---

[28] *The Great Divorce* was first published as a newspaper series in 1944-1945. This is a theological novel that shows the nature of the choices that make us fit for Heaven or fit for Hell.

[29] Dorothy Day, cofounder of the Catholic Worker Movement, repeated this saying often. She attributed it to St. Catherine of Siena (1347-1380 AD), but I have not yet found the original source for it. Evidence of how much it meant to Day is found in "St. Catherine of Siena, a Woman Who Influenced Her Times" (chapter 12 of *The Catholic Worker Movement: Intellectual and Spiritual Origins*, by Mark and Louise Swick [New York: Paulist Press, 2005] 204-211).

- **God's anger is always a function of His love for His People.** God reveals our sins, only so that He can destroy that which would destroy us. **"God is love"** (1 Jn 4:8).
- **God's mercy allows us to make reparation (amends) for our sins.** God does not cancel the debt; He provides everything we need to pay it in full. Those whom we have injured have a right to expect **reparation**, just as we do when we are the injured party. God forgives our sins *and* requires that we make reparation for them—only then will we be reconciled to those whom we hurt. We understand this perfectly well when we are the injured party; we resist this when we are the guilty party.

In the Christian tradition, the reality of Hell was revealed by the one who died to defeat Hell and open the gates of Heaven to all who want to accept mercy and love. The Christian doctrine has many resonances with Hinduism. Both agree that we can have what we want, and that what we really want is unlimited happiness. Hinduism portrays this state as becoming divine ourselves while Christianity sees it as union with the one and only God who created us. The doctrines of Heaven and Hell bear some resemblance to the law of karma, because in both the Christian and Hindu worldviews, we get what we choose and experience the consequences of our own actions, for good or for ill.

Unlike Hinduism, Christianity does not suppose that we have more than one lifetime to make this all-important choice. On this view, God confronts each person with the same challenge that He gave to His Chosen People: "I have set before you life and death, the blessing and the curse. Choose life, then, that you … may live" (Dt 30:19).

The Hindu doctrine of reincarnation softens the law of karma. No final choice is possible. Failure to become divine simply sends jiva back into the finite world to try, try again. From the Christian standpoint, one lifetime is sufficient.

The Sacraments: Seven Reliable Signs of Love

Sacramentum is a Latin word that originally meant a sum of money "set apart" (*sacrare*, "to set apart" or, by extension, "to consecrate") during a legal dispute; the loser of the dispute would lose the deposit. After the Caesars began to call themselves gods and demand worship of themselves as a condition of joining the Roman Legion, soldiers who had worshipped Caesar were given a *sacramentum*, a badge, which indicated that they had fulfilled that obligation. Similarly, in our day, people may not wear military uniforms or police badges unless they have sworn the proper oaths to uphold the Constitution. For those who understand the tradition, the uniforms and badges are *outward signs of inward realities*.

As with the collection and certification of the books of the New Testament, the development of the awareness that some rituals of the Body could be grouped together and classified as "sacraments" took place in the patristic era. Over the next 15 centuries, the concept was elaborated, as

Sacrament	Minister	Outward Sign	Grace Given
Baptism (a bath)	Deacon or any person	Water and Trinitarian formula.	Forgiveness of sins; regeneration (being "born again"); sanctification.
Confirmation	Bishop	Oil, laying on of hands, prayer.	Gifts of the Spirit to intensify faith, hope, and love.
Reconciliation	Priest	Words of absolution.	Forgiveness of sin.
Eucharist	Priest	Bread and wine, prayer of consecration.	Communion with Jesus in the fullness of His divine and human natures.
Marriage	Couple	Vows and sexual intercourse.	Enduring personal union.
Holy Orders	Bishop	Laying on of hands, prayer.	Participation in Jesus' own priestly ministry. Three orders: bishop, priest, and deacon.
Anointing of the sick	Priest	Oil, prayer.	Healing, endurance, assurance of salvation.

theologians debated with each other about what should and should not be classed as a sacrament. Besides endorsing the traditional Catholic canon of the Bible, the Council of Trent (1545-1563 AD) solemnly declared that there are seven sacraments that were instituted by Jesus.

In the eyes of the Church, the sacraments are *signs that cause what they signify*. In all of them, Jesus acts as the High Priest to minister to His People; the human ministers of the sacraments are instruments in His hands to make Himself present to the members of His Body.

The Trouble with "Christ"

Christianity was originally nothing but a form of Judaism. All of its first members were Jews who proclaimed that Jesus was their *Messiah* (Hebrew) or their *Christ* (Greek; in English, "*Anointed One*"), which meant that they were declaring that He was the King of the Jews and, consequently, the King of Israel. Christianity ceased to be a predominantly Jewish religion, because of the decision of the Church not to impose Judaism on its members (Council of Jerusalem; see page 134) and because of the destruction of Jerusalem and the Temple (see page 135). The religion of *the* Christ, *the* King of the Jews, lost touch with its Jewish roots, so that the word "Christian" came to mean the same as "Gentile"—that is, "not Jewish."

Except for scholars, the vast majority of believers are utterly unaware of the original, **Jewish** meaning of "Christ." We tend to make up our own definition of it based upon later dogmatic developments: "Christ"—to us *Gentile* Christians—means **Jesus** and *only* Jesus. Jesus is God, Healer, Lord, Savior, Love, Light, the Way, the Truth, and the Life. Therefore, Christians (understandably) conclude that "Christ" means "God and Savior." This confusion between "Christ" and "Jesus" does not make very much practical difference in the ordinary spiritual life of the Church; the prayers of the Mass always mean "Jesus" when they say "Christ." The trouble begins when we try to understand the *original* meaning of the sacred Scriptures.

To understand what Shakespeare wrote, we need to understand the vocabulary of *his* day. **To understand the meaning originally intended by the human authors of the Scriptures, we need to understand *their* vocabulary and *their* culture.** This is the first commandment of Biblical exegesis (interpretation). Taking a modern meaning of a word and inserting it into an ancient text often produces nonsense. In the following excerpt, the author describes a proposed peace conference between Union and Confederate leaders in the Civil War; note how using a contemporary definition of terms destroys the original meaning of the 19th-century text:

> Grant and Lee could meet for an exchange of views, as could others, not excluding a number of their wives; Mrs. Grant and Mrs. Longstreet, for example, **intimates** before the war, could visit back and forth across the lines, along with their husbands, so that "while General Lee and General Grant were arranging for better feeling between the armies, they could be aided by **intercourse** between the ladies and officers until terms honorable to both sides could be found."[30]

In our day, if we say that we have been "intimate" with someone or have had "intercourse" with them, we mean that we have engaged in a sexually active relationship. In the 19th century, people did not use these words in that restricted sense. Mrs. Grant and Mrs. Longstreet certainly did not have a lesbian relationship before the war, nor was the author of the quotation suggesting that a sexual orgy in the parlor would help bring the negotiations between the generals to a successful conclusion.

Inserting our later meaning of "Christ" into the Scriptures is as absurd as substituting the modern understanding of "intimacy" and "intercourse" into the 19th-century letter quoted above. Christians who really want to understand the Word of the Lord must avoid such anachronisms.

---

[30] Shelby Foote, *The Civil War: A Narrative*, Vol. 3: *Red River to Appomattox* (New York: Random House, 1974) 809.

Union of Church and State: The Age of Christendom (381–1776 AD)

In 381 AD, Theodosius decreed that Christianity would become the official religion of the Roman Empire, and summoned the second council of the Church to meet in Constantinople. For the next 14 centuries, the interests of Church and state would be allied to each other. This was not a new idea. Rome, like all ancient states, had always had an official worldview and prescribed religious rituals for the good of the nation and the empire. Theodosius's decision meant that the pagan (polytheistic) priests and temples were replaced by Christian versions of the same. State funds supported the new religion, just as they had supported the old Roman religion in the past. Just as the pagans had persecuted the Christians during the preceding centuries, so the Christians persecuted the pagans during the next few centuries. In both cases, signs could have been posted at the execution sites: "Your tax dollars at work."

During these 14 centuries, the Church endorsed the state, and the state endorsed the Church. The **Age of Revolutions** (1776-1919, from the American Revolution to the Russian Revolution) was marked by the destruction of this union. The revolutionaries were acting against those whom previous ages had thought ruled by "divine right"—the kings, queens, kaisers, and czars of Christendom (the "Christian kingdoms"). We are still trying to work out the implications of the separation of Church and state in our own day (see page 189).

Christian Sign Language

In the first three centuries of Christianity, while the Roman Empire was still pagan and crucifixion was still a favorite method of terrorizing captive populations, Jesus' followers did not use crosses or crucifixes as a symbol of faith. One popular symbol in the earliest centuries was that of a fish:

The five letters in the Greek word for "fish," *icthus*, stand for the first letter of five words that express the basic act of faith: *Iesous Christos Theou Uios Soter*—Jesus Christ, Son of God, Savior. People will sometimes write the Greek characters inside the fish as a reminder of how the symbol came to represent the Christian faith:

In the age of bumper stickers, advocates of Darwinism have put feet on the icthus and inscribed Darwin's name on it as a symbol of their religious (or irreligious) convictions.

The transition to the cross as the dominant symbol of Christian faith began early in the fourth century. On October 27, 312, Constantine had a vision of a cross surmounted by the first two Greek letters for Christos (χριστος), chi and rho; he heard a voice tell him (in Greek!) that he would win victory using this sign. The next day, Constantine won the battle of the Milvian Bridge, which paved the way for him to become the emperor of Rome. Constantine's legions used the chi-rho as their battle standard for the rest of his reign:

Christians had already been using the chi-rho as shorthand for "Christ"; the adoption of the symbol for the battle-flags and the coins of Constantine's reign increased its popularity. Using "Xmas" as an abbreviation for "Christmas" goes back to these same Greek roots.

The seal of the Society of Jesus (and a great deal of Church art) also goes back to the Greek, using the first syllable of Jesus' name in Greek (ιησους), which has been rendered in the Roman alphabet as *IHS*.

The Fall of "Rome" and the Onset of the "Dark Ages" (476–1000 AD)

Because Constantine had moved the capital of the Roman Empire out of Rome and into Byzantium in Greek territory (see page 139), the sacking of the city of Rome in the fifth century by the Visigoths (410 AD) and the Huns (476 AD) was not really the end of the Roman Empire; the Eastern Empire continued to have emperors, until Constantinople fell to the Muslims in 1453 AD. For western Europe, 476 AD marks the end of the Classical Era and the beginning of the so-called "Dark Ages." This was a term of derision coined by an anti-Catholic historian in the 19th century,[31] and is still used as a stereotype to contrast the alleged darkness of Catholic doctrine as compared to the brilliant light of reason generated by the Enlightened Ones of Europe.

There was undoubtedly a great change in the culture of western Europe after the fifth century. Trade declined; military roads fell into disrepair; the wealthy elite of Rome could no longer

---

[31] Stark, *For the Glory of God*, 133-34.

maintain their palaces and civic arenas; power shifted from the center to local, tribal systems; the nature of literacy and literature changed. The world was unquestionably different from the way it had been, but the people of western Europe did not mourn the death of the Empire or the system of taxation and slavery that made Rome wealthy at the expense of the provinces. Rodney Stark, a contemporary American sociologist, among others, has shown that the "Dark Ages" weren't all that dark. The capital of the Roman Empire—Constantinople!—did not fall to the barbarians. Civilization changed, but did not disappear overnight. Greek ceased to be the dominant language in the western part of the empire; Latin took its place as the main language used by educated people. Monks and nuns preserved the manuscripts that later fueled the Renaissance (14th to 16th centuries). The Christian faith was not the cause of the deterioration in society; the cause of the change was the success of the early French and German cultures in gaining military, political, and cultural independence from Italy and Greece. Europeans—that is, Catholics!—rejected slavery during this period. The Greco-Roman civilization had been based on slavery.

Technology developed at a rapid pace: saddles, stirrups, armor, cannon, clocks, horse collars, agricultural techniques, horseshoes, water wheels, mills, camshafts, compasses, maps, shipbuilding, metalworking, and navigation. Because the people developing the technology were either not literate or not interested in writing about their inventiveness, the immense creativity of the time was invisible to historians who worked from manuscripts. There was no copyright or patent law to motivate keeping records of who invented something first. Inventions spread rapidly from one monastery to another.

In Church history, the Patristic Era, the age of the Fathers of the Church, comes to an end with the fall of Rome. The essential shape of Catholicism was fully formed by this time: the papacy was well established, and the Holy Orders of bishops, priests, and deacons were already ancient; the dogmatic definition of Trinity, Incarnation, and Atonement had been worked out in the first four councils of the Church; the life of the sacraments shaped the lives of ordinary believers. Rome had fallen, but not the Church. Over the next few centuries, Catholicism conquered the conquerors of Rome.

Christian Apocalypticism: "The End Is Near!"

As we saw in the chapter on Judaism (page 90), apocalyptic literature was a *genre* (kind of writing) that arose in the last few centuries BC. In its origin, Christianity is 100% Jewish. It is not surprising, therefore, that there are apocalyptic passages in the New Testament (e.g., Mark 13, Luke 19, Matthew 24-25). The first phrase of the book of Revelation in Greek is "*apocalypsis Iesou Christou*"—"[The] revelation of Jesus Christ" (Rev 1:1). The English word "apocalypse" is derived from a transliteration of *apocalypsis*. Because we are time-bound creatures, we cannot see the future. It is hidden from us. The apocalyptic authors, both Jewish and Christian, canonical and noncanonical, shared the common conviction that God is not bound by time as we are, and that He can "unveil" the future for us.

For people suffering occupation by a much-hated foreign power (the Greek and Roman empires), it was a great comfort to hear that God intended to punish the oppressors and vindicate the faith of His People. At the same time, it was clear that the Day of the Lord (Amos 5:18-20) had not yet arrived, and it was not safe to write or circulate manuscripts that directly named God's enemies. "Plausible deniability" was gained by casting the real history of oppression into a surrealistic, mythical, and symbolic landscape.

> Then one of the seven angels who were holding the seven bowls came and said to me, "Come here. I will show you the judgment on the great harlot who lives near the many waters. The kings of the earth have had intercourse with her, and the inhabitants of the earth became drunk on the wine of her harlotry."
>
> Then he carried me away in spirit to a deserted place where I saw a woman seated on a scarlet beast that was covered with blasphemous names, with seven heads and ten horns. The woman was wearing purple and scarlet and adorned with gold, precious stones, and pearls. She held in her hand a gold cup that was filled with the abominable and sordid deeds of her harlotry. On her forehead was written a name, which is a mystery, "Babylon the great, the mother of harlots and of the abominations of the earth."
>
> I saw that the woman was drunk on the blood of the holy ones and on the blood of the witnesses to Jesus. When I saw her I was greatly amazed.
>
> The angel said to me, "Why are you amazed? I will explain to you the mystery of the woman and of the beast that carries her, the beast with the seven heads and the ten horns. The beast that you saw existed once but now exists no longer. It will come up from the abyss and is headed for destruction. The inhabitants of the earth whose names have not been written in the book of life from the foundation of the world shall be amazed when they see the beast, because it existed once but exists no longer, and yet it will come again. Here is a clue for one who has wisdom. The seven heads represent seven hills upon which the woman sits." (Rev 17:1-9)

It is not hard to unravel the mystery. The Whore of Babylon is a symbol of Rome, known in ancient times as "The City of Seven Hills." The Romans killed Jesus, Peter, Paul, and thousands of other Christians—it is they who were "drunk on the blood of the holy ones and on the blood of the witnesses to Jesus" (17:6). The book of Revelation was clearly written to comfort those who were still living under the threat of persecution. As one evangelical preacher said, "I have looked in the back of the book. *We win!*"

In the meantime, Christians suffer, just as Jesus did. "Do not be afraid of anything that you are going to suffer. Indeed, the devil will throw some of you into prison, that you may be tested, and you will face an ordeal for ten days. Remain faithful until death, and I will give you the crown of life.' Whoever has ears ought to hear what the Spirit says to the churches. The victor shall not be harmed by the second death'" (Rev 2:10-11).

For those suffering persecution, **Judgment Day** promises the joy of complete victory over God's enemies: "Just as weeds are collected and burned (up) with fire, so will it be at the end of the age. The Son of Man will send his angels, and they will collect out of his kingdom all who cause others to sin and all evildoers. They will throw them into the fiery furnace, where there will be wailing and grinding of teeth. Then the righteous will shine like the sun in the kingdom of their Father. Whoever has ears ought to hear" (Mt 13:40-43). The early Church prayed earnestly—and, apparently, with eager expectation—for King Jesus to come and establish His Kingdom on earth: "The one who gives this testimony says, 'Yes, I am coming soon.' Amen! Come, Lord Jesus!" (Rev 20:20).

Waves of enthusiasm about the coming end of everything have washed through Christianity periodically, starting with the apocalyptic passages in the New Testament and continuing to our own day. The Greek word for "end" is *eschaton*, from which we derive the word "**eschatology**," meaning "the study of the end," and "eschatological," which means "related to the end of the world." One of the vexed questions in Christian eschatology (or **apocalypticism**, if you prefer) is the "thousand-year reign" of Jesus and the saints that is portrayed in the book of Revelation:

> Then I saw thrones; those who sat on them were entrusted with judgment. I also saw the souls of those who had been beheaded for their witness to Jesus and for the word of God, and who had not worshiped the beast or its image nor had accepted its mark on their foreheads or hands. They came to life and they reigned with Christ for a thousand years. The rest of the dead did not come to life until the thousand years were over. This is the first resurrection. Blessed and holy is the one who shares in the first resurrection. The second death has no power over these; they will be priests of God and of Christ, and they will reign with him for (the) thousand years. When the thousand years are completed, Satan will be released from his prison. He will go out to deceive the nations at the four corners of the earth, Gog and Magog, to gather them for battle; their number is like the sand of the sea. They invaded the breadth of the earth and surrounded the camp of the holy ones and the beloved city. But fire came down from heaven and consumed them. The Devil who had led them astray was thrown into the pool of fire and sulfur, where the beast and the false prophet were. There they will be tormented day and night forever and ever. (20:4-10)

The Latin word for "one thousand years" is *millennium*; **millennialists** argue with each other about whether the millennium has already taken place (perhaps the first thousand years of Christianity, or the first thousand years of Christendom after the Roman persecutions ended in the fourth century), or is still to come. The *Left Behind* novels and movies by Timothy F. LaHaye (1995-2007 AD) try to picture what the end of our world might be like. Adventists (not just the Seventh Day Adventists!) try to predict when Jesus will "come (Latin, *advent*) again in glory to judge the living and the dead" (Nicene Creed; see page 140). The equivalent Greek word for "advent" is "*parousia*":

> As he was sitting on the Mount of Olives, the disciples approached him privately and said, "Tell us, when will this happen, and what sign will there be of your coming [*parousia*], and of the end of the age?" Jesus said to them in reply, "See that no one deceives you. For many will come in my name, saying, 'I am the Messiah,' and they will deceive many. You will hear of wars and reports of wars; see that you are not alarmed, for these things must happen, but it will not yet be the end. Nation will rise against nation, and kingdom against kingdom; there will be famines and earthquakes from place to place. All these are the beginning of the labor pains. Then they will hand you over to persecution, and they will kill you. You will be hated by all nations because of my name. And then many will be led into sin; they will betray and hate one another. Many false prophets will arise and deceive many; and because of the increase of evildoing, the love of many will grow cold. But the one who perseveres to the end will be saved." (Mt 24:3-13)

From passages like this, many have tried to work out a countdown to kickoff for the beginning of the end of everything.[32] The Catholic Church has made no such calculations about the sequence or timing of events. "But of that day and hour no one knows, neither the angels of heaven, nor the Son, but the Father alone" (Mt 24:36).

We have survived the millennium madness surrounding the year 2000. The dominant apocalypticism as this is being written (2011) is the fear that the world will end when the Mayan Calendar reaches the end of its fifth cycle (December 21, 2012). It is not clear to me why the calendar can't roll over into a sixth cycle, just as our calendars do at the end of every year, but I'm not inclined to dig any deeper into neo-Mayan mysticism. When I was a young man in college, I thought the end of the world would begin in October of 1972. Fortunately, I did not circulate my prediction very widely, and apart from having to write three ten-page papers that I had not expected to have to complete, I did not suffer very greatly from my false prophecy.

Scientists have their own eschatology, though they do not, as a general rule, borrow that terminology from religious studies. The mass, composition, and nuclear processes of the sun are fairly well known. At present, the outward pressure from the fusion reactions in the core of

---

[32] See, for example, Hal Lindsey and Carole C. Carlson's *Late, Great Planet Earth* and Lindsey's sequels, *Satan is Alive and Well on Planet Earth*, and *The 1980s: Countdown to Armageddon*.

the sun keeps the matter in the sun from collapsing on itself in response to the force of gravity. In four to seven billion years (people disagree; scientists are people; scientists disagree), the rate of fusion reactions will decline as the sun runs out of hydrogen; the sun will collapse under the force of gravity, then will become a red giant larger than the orbit of the earth—the planet will be swallowed whole. The transition from hydrogen fusion to helium fusion may make the earth uninhabitable long before then (800 million to 1.3 billion years from now), due to the rise in the sun's temperature. The atmosphere and oceans will boil away, and our goose will be thoroughly cooked.

ISLAM
(JUDAISM AND CHRISTINATY CONTINUED)

• • • • • •

Muhammad[1] (570-632 AD) was born in Mecca but, because of the early deaths of his parents, lived the life of a nomad and trader in his formative years. He married his employer, a wealthy Meccan widow when he was 25; in his late 30s, he found solace from city life by going to pray alone in a cave up on a mountain.

The dominant religious environment of the Arabian peninsula was **animistic polytheism**, very much like that of China. Anything could be occupied by gods, goddesses, and supernatural spirits (Arabic, *jinni*, "**genies**"): trees, rocks, mountains, rivers, regions, and the like. The generic term for a god was "**illah**." Muhammad was especially devoted to *the* God from whom all other gods descended. The Arabic particle that means "the" is *al-*. "Al-" gets attached to the word that it modifies. When it is attached to *illah*, the weak middle vowel drops out, so *Alillah* turns into **Allah**. Its meaning remains "the Illah" or "the God."

Muhammad did not invent the word *Allah*. It was already part of the religious world into which he was born. Muhammad's contribution was to separate the concept of "*the* God" from its polytheistic roots. The pre-Muslim Arabic mythology, like that of Greece and Rome, imagined the illahs being born from the original illah, just as the Titans came forth from Gaia (see page 60); Allah was said to have had sons and daughters, and a multitude of grandchildren. In the fundamental creed of Islam, the first **Pillar of the faith**, called the *Shahada*, Muslims break with that earlier tradition, and make a commitment to radical monotheism:

---

[1] "Muhammad" is the politically and linguistically correct transliteration of the Prophet's name into contemporary English. The Wikipedia article on the name lists almost a dozen other ways of rendering the Arabic into English, Latin, Greek, and Russian. Pious Muslims add "peace be upon him" (abbreviated as "pbuh" in English) when they pronounce the name of the Prophet, and "peace be upon them" ("pbut") when they refer to other prophets or holy people as a group.

There is no god (illah) but *the* God (Allah) and Muhammad is His prophet.

To become a Muslim, all one needs to do is to recite the Shahada with faith in the presence of two Muslim witnesses.

The "Religion of Peace"

Because it is a Semitic language, like Hebrew, Arabic depends upon the consonants as the primary carriers of meaning. The consonants rendered in English as *SLM* mean "peace" in both Arabic (*salaam*) and Hebrew (*shalom*). From this root, a number of other key terms are derived:

- *Aslama*: the act of surrender by which one makes peace with *the* God
- *Islam*: the religion of submission to *the* God
- *Muslim*: a person who has submitted to *the* God

According to the Quran, Abraham became the first Muslim when he showed his willingness to sacrifice (surrender) his firstborn son to *the* God (37:99-106). Muslim commentary on the story tends to favor the interpretation that it was Ishmael, the firstborn son of Abraham and the father of the Arabs, who was the sacrificial victim; the Quran itself does not name the son.

Christian Europe has been at war with the "religion of peace" for 1400 years. European literature is saturated with anti-Muslim stereotypes. The Disney cartoon, *Aladdin*, is filled with them: the fat, wealthy, incompetent caliph; the corrupt, scheming vizier who relies on black magic to pursue his self-serving goals; the beautiful women of the harem wearing seductive lingerie, even in public; the genie trapped in a lamp by another genie's curse; great wealth accumulated by robbery; the use of physical mutilation to punish thieves; the curved swords carried by all of Aladdin's opponents. It is very difficult to step back from the history of the conflict and judge Islam fairly.

From the Night of Power to the Hijra (610–622 AD)

In 610, Muhammad had a life-changing mystical experience while praying in the cave on the mountainside. At first, he did not understand what had happened to him on **the Night of Power**, but with his wife's encouragement, he returned and eventually realized that the angel Gabriel was speaking to him on behalf of Allah. This is the origin of the **Quran** (Arabic, *Qur'an*, "recitation"), the one **miracle of Islam**—that Muhammad faithfully remembered and repeated what he heard from Gabriel.

Muhammad began to recite what he had heard to the warring tribes of **Mecca**. He gained a few followers, but, on the whole, the tribal chieftains resented being told what *the* God thought of their behavior. Muhammad and his followers suffered increasingly intense persecution. In 622 Muhammad led them out of Mecca to Yathrib. This is called the *Hijra*, the migration. Muhammad had so much success in Yathrib that it came to be called *Medinat un Nabi*, "the city of the Prophet," which (as so often happens with names) has been shortened to **Medina**. Mecca and Medina are sacred cities; no non-Muslims may enter them, on pain of death.

The Muslim calendar is oriented around the Hijra, in the same way that the Christian calendar is organized around the birth of Jesus. Because Muslims use a lunar calendar (12 full moons per year) rather than a solar calendar (one full circuit around the sun), they have only 354 days in their year. Their new year begins 11 or 12 days earlier than the previous year when measured against the solar calendar. This means that the months ("moons") of the calendar gradually move from winter to summer, and then back again, over a 33-year cycle. On the Western solar calendar, January always is a winter month in the Northern Hemisphere. The first month of the Muslim calendar will move through every season over 33 years. In solar years, 2011 is 1389 years after Hijra (AH); on the Muslim calendar, which uses the shorter lunar year to mark time, 2011 is 1432 AH.

The Return from Medina to Mecca (630 AD)

Muhammad continued to recite what he heard from *the* God in Medina. He found a much warmer welcome there than he had in Mecca. He conquered the city—by the force of his personality and preaching. In 628 AD, the Muslims defeated a Meccan army outside of Medina. Two years later, Muhammad marched on Mecca with an army of 10,000. The city surrendered to him, and battle was averted. Muhammad ordered the execution of ten of his enemies, but six of them escaped death, most by converting to Islam.

Muhammad was monogamous until his first wife died in 620 AD. In the last 12 years of his life, he married another ten or 12 women (accounts differ; some of the women listed may have been concubines—sex slaves—rather than wives). As with other Oriental potentates (including David and Solomon and their descendants), Muhammad's relationships served many different purposes: sealing alliances, caring for widows, and personal pleasure. The Quran seems to set four wives as an upper limit: "Marry such women as seem good to you, two, or three, or four. But if you fear that you will not do justice, then marry only one" (4:3).

God assured Muhammad that keeping a harem was proper: "Prophet, We have made lawful to you the wives to whom you have granted dowries and the slave girls whom God has given you as booty" (33:50). Muslim men were forbidden to have sex "except with their wives and slave girls, for these are lawful to them" (23:5; 70:30).

Because Muhammad saw himself as God's last and decisive messenger, "The Seal of the Prophets" (33:40), he made no distinction between religious and civil authority. When God speaks, our job is to obey—or else suffer the consequences of disobedience. The name for this form of government is a **theocracy**, a system in which God rules (Greek, *theos* + *kratos*, "rule").[2] The Shahada says that Muhammad is God's prophet. God directly authorized Muhammad to act as a warrior, execute his enemies, take slaves, contract multiple marriages, engage in concubinage, and dictate the proper forms of social life. Because these features are so prominent in the life of the Prophet, it is difficult—if not impossible—to remove warfare, slavery, concubinage, polygamy, and theocracy from the Muslim tradition. It seems to me that a devout Muslim cannot both hold that Muhammad is God's decisive messenger, and also believe that these aspects of Muhammad's own life are in any way offensive to God.

Up until the Age of Revolutions (1776-1917 AD), a consequence of the **Enlightenment** (17th-18th centuries AD), the entanglement of Church and state was theocratic in nature, too. When civil structures collapsed in the West, popes, bishops, and abbots often combined religious and secular authority. In the Middle Ages, popes claimed to have ultimate authority over the kings and queens of Europe. Some Protestant denominations carried on the tradition of the union of Church and state, most notably in England, where the head of state (the king or the queen) is the head of the Church as well.

Sharia, Hadith, Ijma, and Qiyas: Adapting the Prophetic Message

The view that Muhammad is the "Seal of the Prophets" means that with his death in 632 AD, the entire line of prophets, from Abraham through Jesus, comes to an end. Just as the Catholic tradition holds that the Deposit of Faith is closed with the death of the last apostle, so the Muslim tradition holds that the Judeo-Christian prophetic tradition is perfected, and concluded with Muhammad's recitation of God's word. The equivalent in Judaism is the decision made around 90 AD to limit the canon of scripture to TNK, and to reject the additional material that was added in LXX; there is no formal declaration that "no new books may be added to TNK," but that is the way the rabbis have acted for the last 20 centuries. In the Muslim view, the Quran is the third and **Last Testament**.

In all three Abrahamic religions, the body of material that is taken to be revealed by God (TNK, the Deposit of Faith, the Quran) is embedded in a framework of interpretations. The rabbis developed the *Mishnah* and the *Talmud*; Catholicism developed from the writings and decisions made in the Patristic Era; Islam supplemented the Quran with:

---

[2] Other terms derived from *kratos*: democracy, "mob rule"; aristocracy, "rule by the best"; meritocracy, "rule by those who have proved themselves capable" (coined in 1958).

- **Sharia** ("the way"): a body of law based on the principles of the Quran;
- **Hadith/Sunnah**: traditions about the words and deeds of Muhammad that provide guidance in interpreting passages in the Quran;
- **Ijma**: the consensus of the Muslim community (**Ummah**);
- **Qiyas**: reasoning by use of analogies.

In Islam, an **imam** leads a local congregation in prayer, just as rabbis lead synagogue services or priests or ministers lead Christian worship services. Unlike rabbis or priests, functioning as an imam may be a temporary apointment rather than a profession or a long-term state in life. When there is some doubt as to how to apply Sharia to particular situations, an imam or other authority figure may issue a **fatwa** to settle the issue; this is just like a judge's verdict in a court of law in the European tradition. In Judaism, such judgments are made by rabbis, and are only as binding as the rabbi is persuasive. In Catholicism, such judgments are rendered by the councils of the Church (the ordinary teaching authority, or **magisterium**), or by the pope acting on behalf of the whole Church (the extraordinary magisterium).

From its Jewish parent, Islam inherited the idea of **kosher** foods (those that are in accord with God's law). The Arabic term for kosher is **halal**; that which is not halal is *haraam*, "forbidden." The concept of doing what is right and avoiding what is forbidden is, of course, much larger in both traditions than simply the dietary laws. Even those who are not Jewish may sometimes say "That's not kosher!" in order to raise an objection to what someone else is doing.

The Five Pillars of Islam

By far, the largest branch of Islam is called **Sunni**, from *sunnah*, the example set for believers by the words and actions of Muhammad; 90 percent of Muslims follow the Sunni interpretation of the Quran. The **Five Pillars of Islam** were enumerated in the Sunni tradition, but the same elements can be found in **Shia Islam** and among the **Sufis** (those who follow a mystical form of Islam that developed in the Middle Ages). The **Shiites** are "partisans," "followers," or "adherents" of Ali, Muhammad's cousin and son-in-law, who became the fourth Caliph in 656 AD; Ali was assassinated five years later.

1. Creed: The Shahada

Many Muslims claim that the poetry of the Quran cannot be translated into other languages, and as a consequence, they encourage Muslims to learn to read the original Arabic. A transliteration of the basic creed of Islam is *Ashadu ala illaha ill allaah, washadu anna muhammadur wa rasulullah*—"There is no God [*la illaha*] but The God [*ill allaah*] and Muhammad is His Prophet." There is no doubt that the English translation (whether it uses "*The* God" or "Allah") lacks the musicality of the original.

The **Shahada** unambiguously expresses the radical monotheism of the three Western religions. Christians and Jews can—and should—agree wholeheartedly with this aspect of Muslim theology: "Say: He is God, the one and only; God, the eternal, absolute" (112:1); they could also agree that *Allahu-Akbar*: the one and only God is unsurpassably great. Muhammad followed the Jewish unitarian tradition (there is only one Person in the one God), and rejected the idea that there could be other Persons in the Godhead: "He begetteth not" (112:1) is very probably meant as a direct refutation of the Nicene statement that the Son is eternally begotten of the Father.

> O followers of the Book! do not exceed the limits in your religion, and do not speak (lies) against Allah, but (speak) the truth; the Messiah, Isa son of Marium [Jesus son of Mary] is only an apostle of Allah and His Word which He communicated to Marium and a spirit from Him; believe therefore in Allah and His apostles, and say not, Three. Desist, it is better for you; Allah is only one God; far be It from His glory that He should have a son, whatever is in the heavens and whatever is in the earth is His, and Allah is sufficient for a Protector. (4:171)

In this passage, "the followers of the Book" are Christians, but Muhammad gave the same title to the Jews. He saw himself and the Quran as the fulfillment of both the Jewish and Christian traditions. The Christian doctrine, that Original Sin places all humans in a condition from which only God can save them, does not have a parallel in Islam (or Judaism, for that matter; see page 63). For Muhammad, the human race has forgotten the one God, and only needs to submit to God's self-revelation in the Quran to be restored to God's favor. The Quran calls Jesus the Messiah, but denies that He was crucified or raised from the dead:

> [The Jews] said (in boast), "We killed Christ Jesus the son of Mary, the Apostle of Allah"; but they killed him not, nor crucified him, but so it was made to appear to them, and those who differ therein are full of doubts, with no (certain) knowledge, but only conjecture to follow, for of a surety they killed him not. Nay, Allah raised him up unto Himself; and Allah is Exalted in Power. (4:157-158)

In this reinterpretation of the Jewish and Christian Scriptures, there is no need for Atonement, and hence, no meaning in the claim that Jesus died for our sins.

2. Prayer: "In the Name of Allah, Most Beneficent, Most Merciful"

Muslims pray five times each day: before dawn, at noon, in the afternoon, at sunset, and in the evening. Prior to the Hijrah from Mecca to Medina in 622 AD, Muhammad originally prayed facing toward Jerusalem. After Hijrah, Muhammad and his followers prayed toward the

Kaaba ("cube") in Mecca (2:142-150). According to the Quran, Abraham and his firstborn son, Ishmael, built the original Kaaba (2:125-127).

Although it was displaced by Mecca as the focus of prayer, Jerusalem is the third holiest city in the world, after Mecca and Medina. Muhammad is said to have been taken by God from Mecca to Jerusalem on a winged horse in the Night Journey (620 AD, two years before the Hijra): "Glory to (Allah) Who did take His servant for a Journey by night from the Sacred Mosque to the farthest [*al aqsa*] Mosque, whose precincts We did bless, in order that We might show him some of Our Signs: for He is the One Who heareth and seeth (all things)" (17:1).

3. Alms

All Muslims are obliged to give one-fortieth (2.5%) of their assets to the poor each year. "Alms are only for the poor and the needy, and the officials (appointed) over them, and those whose hearts are made to incline (to truth) and the (ransoming of) captives and those in debts and in the way of Allah and the wayfarer; an ordinance from Allah; and Allah is knowing" (9:60).

4. Fasting (Ramadan)

The Night of Power (610 AD) took place during the ninth month of the year, Ramadan. The entire month is devoted to fasting, in honor of the giving of the Quran to Muhammad. Devout Muslims abstain from all food, drink, and sexual activity from dawn until sunset for the whole month. There is usually a feast each evening after sunset and a pre-dawn meal in the morning.

5. Pilgrimage (Hajj)

Every able-bodied male is supposed to make a pilgrimage to Mecca at least once in his lifetime, ideally during the solemn pilgrimage during the 12th month of the year. The pilgrims (*hajji*) dress in the same simple garments and engage in a series of ritual activities together, the most important of which is circling the Kaaba seven times. A man who has made the pilgrimage may be honored with the title "Hajji" or "al-Hajj" for the rest of his life.

The Religion of Peace Goes to War (Jihad)

In and of itself, *jihad* means "struggle." There are many spiritual interpretations of this word that are perfectly consistent with the Christian ascetic tradition of struggling to overcome sin within one's own heart and mind; Muslims call this "the greater jihad." The same idea is found in TNK: "A patient man is better than a warrior, and he who rules his temper [is greater] than he who takes a city" (Prov 16:32). Jihad may also mean the struggle against aggressors, which the Christian tradition also accepts as legitimate self-defense, both for individuals and for communities.

The third form of jihad is against nonbelievers:

> Therefore, when ye meet the Unbelievers (in fight), smite at their necks; At length, when ye have thoroughly subdued them, bind a bond firmly (on them): thereafter (is the time for) either generosity or ransom: Until the war lays down its burdens. Thus (are ye commanded): but if it had been Allah's Will, He could certainly have exacted retribution from them (Himself); but (He lets you fight) in order to test you, some with others. But those who are slain in the Way of Allah,—He will never let their deeds be lost. (47:4)[3]
>
> Fighting is prescribed for you. (2:216)
>
> Fight those who believe not in Allah nor the Last Day, nor hold that forbidden which hath been forbidden by Allah and His Apostle, nor acknowledge the religion of Truth, (even if they are) of the People of the Book, until they pay the Jizya with willing submission, and feel themselves subdued. (9:29)

The *Jizya* is a penalty tax paid by "the People of the Book" (Jews and Christians) who live in territories conquered by the Muslims.

Muhammad exemplified this form of jihad when he led ten thousand troops prepared to wage war against the polytheists in Mecca. The Meccans surrendered in the face of the threat of a battle that they knew they could not win. Muslim armies rapidly spread out from Arabia, conquering Christian territory from the Middle East, across the north of Africa, and up into the Iberian peninsula (the territory of Spain and Portugal). By 732 AD, one century after Muhammad's death, the *mujahaddin* (warriors, jihadists) were at war with the Christians at the Battle of Tours in southern France. The Christian armies (somewhat surprisingly) were able to stop the Muslim invasion, but the Moors (North African Muslims) remained in Al Andalus, until they were driven out by Ferdinand and Isabella in 1492 AD.

Al Andalus (or Andalusia) was the western end of the Muslim world. Over the centuries, Muslim armies marched eastward as well, all the way to Indonesia; the Muslim empires circled the globe close to the equator. After Christian Turkey fell to the Muslims, the Turks waged war on the eastern half of the Roman Empire, eventually conquering Constantinople in 1453 AD, and twice laying siege to Vienna (1529 AD and 1683 AD).

The **Crusades** were a series of wars intended to take back the Holy Land from the Muslims. They lasted less than two centuries (1095-1291 AD), and were ultimately won by the Muslims. The tiny patch of land taken and briefly held by the Crusaders is nothing compared to the lands conquered by the Muslims, particularly Constantinople (now known as Istanbul, and still occupied by the Turks).

---

[3] *http://www.muslimaccess.com/quraan/arabic/047.asp*

Triumphs of Muslim Culture

When the Muslims conquered the Christian city of Alexandria in 641 AD after a siege of 14 months, they took possession of the world's greatest library. Muslim scholars absorbed the philosophy and mathematics of the Greco-Roman civilization. They made dramatic advances in number theory, inventing the Arabic numerals (1–9) to replace the Roman numerals (i–ix), creating and naming the concept of zero, which allows organization of numbers in columns (a tremendous aid to calculations of all kinds), and, of course, developing algebra. The art and architecture of the Muslim Empire far surpassed that of Europe in the Dark Ages. While western Europe struggled against the barbarian invasions, the Muslims profited from trade with India and the Far East, and created many centers of sophisticated learning.

Western Europe became reacquainted with Greek thought through Muslim translations of Plato and Aristotle. Muslim philosophers used Greek philosophy to defend and explain their religious worldview. The rediscovery of Plato and Aristotle helped to fuel the development of universities in Europe during the high **Middle Ages** (1000-1300 AD) which, in turn, helped to inaugurate the **Renaissance** (French, *re-* "again" + *naitre*, "to be born" = "rebirth" (14th to 16th centuries). Our universities in the West are direct descendants of the medieval universities; we still use medieval costumes and language in our school rituals.

The medieval universities, inspired by the example of Muslim scholars, used Greek philosophy to synthesize (combine) **faith and reason**, philosophy and theology. This integration of the two realms of knowledge is called **scholasticism**. One of the greatest of the scholastics was Thomas Aquinas (1225-1274 AD), a member of the Order of Preachers (also known as the Dominicans). The Catholic Church continues to defend the basic scholastic position: Truths known from God's gift of reason cannot contradict truths known from God's revelation.

The Great Schism: Roman Catholicism vs. Eastern Orthodoxy (870–1054 AD)

Religious, cultural, military, economic, and linguistic forces caused the Roman Empire to split into two parts, and eventually contributed to a break (schism) between western and eastern Catholicism. The western half of the empire was preoccupied with a series of barbarian invasions from the North. Latin evolved into the Romance ("Romanic") languages, such as Italian, French, Spanish, and Portuguese. The Roman system of domination and tax collection collapsed, along with the system of slavery that had made the system work. Trade, justice, military issues, and governance became local and regional concerns, giving birth to the feudal system.

In the East, Constantinople continued to be the center of wealth and power for almost a full thousand years after the "fall of Rome" in the west (476 AD). Greek remained the language of the Eastern Empire. With the rise of Islam (622 AD), the Eastern Empire was fully preoccupied with defending itself against jihad for the next eight centuries, until at last Constantinople fell to the Turks (1453 AD). The trading partners who made Constantinople rich were to the East—India and the Orient. The difficulties being faced by the western, Latin half of the empire were of little concern to the eastern, Greek half of the empire, and vice versa.

When Constantine moved the capital of the Roman Empire from Rome to Byzantium, "the new Rome," early in the fourth century AD, the papacy remained in the old Rome. The first eight councils of the Church were held in Greek territory, in or near Constantinople. The Roman emperor participated in all of the councils from the beginning, either by summoning them (as Constantine did at Nicaea in 325 AD), or by having legates (representatives) in attendance. Catholicism was the official religion of the empire after 381 AD.

In 870 AD, the eighth council of the Church, Constantinople IV, asserted that the pope exercised **primacy** (supreme jurisdictional authority) over the other bishops of the Church. Although this council was summoned and conducted in the same fashion as the first seven councils of the Church, the eastern **patriarchs** (heads of local regions of the Church) did not recognize the validity of this claim. Over the course of the next two centuries, relationships between the eastern and western Church continued to deteriorate, until the Pope and the Patriarch of Constantinople mutually excommunicated each other in **1054 AD.** The eastern Catholics have come to be known as **Eastern Orthodox Churches**.

Roman Catholics and the Eastern Orthodox are nearly twins. Both have seven sacraments, and share the same dogmatic theology of Trinity, Incarnation, and Atonement. Both accept the teachings of the first seven councils of the Church. Roman Catholics recognize the authority of another 14 councils; for the Orthodox, the conciliar process came to an end with the seventh council. The Roman Catholic Church acknowledges the authenticity of all seven sacraments in the Orthodox Churches, and endorses the unbroken apostolic succession of Orthodox bishops, from the apostolic era to the present.

The Eastern Orthodox view the pope as a bishop and patriarch on a par with their own bishops and patriarchs, with no special power over other bishops (no primacy), and with no special gift of teaching infallibility (a doctrine defined by Vatican Council I in 1870 AD). There are other theological issues as well, especially concerning the relationship between the Son and the Spirit in the Trinity.

The Renaissance (14th–16th Centuries AD) and the Rise of Protestantism (1517 AD)

As noted above, "**Renaissance**" literally means "rebirth." The leading thinkers of the Renaissance thought of themselves as "born again" Romans and Greeks. They were conscious of the fact that western Europe had lost touch with its Greco-Roman roots for many centuries. It was Renaissance scholars who coined the term "Middle Ages," to classify the centuries that had elapsed from the fall of Rome until the rise of the Renaissance.

The orientation of the Renaissance was backward-looking. The "grandeurs that were Greece and the glories that were Rome"[4] seemed to set the right standard by which to judge human excellence. The Renaissance led to a quest to uncover the lost documents of the past; the libraries of the monasteries were studied intently. Scholars trained in Hebrew, Greek, and Latin so that they could get closer to the original meanings of the texts. Poets, painters, sculptors, architects, orators, politicians, and jurists imitated the models provided by the Classical Era.

The **Protestant** objections to Catholicism were largely made possible—and inspired by—Renaissance scholarship. The idea that the earlier, classical ages were better than subsequent ages of apparent or alleged corruption and decay was a typical Renaissance mind-set. When scholars read the Scriptures with that mentality, they noticed the vast differences between the images of the original Christian community captured in the New Testament, and the theology and culture of Catholicism that had developed over the 14 centuries that followed the era of the New Testament.

As I noted in the introduction, it is an unassailable fact that people disagree. There have been disagreements about how to interpret who Jesus is since He began His public ministry at the Jordan River. Every age saw **heretics** select some part of the tradition to keep, and reject other parts of the tradition. What made the Protestant era different from preceding times of dissent and protest was the collapse of the union between the Catholic Church and the royalty of Europe; Protestants formed successful alliances with many of the nobility and gained territory the old-fashioned way, by royal edict. The Peace of Augsburg (1555 AD) was based on the idea that the ruler's religion determined the religion of the region that was ruled (Latin, *cujus regio, ejus religio*, "whose region, his religion"). In times past, the union of Church and state had helped to exterminate heretical sects; now the union helped to preserve them.

Many Protestants celebrate October 31, 1517, as "Reformation Day." This was the day that Martin Luther nailed a list of 95 objections to Roman Catholic doctrine and practices to the door of a church in Wittenberg, Germany. Luther's protest was characterized by three "solas" (Latin, *sola*, "alone"): **sola fide**, we are saved "by faith alone" and not by good works; **sola scriptura**, we know the mind of God "by scripture alone," and not by the tradition of the Catholic Church; and **sola gratia**, everything is given "by grace alone," and not by human merit. "Sola fide" and "sola scriptura" are themes common to many forms of Protestantism. There is no pope of Protestantism, no councils, no universal catechism, no dogmas binding on all; each individual and group enjoys the freedom of private judgment to interpret and apply the Scriptures as they please.

---

[4] Edgar Allan Poe, "To Helen." Although this was written in 1831, the line captures the flavor of the Renaissance.

Reformation vs. Deformation

Since the day that Luther publicized his protests against the Church, the number of objections to Catholicism has multiplied beyond counting. There is no true statement that can be made about all Protestants, except to say that they are non-Catholic Christians. Protestants disagree with one another, as well as with the Catholic Church. I have seen estimates that there may be as many as 33,000 different varieties of non-Catholic Christianity. The number is indefinite, because anyone may take the Bible in hand, read it piously, come up with their own unique interpretation, and open a new church later this afternoon. Some Christians are so tired of the endless multiplication of denominations that they have started a brand-new movement called "nondenominationalism." Such groups want to have no association with any other form of historical Christianity—not Catholic, not Orthodox, and not Protestant.

There are no nonjudgmental terms for the rise of Protestantism. Those who call it the **Reformation** are taking the anti-Catholic view of the founders of the movement; those who call it Protestantism are taking the Catholic view. Christianity certainly changed after 1517, and in that sense, was re-formed. Whether one judges that the changes were positive or negative depends on one's own religious convictions. Many of the protests against the leaders and members of the Church were unquestionably valid, and did lead to changes for the better in pastoral administration. Some of the Renaissance popes were among the most shamelessly sinful and corrupt criminals ever to occupy the chair of St. Peter.

Without giving up the doctrine of Purgatory and the need to pray for the repose of the souls of our brothers and sisters, the Church did stop the scandalous practice of using the sale of indulgences (formal declarations that sins were to be forgiven) as a fund-raising gambit. The training of priests was dramatically improved through the establishment of seminaries that helped the candidates to understand the faith that they were meant to cultivate in their parish work. The **Council of Trent** (1545-1563 AD) painstakingly sorted through the questions raised by the protestors, and provided dogmatic clarity about the Catholic vision of reality and sacramental life. The **Tridentine**[5] formulas dominated the life of the Catholic Church for the next four centuries, up until **Vatican Council II** (1962-1965 AD).

Measured by these changes, the protestors did motivate the Church to reform its teaching and its religious practices; such reforms had been called for by the fifth Lateran Council (1512-1517), but it took the sting of the defection of the Protestants to motivate the Church to truly reform its way of life.

If we measure the goals of the Protestants by the kinds of churches they founded, they unquestionably gave Christianity a new form. The Protestant bodies rejected the teaching and pastoral authority of the Pope, placing the Bible at the summit of teaching authority (very much like the

---

[5] "Trent" is a contraction of the Latin word *tridentum*, trident; the Latin adjective, *Tridentinum*, "things related to the town of Trent," is the root of the English word Tridentine, which means "things related to the Council of Trent."

Muslim relationship to the Quran); changed the theology of the sacraments (often reducing the number to two: Baptism and the Eucharist); favored the individual and private interpretation of the Bible over the teaching of tradition; and (like the Orthodox) set aside the teachings of some or all of the councils of the Church. These changes were not made *in* the Catholic Church, but outside of it. If their goal was to re-form the Catholic Church itself along these lines, the Reformers failed to reach their objectives; they produced new forms of Christianity outside the Catholic Church.

If the intention of the Reformers was simply to cut the cloth of the Christian tradition to suit their own tastes and interpretations, they succeeded admirably. The Catholic Church, and many of the Protestant churches, continued the tradition of seeking an alliance with secular authorities, producing "established" (that is, state-sanctioned) churches. Many subsequent Protestant groups withdrew from the established churches and were persecuted as a consequence; such religious persecution of some Protestants by other Protestants was, of course, one of the contributing factors in the colonization of the United States.

As we approach the 500th anniversary of the Protestant era, a new form of Protestantism has become very popular. Whereas the classical Reformers achieved their goals by leaving the Catholic Church and creating new churches of their own design, many Catholics are adopting Protestant principles—consciously or unconsciously—but continue to think of themselves as Catholic. Those who do so consciously want to see the Protestant program adopted *in* the Church itself. Those who do so unconsciously tend to say, "I am Catholic, but I disagree with some of the teachings of the Church." The technical term for the movement to refashion the Church to align it with contemporary culture is **Modernism**. Modernists, like Protestants, do not possess a monolithic or dogmatic standpoint. Not all Modernists would subscribe to all of the points in the following table, but the table does give some sense of the Modernist mentality: that the Church should change, in order to keep step with modern times.

Every change desired by the Modernists is readily available in non-Catholic Christian traditions: endorsement of sincerity rather than marriage as the proper framework for sexual activity; acceptance of same-sex relationships (whether in or out of marriage); contraception, sterilization, abortion, and divorce; and ordination of women as bishops, priests, and ministers. My impression is that the Modernists far outnumber the traditionalists in the American church. I cannot predict whether this will lead to a new schism or set of schisms, or whether the Modernists will eventually join the existing varieties of Protestantism—or both.

Sikhism: Child of Hinduism and Islam (1507–1708 AD)

The world's fifth largest religion arose in the Punjab region of India just 500 years ago. Nanak (1469-1539) became a **guru** (an "enlightened teacher") in 1507; another nine gurus continued his teaching about devotion to the one and only God, **Waheguru** (or Vahiguru, "the wonderful

Traditional Roman Catholicism	Modernism
The faith is defined by the Magisterium, the living teaching authority of the Church (the pope and bishops acting in union with each other).	The faith is defined by one's own conscience and inner light.
The Scriptures are part of tradition, and must be interpreted according to tradition.	One's own personal interpretation of the Scriptures is what is decisive.
Our consciences must be informed by the teaching of the Church.	We should make up our own minds about what we think is right. If we think it's right, it's right.
The prohibition of adultery excludes all sexual acts outside of marriage.	People may do what feels right to them, as long as their motives are sincere.
Marriage can only take place between a man and a woman.	People with same-sex attractions should be allowed to be married.
A valid, consummated marriage creates a bond between husband and wife that cannot be broken. Couples may separate, but neither one may remarry; they must be faithful to their vows until their spouse dies.	When marriages break down, the partners should be allowed to divorce and marry someone else.
Couples may use only natural methods of family planning.	Couples should be allowed to use any form of contraception and/or sterilization that they please.
All deliberately procured abortions are the murder of an innocent human being.	Mothers should be allowed to kill the child within their womb if they feel that it is the right thing to do.
Children must be conceived through the means given by nature (sexual intercourse between a man and a woman).	The Church should endorse all forms of *in vitro* (test-tube) fertilization, artificial insemination, surrogate motherhood, and genetic engineering.
Candidates for priesthood in the Roman rite must personally desire and freely choose celibacy.*	Priests should be allowed to marry.

* Note well: *The union of ordination with celibacy is only required in the Latin rite of the Roman Catholic Church. In the 22 Eastern Churches in union with the Roman Catholic Church (also known as the Eastern rites), the tradition of ordaining married men prevails. This means that there are married priests in the Roman Catholic Church. Few American Catholics are aware of the fact that there already are—and always have been—"married priests" in the Roman Catholic Church. Simon Peter had a mother-in-law (Mk 1:30), which means that he had to have been married before he was chosen as an apostle by Jesus.*

Only men can be ordained.	The Church should ordain both men and women.
The faithful are required to attend Mass on Sunday.	There is no need to attend Mass at all. Those who wish may accomplish all the purposes of the Mass all by themselves.
We may not commit suicide, nor may we murder the sick.	Suffering is an intolerable evil; therefore, the sick may murder themselves, or may require their doctors to murder them.
Bishops should be chosen because they have demonstrated fidelity to the Deposit of Faith.	Church leaders should be elected democratically.

guru") until 1708, when the tenth guru declared that, from then on, the book of the teachings of the gurus would be the guru for the Sikhs: "All the Sikhs hereby are commanded to obey the Granth as their Guru."[6] The name of the sacred writings is *Guru Granth Sahib* (literally, "Master Guru Book").

It is clear that Sikhism inherited its monotheism and devotion to a sacred book from its Muslim parent. In that same vein, the Sikh gurus rejected the Hindu stories about **avatars** (gods come in human form, like Krishna), the caste system, the use of "graven images" to represent God (from the Muslim interpretation of the first commandment in the Decalogue), and the magical chants of the Vedas. From its Hindu parent, Sikhism inherited the belief in the need to be continually reincarnated until one attains salvation by union with the one God. Guru Nanak also rejected key elements of Islamic life: the Ramadan fast, polygamy, and pilgrimages to Mecca.

Every boy is given the name **Singh** as a middle or last name, which means "lion," and every girl is similarly given the name **Kaur**, which means "princess." All males who have undergone the baptism and purification ritual are required to follow the tradition of "the five Ks"; the word for each of these traditions begins with a "K" in Punjabi:

- uncut hair: as in the story of Sampson, the uncut hair represents an unbroken commitment to God, and is normally wrapped in a turban (a sixth "K");
- a comb to keep one's hair in good condition;
- a circular iron bracelet that is a symbolic shield;
- a sword (usually represented by a short dagger);
- battle dress (shorts worn under the normal flowing garments of the region).

As with the Muslim traditions about jihad, all of the warlike aspects of the five Ks may be seen as reminders of the spiritual battle that all must fight in order to pass from *Manmukh*, selfishness, to *Gurmukh*, God-centeredness and selflessness.

Western Enlightenment (17th–18th Centuries AD)

The kind of thinking that today we call "science" was originally known as "natural philosophy." It was one of the branches of medieval scholastic study. Starting with the questions raised by the Greeks and preserved in the treatises studied by the scholastics, Western thinkers slowly laid the groundwork for the successes that have come from empirical (observational) and experimental science. Renaissance scholars contributed to these developments too. Astrologers studied the movement of the planets because of a classical, Greco-Roman religious superstition that our fates were determined by the location of the planets at the moment of our birth. Accurate tables

---

[6] "Guru Granth Sahib," *Wikipedia*.

of planetary motion were therefore necessary to determine what those fateful planetary conjunctions were, and to provide guidance for heads of state. Our science of astronomy emerged from those superstitiously motivated studies.

Similarly, Renaissance alchemists were persuaded that there might be a "philosopher's stone" that could grant immortality or a method to change lead into gold. Their desire for life and wealth led them to acquire skills in the purification and combination of elements, thus laying the foundations for our science of chemistry. Although we now know that their objectives were foolish—it is fetal tissue research that promises us unendingly renewed life, and lead can be turned into gold only through prohibitively expensive nuclear reactions—the alchemists were, in fact, doing chemical experiments and learning from the results, just as modern chemists do.

The successes of observational and experimental methods led to the **philosophy of the Enlightenment**, which held that our lives are meant to be governed by "pure reason," the kind of reason employed in the scientific laboratory. This kind of enlightenment is very different from Eastern enlightenment. Western science, the light in our Enlightenment, depends on logic, mathematics, measurement, precision, clarity, and accuracy. Eastern enlightenment means escaping from this world entirely, and ceasing to care about the restrictions of language.

Where the people of the Renaissance were, as a general rule, backward-looking (due to their assumption that the Greeks and the Romans had reached the pinnacle of human development), the people of the Enlightenment tend to be forward-looking, trusting in human reason to deliver ever greater progress and prosperity. The United States is an Enlightenment nation. The Declaration of Independence (July 4, 1776) says that "We hold these truths to be *self-evident*." That is the tone of the Enlightenment: All that is needed is purity of thought and reasonable discourse; if we just stick to the principles of reason, all will be well.

Emancipation of the Jews

During the age of Christendom (381-1776 AD), when Christianity, in either its Catholic or Protestant forms, had been united with the state, Jews were confined to isolated communities within the Christian culture, partly by the precepts of the Torah, which favored living within a Sabbath's walk of a synagogue and marrying one's own kind, and partly by the laws of Christian polities that discriminated against Jews and forced them to live apart. In Venice, the walled-off Jewish quarter was called the "ghetto." With the rise of the Enlightenment philosophy that "all [humans] are created equal and are endowed by their Creator with inalienable rights" (that is, rights that cannot be taken away or "alienated"), and with the increasing detachment of the state from its long union with Christianity, Jews gained the freedom to leave their closed communities, and to enjoy equal human rights as full members of society.

This emancipation (liberation) of the Jews from the ghettos of Europe gave rise to three new forms of Judaism: **Orthodox Jews** continue to live in tight-knit, distinctive communities gathered

Islam (Judaism and Christinaty Continued)

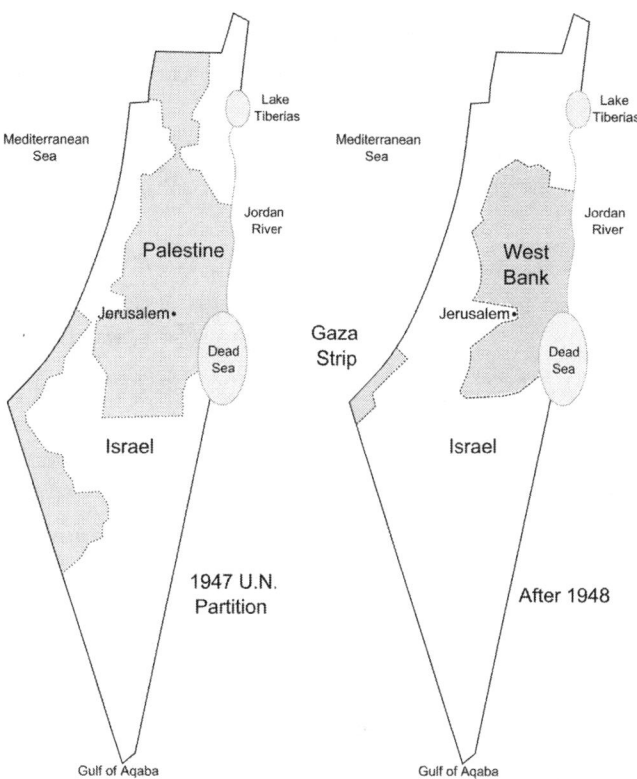

around a synagogue. They observe all of the principles of the Torah that apply to home life and social relationships with other Jews. So, for example, because the Torah prohibits kindling a fire on the Sabbath (Exodus 35:3), Orthodox Jews will not turn on any electric appliances, not even lights, or drive a car on the Sabbath—they must live within a "Sabbath walk" of the synagogue.

Conservative Jews maintain some distinctive aspects of the Torah (some of the dietary laws and some aspects of Sabbath devotion) but have abandoned others, in order to adapt to the modern world (e.g., use of electricity and cars on the Sabbath).

Reform Jews keep the ethical worldview of the Torah—the essential principles of justice embedded in the Decalogue—but feel free to imitate Gentile manners, dress, and customs in their daily life.

The Rise of Zionism (1898 AD) and the Restoration of Israel (1948 AD)

In 1898, Theodor Herzl founded the **Zionist movement**, which was intended to create a new state of Israel. Herzl was not Orthodox; he was open to the idea of locating the new nation of Israel in Argentina or on Grand Island, New York, or anywhere else that seemed convenient. The people who responded to his idea of returning to Zion, the holy hill in the city of Jerusalem (Ps

2:6), were more Orthodox than Herzl, and wanted to see the original Promised Land returned to them—not some substitute acreage elsewhere. They began to move to **Palestine**, a name derived from the consonants for the biblical **Philistines** (PLSTN—see the footnote on page 81). The original Philistines (or Palestinians) had long been replaced by Arabs who came in the wake of the jihad across the Middle East and North Africa that took place shortly after Muhammad's death (632 AD).

Because the Ottoman Turks allied themselves with Germany and Austro-Hungaria in World War I, their territory in the Middle East came under British control in the aftermath of the war. In order to gain their support against the Turks during the war, the British promised independence to the Arabs and the creation of a new state of Israel to the Jews (the famous—or infamous—Balfour Declaration of 1917). Zionist Jews continued to move into the British Mandate of Palestine, anticipating the fulfillment of the promise that had been made to them.

Nothing was done until after the Nazi Holocaust in World War II (1939-1945 AD). The white, Christian, European, colonial powers who won the war organized the United Nations. The United Nations then called for the end of British rule over Palestine and the formation of two new states in that area, Palestine and Israel (1947 AD). This was a unilateral decision by the United Nations; the people living in Palestine at that time were not given a chance to accept or reject the new form of government being imposed on them by foreign powers—an act that is the very essence of colonialism!

War broke out within a few months of the passage of the UN resolution. The Israelis won the war, and took over a great deal more territory than had been envisaged in the original plan. The largest piece of Palestine is called the "West Bank," because it is on the west bank of the Jordan River, which runs from the Sea of Galilee in the North to the Dead Sea in the South. The smaller piece is the "Gaza Strip." Although Palestine was supposed to be an independent nation (according to the original UN resolution), Israel has ruled the West Bank and the Gaza Strip since 1949, keeping the Arab population in those areas in a state of **apartheid** (Afrikaans, "apartness," a state of separation from the rest of the population). The Palestinians who live under Israeli jurisdiction do not have human rights equal to those of Israeli citizens, and are governed and taxed without representation; if the United States' War of Independence was justified by "taxation without representation," so, too, would a Palestinian War of Independence be equally justifiable.

Israel has been in a constant state of war since it declared independence from Palestine in 1948. Hostilities were renewed in 1956, 1967, 1973, and 1982; it also came under missile attack in the Gulf War of 1991. Although Israel is surrounded by enemies and is tiny when compared to the territory of the Arabs, it has prevailed in all five wars. From the beginning, Israel has relied on funding and technological support from the citizens and government of the United States. Without the backing of the United States, Israel would not have been created by the United Nations, nor would it have survived the efforts of its Arab neighbors to overthrow it.

The United States plunged itself into a sea of profound religious hostilities when it decided to help create and sustain the modern state of Israel. Faced with the horror of what Hitler had done to the Jews in Europe—and undoubtedly feeling guilty for not allowing more Jews to escape from territories threatened or occupied by the Nazis in the late 1930s and early 1940s—the coalition of colonial powers, led by the United States, seems not to have given much thought to the religious and cultural consequences of imposing a Jewish state on the people of Palestine. In this act, the United Nations achieved the original objective of the Crusades: *it took the Holy Land away from the Muslims*. What the United Nations understood as a noble act of reparation to the Jews is interpreted as an act of aggression against Islam by many Arab Muslims.

The Palestinian Refugee Problem (1948 AD to the present)

When the first Arab-Israeli war broke out in 1948, 500,000 to 800,000 Palestinians fled from the region,[7] either voluntarily and in expectation of a short, decisive Arab victory, or else involuntarily as the Jewish forces took possession of their lands. Israel declared the refugees to be allies of the combatant nations, and has steadfastly refused to allow them to return to their homes; the Arab nations seem content to let 1.3 million Palestinians languish in 58 squalid refugee camps in Gaza, the West Bank, Jordan, Lebanon and Syria.[8] There is not much else to do in the camps but raise children to hate Israel (and, of course, its Western, Christian, European, colonial allies), and to hope and pray for a reversal of fortune.

Israel offers the "right of return" to all Jews living anywhere in the world. They may move to Israel and become full-fledged citizens of the nation. This was one of the purposes for creating a Jewish homeland, and it remains an essential feature of Israel's constitution. Israel cannot afford to allow the 4.6 million Palestinian refugees and their descendants the "right of return" to their native land. Israel is a democracy only for its Jewish citizens; no other ethnic group need apply, especially not the Arabs from Palestine. If the refugees and all of the Palestinians living in apartheid under Israeli jurisdiction were accepted as equal citizens with equal voting rights, they would outnumber the 5.4 million Jews living in Israel,[9] and would almost certainly exercise democratic power vindictively so as to do unto the Jews what has been done unto them for the last 60 years.

---

[7] People disagree in general; the Jews and Arabs disagree passionately about the demographics of the Palestinian refugee problem, and the proper way to describe how the Palestinian refugee problem developed.

[8] The numbers and locations come from the UNRWA, the United Nations agency created in 1949 to assist the Palestinian refugees (*http://www.un.org/unrwa/refugees/wheredo.html*). The judgment that the camps are no place for humans to live is my own. UNRWA estimates that there are 4.6 million refugees and their descendants (*http://www.un.org/unrwa/refugees/whois.html*).

[9] "Demographics of Israel," *Wikipedia*.

The only way that the Jews can maintain control of Israel—and to preserve it as homeland for Jews—is to treat all other ethnic groups, and especially the Arab Palestinians, as second-class citizens. Because of security concerns, it is highly unlikely that Israel would ever allow the West Bank and the Gaza Strip to form a truly independent Palestinian nation.

This is the quagmire that we decided to enter in 1947.

Because the United States is a predominantly Christian nation, and because Christianity is a child of Judaism (even if unwanted and unacknowledged), there is a profound bias on the part of most U.S. Christians in favor of Israel. The survival of the Jews in diaspora is a moral miracle, made possible by the rabbis who found a way to preserve the spirit of the Torah, even when the Promised Land, the Kingship, and the Temple were destroyed; the resurrection of the Holy Land from the dead and the victories of Israel over its enemies since 1948 are equally astonishing, and in the eyes of many Christians, seem to be the fulfillment of ancient biblical prophecies. Many fundamentalist Christians are as eager as the Orthodox and ultra-Orthodox Jews to see the Temple in Jerusalem restored. Just as the reconstruction of the Temple in the sixth century BC completed the return from Exile in Babylon, so too the reconstruction of the Temple in this century would complete Israel's return from the diaspora that began in 70 AD. Both biblical Christians and Orthodox Jews anticipate that the restoration of the Temple would prepare the way for God to raise up the Messiah promised to David so long ago (Ps 89).

Al-Haram Al-Sharif: Whose God Will Rule on This Mountain?

Herod the Great (73-4 BC) began the complete reconstruction of the Second Temple in Jerusalem in 19 BC;[10] work was completed in 65 AD—just prior to its destruction by the Romans in 70 AD. Herod's project created a 28-acre site on the top of Mount Moriah by constructing huge retaining walls; they alone survived after 70 AD. When Catholics dominated Jerusalem, their efforts were focused on building churches to memorialize scenes from Jesus' suffering, death, resurrection, and ascension; the Temple Mount was used as a trash dump. When the Muslims took control of Jerusalem in 638 AD, they venerated the Temple Mount as the focus of Muhammad's Night Journey (17:1). The **Dome of the Rock** (also known as the Mosque of Omar) was constructed in 691 AD on the rock that presumably was the foundation for the Holy of Holies (Hebraism meaning "the holiest place") in the Temple (see page 84).

The Muslims also built the Al-Aqsa ("The Furthest") Mosque on the Temple Mount, shortly after the Dome of the Rock was completed. For them, the mountaintop with its mosques is

---

[10] John's gospel reports that the Temple had been under construction for 46 years when Jesus and His disciples first visited it together (Jn 2:20). The *New American Bible* says that this may indicate a date of 28 AD for the Cleansing of the Temple. If we follow John's chronology (a two-to-three year ministry), that would put the death of Jesus in 30 AD.

known as *Al-Haram Al-Sharif*, "The Noble Sanctuary" (land that is set aside for or consecrated to God is "haram," prohibited from being used for ordinary purposes).

For Orthodox and ultra-Orthodox Jews and their Christian fundamentalist supporters, God's word in the Old Testament not only gives the Jews title to the whole of the territory of ancient Israel, but most especially to the Temple Mount; if they were religiously justified in resurrecting Israel by taking land from Muslims, they would be religiously justified in taking the Noble Sanctuary from them, too.

Muslims understandably see things differently. For them, Muhammad is the last in the line of the Jewish and Christian prophets. He completes and perfects the revelation that began with Abraham and continued through Jesus. From their perspective—and on the basis of *their* sacred Scripture and tradition—the God of Abraham has commissioned them to rule the whole world. There is only one God, one final prophet, one Quran, and one Way (Sharia). The Last Testament (Covenant) made through Muhammad displaces the Jewish and Christian Testaments. Muslims, therefore, see themselves as occupying and controlling the Noble Sanctuary by divine right.

The government of Israel has so far resisted all efforts to complete the restoration of Israel by taking control of the Temple Mount and clearing the ground for the construction of a new Temple. How long it can resist the religious pressures to do so remains to be seen.

For now, as for the 18 centuries since the Temple was destroyed, all the Jews can do is visit the Wailing Wall, the western retaining wall built by Herod, and lament: "O God, the nations have invaded your heritage; they have defiled your holy temple, have laid Jerusalem in ruins" (Ps 79:1).

If God Himself gave me power and authority to settle this dispute, I would not know how to do so. The religious principles of Judaism demand that the Holy of Holies be built on the rock on the Temple Mount, and that no one except the high priest enter the sanctuary, to offer animal sacrifice on Yom Kippur. The religious principles of Islam would prevent me from acting as God's prophet (*Muhammad* is His Prophet!) to command the Muslims to relocate their mosques.

If there is a God, we need Him now more than ever to bring peace to the children of Abraham.

Forswearing Stereotypes of Islam

Dr. Christopher Lee of the Canisius College Department of Religious Studies and Theology has taught me to be wary of falling victim to, or continuing to perpetuate, false images of Islam.

- **Islam must not be identified with violence.** The vast majority of the world's 1.5 billion Muslims are not violent. Violent extremists make up only a fraction of Islam.
- **Islam must not be identified with Arabs or the Middle East.** The religion originated in Saudi Arabia among Arabs, but has spread around the world. The vast majority of Muslims are not Arab, and do not live in the Middle East. The largest Muslim nation in the world is Indonesia, with a population of about 220 million people.

- **Not all Arabs are Muslims.** One of the most ancient forms of Christianity is Arabic. Arab Christians have suffered greatly in the Middle East wars, especially in Palestine and Lebanon.
- **Islam is not a monolithic religion.** There are many varieties of spirituality and devotion in Islam that have only been hinted at in this brief treatment. Just as pious Christians naturally assume that their variety of Christianity is the standard by which all others are to be judged, pious Muslims naturally see their own form of Islam as normative. This is not inherent to Islam, but is the logical consequence of making any kind of commitment to a religious worldview.

Part III

• • • • •

Taking a View

Judgment Day

· · · · · ·

What Right Do We Have to Judge Others' Beliefs?

"Judge not lest ye be judged" (Mt 7:1, KJV) is one of Jesus' most famous sayings. I am amazed at how much reverence is given to this precept by those who have rejected every other part of the Christian tradition: "I have the right to my opinion, just as you have the right to yours. Leave me alone. Stop trying to force your religious views on me."

There is a proper and an improper interpretation of Jesus' prohibition of judgment. On the one hand, Jesus forbids us to think that we are in a position to judge another person's behavior in a condemnatory fashion. We are not God. We do not know the secrets of the heart. We do not know what mercy God has shown, can show, or will show to our errant brothers and sisters. We do not know who will go to Hell, nor who, by the mercy of God, will go to Heaven. That kind of judgment about where others stand in God's sight is none of our business.

On the other hand, every meaningful choice we make in life is a matter of judgment. Jesus requires that we *make up our minds about Him*: "Stop judging by appearances, but judge justly" (Jn 7:24).

> Then Jesus said, "I came into this world for judgment, so that those who do not see might see, and those who do see might become blind." Some of the Pharisees who were with him heard this and said to him, "Surely we are not also blind, are we?" Jesus said to them, "If you were blind, you would have no sin; but now you are saying, 'We see,' so your sin remains." (Jn 9:39-41)

Jesus promised that we would know the truth and that the truth would set us free (Jn 8:32). Knowledge of any truth whatsoever is a matter of sound judgment, whether it is about ideas (notional assent) or realities (real assent).

Jesus' instruction not to judge the spiritual standing of others in God's eyes does not mean that we should think or act unintelligently. We have an obligation to discriminate between good and evil. We must not stand idly by while evildoers injure the weak. We must condemn assault; murder; hatred; genocide; the actions of terrorists; adultery; rape; incest; the sexual abuse of children by adults (especially if the adults were priests or bishops!); irresponsible parenting; lying; theft; bigotry; the abuse of power by corrupt judges and politicians; the wanton destruction of ecosystems; and every other kind of crime against humanity. We must not call evil good, or good evil.

Those who say "you must not judge others" or "you cannot judge others" in the sense of forbidding another person to evaluate others' beliefs are being judgmental *in exactly the same way they are reprehending in others*. What gives them the right to judge all who judge others? Why are they exempt from their prescription against judgment? They are hypocrites—they do what they say must not be done.

A very popular anthem among atheists is John Lennon's "Imagine" (1971). The song implies that religion is the cause of the world's problems. Lennon imagines that if there were no Heaven, no Hell, no religion, and "nothing to kill or die for," then there would be a "brotherhood of man" and "the world [would] live as one." Because the melody, arrangement, and vocals are sweet, the song is a rhetorical masterpiece—it seems so gentle, calm, and sweetly reasonable, that it's easy to ignore the fact that it is utterly judgmental. Lennon's view that *all religions are evil* and that the world would be better off without them is certainly not a formula for tolerance and acceptance of diversity of belief. It is an absolute judgment on all religions other than his own.

In my view, the declaration that all religious worldviews are false and destructive is itself a religious worldview; it comes from comprehensive view of reality, and establishes standards of conduct for our lives. "No one has the right to impose religious ideas on others" is a religious ideal imposed on others, by those who propose it as a dogma and as an ethical ideal.

Passing judgment on what is true or false, good or evil, worthwhile or worthless, appropriate or inappropriate, and the like is what our minds do all day long. We cannot function without judgment. Every sentence to which we assent is like the sentences issued by a judge in court; we are judges who have an obligation, like the judges in court, to *judge justly*.

I cannot compel you to believe this. I have jurisdiction only over my own thoughts, words, and deeds. In judging that I am sovereign over myself, I accept that you are sovereign over yourself. You may accept or reject my view—but you can do so only by passing judgment on what I have said.

There is no way to escape this intellectual obligation to make up our minds and pass sentence on the claims made by people around us. This is part of the predicament noticed by the existentialists. Their focus was on the fact that we are obliged—whether we like it or not—to make choices. Choosing not to choose is a choice. Similarly, the decision to adopt the standpoint that passing judgment is evil is a judgment. We may ask critical questions of the speaker in Lennon's song "Imagine": How do you know that all religion is evil? By what authority do you say this? What makes you so sure? Are you right that there is no Heaven or Hell? Are you telling the truth? What evidence supports your view? What evidence might contradict it? How is it that you are allowed to declare others' views evil? Would abolishing all other concepts of good and evil other than your own *truly* bring about a "brotherhood of man"? Would abolishing all religious doctrines *really* cause the world "to be as one"?

I don't say that Lennon (or the speaker in the song) is a dreamer. I say that he is doing *exactly* what he condemns in others—he is defining what is and is not real, what is good and evil, and what will make us happy forever. If that is an evil thing to do, then he is guilty of evildoing; if it is acceptable for him to make sweeping religious generalizations, then it should be acceptable for other human beings to do so, too. He doesn't get a pass, because he hates all worldviews other than his own.

Our culture is permeated with the hatred of organized or institutionalized religion. The Roman Catholic church is the most organized religious institution in history. The dream of abolishing all organized religion breeds hatred of Catholicism, even among Catholics themselves. Disorganized, nondogmatic, antiauthoritarian, privatized Christianity (spirituality without religion) that takes no stance on public policy, and never criticizes the will of the majority, is what our culture favors. The Catholic Church claims to be prophetic, making known God's own mind on the nature of good and evil. When the modern world hears this claim, it replies, "Shut up! Who are you to claim God's own authority over me?"

We Should Disagree with What Is False

If someone decides to object to what I have written, they can do so only by appealing to the principle that truth should be accepted and falsehood rejected. If a reader says, "Your view of the nature of the human mind and our existential obligation to act as judges of ideas and reality is wrong," then they are asserting that I ought to change my mind about the nature of reality. If a reader says, "I don't care about religious disagreements," then they are judging that such debates are fruitless and not worthwhile.

Some students play a hit-and-run game. First they reveal their judgment that all religious discourse is absurd, then run away from further discourse by concluding, "But this is just my opinion"—as if that tagline somehow absolved them from responsibility for the judgment that all religions are absurd, meaningless, and irrelevant to real life.

All religious opinions are about *you and me*. All statements people make about reality are statements about the reality that *you and I* inhabit. All humans are necessarily in dialogue with each other and in conflict with each other, where our judgments about ultimate reality differ.

We Should Condemn What Is Evil

In my view, it is evil to call good things evil, and evil things good. There is a difference between what is right and what is wrong, and it is often not hard to tell the difference. There are a multitude of evils that have been done by people claiming religious inspiration. I think it is the duty of all right-thinking people to condemn evil in no uncertain terms, and not to tolerate religious rationalizations of evildoing.

Murder "in the name of the Lord" is murder. I condemn the murder of abortionists on the same grounds that I condemn the murder of innocent children in their mother's womb. Society may punish evildoers for just cause after due judicial processes, but vigilantism, alone or with others, is evil. I grieve the suicides and murders that have taken place in cults like Jonestown, Heaven's Gate, and Waco.

I condemn all of my fellow Christians who have committed crimes of murder, rape, robbery, and every kind of injustice against Jews and other ethnic minorities. I condemn those who twisted the Scriptures to justify the enslavement of blacks and the murder of native Americans in the United States.

I condemn the use of weapons of mass destruction, both those used by the United States and its allies in World War II (firebombing and nuclear weapons), and those used to attack the United States on 9/11/2001. A just war may only be fought to defend those unjustly attacked, and the means of waging war must also be just.

I abhor the use of violence to force conversions, whether it be the violence of the Spanish Inquisition against Muslims and Jews, or the violence of jihad against Christians and Jews.

I am deeply ashamed by the sins of priests and the sins and stupidity of bishops in the Catholic Church (see "The Judas Factor," page 127). What they did was wrong and inexcusable. I do not think that Jesus would object to our saying that such people deserve to be cast into an unquenchable fire with a millstone around their necks (Mk 9:42-43).

Evil is evil. Bad religions are bad. Sin happens. But, in my view, we should not throw out the baby with the bathwater. Good religion is the antidote to bad religion. Worship of God; repentance for sin; reparation of the evils done by others; tenderness and compassion for the oppressed; consolation for those who are suffering; healing for the broken-hearted; fresh strength for the weak; and hope for those in despair are also to be found in any fair account of the history of religion.

It is a sin against religion to use religion to rationalize evildoing. Religion is not the root of all evil—nor is civilization (as suggested by *Huckleberry Finn* and the Tarzan myths), nor money (1 Tim 6:10), nor private ownership of the means of production (Marx). **Self is the root of all evil.** In every crime against God and against humanity, criminals put themselves first, and refuse to love God and love their neighbor. "Me first" is the structure of all evildoing, regardless of the specific form it takes.

It is not just religious people who do evil. So do professed atheists like Hitler, Stalin, Mao Zedong, and Pol Pot. The hundreds of millions of people killed—directly and indirectly—by atheist regimes in the 20th century far outnumber all the people killed in all the wars of Christendom.

All humans are capable of evil, whether they are religious or not. All people are capable of self-centered stupidity. It is a hasty and lazy generalization to say, "Because some people who claim to be religious are evidently evil, all religions are evil."

The Triple-A Stew: Apathy, Agnosticism, and Atheism

For our minds to work correctly, we need to be motivated to pay attention to the data, ask questions, seek insight, and pass judgment.[1] We cannot think or know unless we *want* to do so. It is very easy to drop out of the dialogue. It is easy to put other things in the foreground of consciousness—health; success; pleasure; power; money; entertainment in a multitude of forms—and shut out questions about God; the spiritual realm; life after life; truth; meaning; suffering; justice; the conflict between good and evil; and the clash of conflicting worldviews.

No one can make you care about these things. You are the sovereign of your heart and mind. It's your choice. Modern culture provides thousands of myths about how to find happiness in a godless world. Let the good times roll!

In Freudian theory, religion is just a projection of an idealized father figure on the screen of the universe; it is *nothing but* wishful thinking. With or without Freud's help, this view of religion can form the foundation for a kind of tolerance for—although it is really indifference toward—all religions: "They're all equally absurd. Whatever. If they think it's good for them, it's good for them."

Indifferentism is found even within the field of religion, as in the case of Ramakrishna (page 30). "No one knows anything for certain about God. Any religion is as good as any other. They all say pretty much the same thing. Let's all play 'Pin-the-Tail on the Donkey'! Whatever we say about God is as good as anything anyone else has ever said about God." This kind of thinking may lie behind the invention of New Age religions and the resurrection of paganism and witchcraft. New Agers and neo-pagans tend to be syncretistic, which means that they collect materials from many religious traditions and jumble them together, according to standards not drawn organically from any of those traditions.

If you find yourself unable to stay apathetic, the next easiest dodge is **agnosticism**. There are two forms of this worldview: personal and dogmatic. If someone says of himself or herself, "I am ignorant and cannot decide whether there is a God, whether there is a real difference between

---

[1] In this paragraph, I combine Michael Polanyi's idea of intellectual passions (Chapter 6 in *Personal Knowledge*) with Lonergan's epistemology in *Insight*.

good and evil, or whether life is meaningful," then I have no argument with that person. Telling the truth about one's own ignorance and confusion is a noble act, and deserves to be treated with respect.

Dogmatic agnostics go beyond admitting the limitations of their own minds to asserting the limitations of *all human minds*. It is one thing to say, "I don't know." It is entirely different to say, as Bill Maher does at the end of the movie, *Religulous*, that no human beings can ever know anything more than he does:

> How can I be so sure? Because I don't know, and you do not possess mental powers that I do not. The only appropriate attitude for man to have about the big questions is not the arrogant certitude that is the hallmark of religion, but doubt.[2]

The person who makes the this kind of claim is pronouncing a dogma about all people at all times in all places, past, present, and future. It is not a modest or humble statement. It is judgmental in the highest degree. The dogmatic agnostic claims to know that no one can know anything about religious questions. I find this self-referentially inconsistent. The dogmatic agnostic is *answering all religious questions by declaring that they are all unanswerable*. That doesn't make any sense to me. It seems to me to be pretty arrogant to condemn all religious discourse, on the grounds that one knows for certain that no one can know anything for certain about religion.

Dogmatic agnosticism is just **atheism** in disguise. If one knew for sure that there is no God, then it follows immediately, and with perfect logical consistency, that all forms of theism (pantheism, polytheism, monotheism) are absurd; along the same lines, if one knew for certain that there are no powers other than the powers of nature, then all forms of animism are also absurd. From this materialist standpoint, one may judge—must judge—that no one can know anything about religious realities, because they do not exist; religion is necessarily nothing but a dream or wish fulfillment, or a projection of human fictions onto the screen of the natural order. For the atheist, religion is a figment of human imagination that stands in the way of understanding the only reality there is, the physical universe. Religion is, therefore, a form of darkness that must be banished by the light of reason.[3]

Atheism has a history of its own. One of the charges brought against Socrates (470-399 BC) was that he was an atheist.[4] Rather than recant the questions he had raised, Socrates committed suicide by drinking poison, as had been ordered by the court that sentenced him to death.

---

[2] *Religulous*, http://www.imdb.com/title/tt0815241/quotes

[3] Carl Sagan's last book, *The Demon-Haunted World: Science as a Candle in the Dark*, contrasts the light of scientific reason with the darkness of religious worldviews; see also page 149.

[4] *Apology*, 26a-28a.

Atheist philosophies of science played a prominent role in the Enlightenment and in the French Revolution (1789-1799 AD):

> [The Goddess of Reason was a] personification of those intellectual powers which distinguish man from the rest of the animal creation; deified in 1793 by the revolutionists of France, and substituted as an object of worship for the divine beings of the Christian faith. It was decreed that the metropolitan church of Notre-Dame should be converted into a Temple of Reason; and a festival was instituted for the first day of each decade, to supersede the Catholic ceremonies of Sunday. The first festival of this sort was held with great pomp on the 10th of November. A young woman, the wife of Momoro, a well-known printer, represented the Goddess of Reason.[5]

The "decade" referred to above was the new ten-day week for the new secular calendar, designed and adopted by the revolutionaries. In the 19th century, Auguste Comte (1798-1857 AD), a French philosopher, declared himself the prophet of the Religion of Humanity.[6]

Carl Sagan (1934-1996 AD), an astronomer and exo-biologist (a person who speculated about life on other planets), may be the best-known atheist of the 20th century; he appointed disciples to observe him carefully as he died, so that they could testify afterward that he had not undergone a deathbed conversion: "Contrary to the fantasies of the fundamentalists, there was no deathbed conversion, no last-minute refuge taken in a comforting vision of a heaven or an afterlife. For Carl, what mattered most was *what was true*, not merely what would make us feel better."[7]

If I was convinced that atheism is true, I would be duty-bound to follow Sagan's cult of materialism, and join him and his disciples (whom I call "saganists") in their steadfast resistance to every other form of religion. If there is no God, then he and other like-minded atheists are right: the universe exists merely by chance, has no meaning whatsoever, and will leave nothing behind but cosmic ashes when the fires lit by the Big Bang burn out. We are nothing but random mutations preserved by natural selection—and when we die, we are dead and gone.

I can see why many people would rather drink beer, watch TV, and hook up when they can, rather than think about things like this.

---

[5] William Adolphus Wheeler and Charles Gardner Wheeler, *An Explanatory and Pronouncing Dictionary of the Noted Names of Fiction* (Ticknor and Fields, 1865); http://books.google.com/books?id=GL0OAAAAYAAJ

[6] "Religion of Humanity," *Wikipedia*.

[7] Ann Druyer, Sagan's third and last wife, in her epilogue to Carl Sagan's posthumous work, *Billions and Billions: Thoughts on Life and Death at the Brink of the Millennium* (New York: Ballantine Books, 1997), 270; emphasis added.

The Myth of Mr. Spock (Scientism)

Gene Roddenberry, creator of the *Star Trek* franchise, was an atheist who imagined a future, in which science had completely eradicated all forms of religion. The Vulcan race in general, and Mr. Spock in particular, were icons of devotion to "pure reason." Formal reasoning (logic) is a beautiful tool and an amazing accomplishment, but it operates solely at the level of ideas. Logic has an "if-then" structure. It shows correlations between abstractions. *If* one idea is true, *then* something else follows from that idea.

> **Abstract generalization**: "All humans are mortal."
> **Arguable assertion**: "Fr. Moleski is a human being."
> **Logical conclusion**: "*If* Fr. Moleski has not yet died, *then* he will die later."

In and of itself, logic is noncommittal about the nature of reality. It shows that there are options for belief, but logic does not specify any particular belief about ultimate reality and meaning:

> **Abstract generalization**: "Science provides excellent resources for the study of physical things that can be observed by the senses, measured, and manipulated in experiments."
> **Arguable assertion**: "All of reality is physical; there are no metaphysical realities."
> **Logical conclusion**: "*If* all of reality is physical, *then* science provides excellent resources for the study of the whole of reality."

The materialist belief that "all of reality is physical" is an unproven assertion. It is not self-evident, nor is it a conclusion from a self-evident principle. It is not dictated by "pure logic." It is a generalization that may—or may not be—true.

Nothing Buttery[8]

The central dogma of materialism provides a sword with which to slay all religious beliefs.

Religion is *nothing but* wish fulfillment.
Human beings are *nothing but* atoms and molecules.
The mind is *nothing but* a by-product of random events.
Marriage is *nothing but* a social convention.

Of course, *if* materialism is true, *then* it follows that materialism itself is *nothing but* wish fulfillment, produced by social conventions, based on *nothing but* the random interaction of atoms and molecules.

Religions Disagree

Never before in history have humans had as deep a knowledge of the multiplicity of cultures and religions as we have in our day. The whole globe has been mapped, not only geographically, but also anthropologically. Our maps extend into the past, too. We know about past cultures and religions, as well as those that exist today. A common—and culturally reinforced—reaction to the diversity of religions is to say, "None of them can be true; if there were one true religion, everyone would have adopted it by now; no religion has prevailed over all others; therefore, there is no true religion."[8]

The hidden premise of this argument is that people are purely rational beings, who always choose what is true and always do what is good. There is, I think, a fair amount of evidence that this is not the case. The absurd, self-contradictory, self-destructive, and irrational behavior of human beings is fairly well documented, even if one does not accept the Catholic teaching on the universality of Original Sin. Things that seem blindingly obvious to one person seem utterly absurd to another. Sin and stupidity seem to me to be sufficient reasons for the multitude of conflicting opinions about God and humanity.

While it is true that not all religious claims can be true (because they contradict each other), it does not follow that there cannot be one that is true and trustworthy. Just like John Lennon, I wish all men and women would adopt my worldview and my spirituality. I think "the world would be a better place" if we all were of "the same mind, with the same love, united in heart, thinking one thing" (Phil 2:2). It is by accepting Jesus as "the Way, the Truth, and the Life" (Jn 14:16) that I acquire a standard by which to judge what is true, beautiful, good, noble, and praiseworthy in other religious traditions—and what is not.

Freedom of Religion, Not Freedom from Religion

The first Amendment to the Constitution of the United States is entitled "Freedom of Religion, Press, Expression" and reads in its entirety:

> Congress shall make no law respecting an establishment of religion, or prohibiting the free exercise thereof; or abridging the freedom of speech, or of the press; or the right

---

[8] I have used this same argument in Chapter 1, p. 12.

of the people peaceably to assemble, and to petition the Government for a redress of grievances.

This amendment is tacitly critical of the European nations, from which the colonies of the United States descended. From time immemorial, what we in our day call "church" and "state" were intertwined with each other (Greek and Rome both had state-sponsored religious creeds and practices; in local religions, all authority has a religious dimension). The Catholic Church became the established religion of the Roman Empire in 381 AD and remained the dominant state-sponsored religion in Europe, until the rise of Protestantism in 1517 AD; just like Catholics, the classical Protestant denominations allied with the power of the state, and enjoyed the status of being established religions. The King or Queen of England still rules the Anglican Communion by right of royal birth. Remnants of established religions still exist in many other European countries, as well.

The framers of the First Amendment wanted to prohibit the government from interfering in the free exercise of religion on the part of the citizens of the United States. The phrase "separation of church and state" is not in the Constitution; it is found in a letter from 1802 that Thomas Jefferson wrote, 11 years after this amendment was ratified. In contemporary culture, some seem to think that the Constitution requires that religion be walled off from secular, state concerns, as if the amendment prohibited religious people from criticizing the actions of the government on religious grounds. Nothing could be further from the text or spirit of the Constitution. The government may not forbid its citizens to be religious, or to think religiously about what is right for our nation. To do so would be to prohibit the "free exercise" of religion.

Doubting the Atheist Religion

Atheism qualifies as a religion in my book, because it is a comprehensive view of ultimate reality and meaning, and answers all the questions posed by all other religions (see pp. 9-11). Since it competes with all other religious worldviews, it exists in the same ecological niche, and belongs in the same class as its competitors.

Skeptics recommend doubting everything and questioning authority. I doubt that atheism has been established on rational grounds, and question the authority of those who assert that it is superior to theism. In order to assert on one's own personal authority that there is no God, one would have to be all knowing and eternal—one would have to *be* God to have such godlike knowledge of the whole of reality.

If the case against God is not made on the basis of one's personal knowledge of the whole of reality, then it can only be advanced as a matter of argument from evidence. Atheists rarely attempt to provide disproofs of the existence of God. Authoritative assertions take the place of argument. Some atheists claim that they cannot be obliged to prove that God does not exist on the alleged principle that "no one can prove a negative." This is itself a negative proposition, and if it is true, it cannot be proved; if it is something believed without proof, then it is a mere assumption or an irrational and unjustified act of faith, no more worthy of respect than a groundless belief in the existence of God.

In fact, pure logic and mathematics make no distinction between positive and negative statements. It is not an axiom of thought that "no one can prove a negative." There are various kinds of negatives, and various forms of proof for each kind. I can prove to myself that there is no 1954 Pontiac Star Chief in the room where I am typing this, simply by using my senses to search the space around me. Scientists call this "observation," and many of the truths of science depend upon the use of our senses in precisely this fashion. Others who wish to verify that there is no automobile in this room would have to come and see for themselves; there is no *logical* reason why I couldn't be working in a garage large enough to hold such a big car, nor is there any *logical* reason why I shouldn't be working in a different kind of room than I am. Logic cannot decide the question. This particular matter of fact can only be settled by a judgment based on the proper kinds of observation (finding out what room I am in, then inspecting the room for the presence of the Star Chief).

Judging whether God is in the room where I am writing—or with you where you are when you read this—is a much more difficult proposition than counting the number of Star Chiefs nearby. In the radical monotheistic religions of the West, God is held to be a pure spirit, with no physical limitations. God is not composed of form and matter, is not located in space and time, and cannot be observed by the senses, or by instruments that extend the range of the senses. We can't tell God's presence or absence by seeing, hearing, tasting, touching, or smelling; to say that there is a God, or else that there is no God, is a metaphysical judgment.

Perceiving Metaphysical Realities

The claim that God is an invisible friend (also inaudible, untasteable, untouchable, and unsmellable) causes some materialists to foam at the mouth. To mock the metaphysical and religious standpoint, they invent dragons in their garage (Sagan), dream up absurd versions of religion (*Men in Black*, *The Hitchhiker's Guide to the Galaxy*, and a multitude of other science fiction works), or explain the power of religion as a con game (*The Wizard of Oz*).

If there is no God—and if we can *know for certain* that there is no God—then, of course, religion deserves all the abuse that people have heaped on it.

The first level of metaphysical realities to which we may pay attention are things like beauty; truth; goodness; justice; reality; reason; science; mathematics; logic; music; or history. None of these are physical, sensible realities. They are at least mental realities. Of course, the dogmatic materialists have already taken cover under the Shield of Nothing Buttery, lest they be forced to concede that there are kinds of non-sensible realities that make a great deal of sense. But once they've crawled under the Shield, they have nothing more to say. because they cannot defend their interpretation of science, truth, logic, or reason—anything they could say would be *nothing but* a random output from a meaningless physical reality. They cannot say, "You are wrong about materialism," because wrongness is not an observable physical reality; it is a metaphysical quality that can only be perceived by reasoning metaphysically.

Reasoning from Effect to Cause

I would not worship a God whose reality is no greater than that of mathematical truths or musical theory. The Western religions claim that God is *the cause of all that is*. "Ever since the creation of the world, his invisible attributes of eternal power and divinity have been able to be understood and perceived in what he has made" (Rom 1:20).

In the Catholic tradition, looking at the universe philosophically to recognize the "invisible attributes of eternal power and divinity" is called "**natural theology**." Please note well that the kind of knowledge that can be gleaned from this kind of reasoning falls short of what can be known from God's self-revelation in salvation history. There is a huge difference between what we can find out about God philosophically and what God tells us in revelation.

Before we turn to God, let's consider a simpler example of reasoning from effect to cause. Take any human artifact you please, and consider what you can understand about the makers of that artifact. I'm surrounded by such things at this moment: the keyboard, mouse, monitor screen; a microphone, camera, and earphones for Skype; pens, pencils, Sharpies, CDs, DVDs, paper clips, lighters, a stapler, matchbooks, Kleenex; the chair on which I'm sitting, a fan, lights in the room; the clothing I'm wearing; pads of paper; statues, knickknacks, clocks; a stereo system; a teaspoon and coffee mug; a briefcase, filing cabinet, and dozens and dozens of books and some bookends; a two-ounce fishing weight; a magnifying glass; a flashlight; etc., etc. Of all these things around me, I only know the story of the making of a few of them. I built the copy stand and the table and shelves on which my keyboard, monitor, and printer rest. Everything else around me was made by someone else.

I know that all of these things were made by intelligent human beings. Sony amplifiers don't grow on trees. Everything that I see around me right now was made on purpose by intelligent people. I know that they acted to create these things to make money because, apart from the few crude things I made myself, all of them were sold to me or given to me by people who purchased them. I know that the makers wanted money for the sake of the things that money can buy, and I know that they wanted those things, in turn, because they wanted to be happy.

What I can't tell from the works of human hands that surround me is the names of the designers, workers, and marketers who made these things for me. I do not know whether they were men or women; what their cultural background was; their age, height, weight, appearance, or the condition of their health; their marital status; their scholastic achievements; the mood that they were in when they did this work for me. I do not know whether they found the happiness they sought, or whether they are alive or dead today. I know how little I know about them, even though I know something of their talent and ingenuity from their works and something of their motivation to find happiness from an understanding of human nature.

In a similar way, natural theology (if it is valid) can disclose some truths about God: His existence, unity, eternity, infinitude, omnipresence, intelligence, goodness, and beauty. The works of God's hands tell us something about the Worker, but not all that there is to be known.

Reasoning from effects to causes is a perfectly normal part of scientific reasoning. We cannot see gravity, electromagnetic fields, or quantum particles; we assert that such things exist, because we can show the effects that they have on observable realities.

Some people argue against the existence of God using a kind of effect-to-cause reasoning. They say that if there were a God, then:

- scientists would have seen Him;
- there would be no evil in the world;
- animals would not be so goofy;
- everyone would believe in Him;
- there would only be one form of religion.

Since none of these things is the case, it seems that there is no God *such as the one envisaged in the objections*.

The reply to the first objection is, of course, the point already made above: God is not an object of science (an observable physical reality) and is never an answer to any proper scientific question. Science deals with the observable universe. If there is a God, He is not part of physical reality.

Moral evil, unbelief, and the multiplicity of religions can be understood in terms of the gift of human freedom and its misuse (see the section on theodicy, page 63). If there is a God, He is tolerant of sin and stupidity in His creatures.

The existence of natural evil (fire flood, famine, pestilence, disease, and other natural disasters) is a function of God's decision to give us a stable universe, within which we can tell what the consequences of our actions will be; the laws of physics, chemistry, and biology are not suspended when a human might be hurt by their operation.[9]

If things were otherwise, such that the law of the universe was "no harm may come to any human being from natural activity," then there would be no science, and no awareness of the consequences of our actions. People could walk to the top of Mount Everest barefoot; they could leap off of tall buildings—or throw their siblings off them—without harm; they could swim to

---

[9] C. S. Lewis, *The Problem of Pain* (New York: Touchstone, 1996), 25-32.

the bottom of the ocean without needing a submarine; they could never die of starvation due to poor harvests. There would be no suffering, disease, or death—but there would be no stable frame of reference for moral or physical knowledge, either. If there is a God, He allows human beings to be hurt, both by the operation of the laws of nature, as well as by the sins of other human beings.

The remaining difficulty is the thought that if there were a God, there would be no evolution. Animals would appear immediately in a perfect form that would last forever. There would be no huge waves of extinction of strange (and ugly!) animal species. Every part of every animal would be perfect, and there would be no leftovers at all in the genetic code or in animal forms. It is inconceivable that God would be haphazard in creation. On this assumption, it seems that if there were a God, there could be no evolution and (by a purely logical inference) if there is evolution, then there is no God.

Both biblical literalists and those who interpret science atheistically back the idea that one must choose between God and evolution. As noted above in the discussion of the Genesis stories (p. 47), the Catholic tradition does not require us to take every proposition in the Bible literally. If biology shows that evolution is a matter of fact (in the sense that one form of life derives from earlier forms of life), as seems to be the case, then we have to accept that God created an evolving universe. The Catholic Church does not accept the *atheistic interpretation* of this fact, which is an entirely different matter altogether. The Church rejects the idea that God could not achieve His purposes by working through an evolving universe.

It is hard to imagine how God can give the universe so much freedom that millions of species come into being and pass out of being through random mutation and natural selection. When I write programs for my computer or my websites, I don't want them taking on a life of their own and changing at random; I want every bit in every byte of the programs or documents I write to stay the same as it was the day I finished compiling the executable or installing the script. In my little universe, everything is under my control and, as the song says, "That's the way I like it, uh huh!"

When I am confronted with the bewildering variety of species in the universe, both extant and extinct, I conclude that God is not like me. He seems to have the power to turn things loose, to give them their own nature and their own kind of freedom. Although it is hard for me to imagine how this can be, it is not the only aspect of reality that is hard to imagine. It is hard to imagine how electromagnetic phenomena can have both the properties of waves and particles; it is hard to imagine that everything we see in the universe came from the Cosmic Egg or the God Particle; it is hard to imagine how neutrinos pass through most of matter without any interaction, how there could be dark matter and dark energy, and how space itself may be expanding at an accelerating rate. Here again, it is another assumption that must be jettisoned, not belief in God. The assumption that we have to give up is that "anything that is hard to imagine cannot be real." If there is a God, and if the evolution of one form of life from other forms of life is a matter of fact, then—hard as it may be to imagine—we have to accept that God intended, and accepts, the vagaries of evolution.

Arguments for the Existence of God

Long before the birth of Jesus and the rise of Christianity, the pagan Greek philosophers, **Socrates** (470-399 BC), **Plato** (427-347 BC), and **Aristotle** (384-322 BC), criticized the polytheistic worldview of their culture, and argued that there could only be one real God Who was the cause of all that is. Socrates was executed, in part because his questions about Greek mythology caused the youth of Athens to lose faith in the gods and goddesses. Aristotle outlined Five Ways to show that there must be a God. Thomas Aquinas (1225-1274 AD) made those Five Ways the cornerstone of his natural theology.

It is a dogma (irreversible teaching) of the Roman Catholic Church that the existence of God can be known with certitude through the use of reason (philosophy): "The Catholic Church believes that there is one true and living God, the Creator and Lord of heaven and earth, Almighty, Eternal, Immense, Incomprehensible, Infinite in intellect and will and in all perfection; who, being One, Individual, altogether simple and unchangeable Substance, must be asserted to be really and essentially distinct from the world, most happy in Himself, and ineffably exalted above everything that exists or can be conceived. … Holy Mother Church does hold and teach that God, the Beginning and End of all things, can certainly be known from created things by the natural light of reason, 'for the invisible things of Him from the creation of the world are clearly seen, being understood by the things that are made' (Rom. 1:20)."[10] The council that proposed this teaching (Vatican I, 1870) did not specify any particular philosophy or set of arguments by which such certitude could be obtained; the council was essentially upholding Paul's statement, that such natural knowledge of God is possible without making any commitment to a particular system of reasoning.

I have studied the Five Ways of Aristotle and Aquinas for more than 40 years, ever since I took Aquinas as my confirmation sponsor in seventh grade. I know how hideously complex the arguments *about* the arguments become in very short order; simply to chart all of the objections and replies that have been given to Aristotle's view over the last 2300 years would take a huge book, and wouldn't necessarily help people gain confidence in the arguments.

For me, seeing the universe as filled with God's glory (Ps 8, Ps 19) is a Gestalt switch (a change in perception of the data). God is the Gestalt (interpretation) that makes sense of all sense-making. Once some realizes that there is a God, then everything else in the universe looks different from the way it did before. As with the Magic Eye puzzles, which look like completely random scraps of graphics until one learns to view them properly, "those who have eyes to see

---

[10] "Dogmatic Constitution on the Catholic Faith" (Vatican I, 1870), Chapters 1 and 2. See CCC 36 and 47.

	NATURE DOES NOT EXIST	**NATURE EXISTS**
GOD EXISTS	**Pantheism** Involuntary theocentrism. God is immanent with, and indistinguishable from, the cosmos. E.g., various forms of Hinduism, Buddhism, Taoism.	**Theism** Theocentric: worship. God transcends the cosmos. Polytheism (some Hinduisms) vs. monotheism of Abrahamic religions: Judaism, Christianity, Islam.
GOD DOES NOT EXIST	**Nihilism** Denial of all reality and meaning. Eccentric? *[Something no one can consistently assert.]*	**Atheism, neopaganism, materialism, modernism, secular humanism, saganism.**[11b] Cosmocentric, anthropocentric. Popular philosophy of science in our culture.

[11b] "Saganism" is a term I have coined for Carl Sagan's metaphysical philosophy of science, which holds that the methods and results of science logically entail atheism; see page 187.

will see, those who have ears to hear will hear" (Ez 12:2, Mk 8:18). I can't force anyone to open their eyes to God as the Cause of all that is; I can't force people to *see* the force or *feel* the weight of the arguments against their will. The Five Ways all make sense to me, even though I know that I have not found or answered every possible objection to them that has been, or could be, raised by philosophers.

1. There must be an Unmoved Mover

Every thing in the physical universe is in motion. Nothing that is in motion set itself in motion; its motion and power to move (if it is alive) comes from other things. But the chain of things that causes motion or gives the power to move cannot be infinite. There must be an Unmoved Mover that is an entirely different kind of being from things that are moved, or empowered to move, by others; it must be outside of space and time, and have infinite power at its disposal, because it is self-sufficient to make other things move.

Because of the Second Law of Thermodynamics (entropy increases: some energy becomes unavailable whenever work is done), it is not possible to have a perpetual-motion machine. People who deny the argument from motion believe in a perpetual-motion universe.

2. There must be an Uncaused Cause

Every thing that is in the physical universe is a form of matter that has been formed by some other agent; no thing in the universe forms itself. The line of agents-caused-by-other-agents cannot be infinite. There must be an Uncaused Cause that gives all other agents the power to act. The Uncaused Cause cannot be part of the physical universe, and cannot be limited in its power to act, because it is self-sufficient. It must be an entirely different kind of being from what we see in the physical universe.

3. There must be a Necessary Being

Every thing in the physical universe is a "contingent being." That means that it comes into being, exists for a while, then ceases to exist. It is possible for such things "to be or not to be" (*Hamlet* III, i). Such things come into being through other contingent things. Things do not come into being out of nothing. There cannot be an infinite regress of beings caused by other beings. The matter and energy in the universe, from which all other beings come, cannot have come into existence out of nothing. There must be a different kind of being from the kind of things we find in the universe, a being whose existence is necessary, not contingent; this is a being whose being is to be. That kind of being cannot be part of the physical universe, and cannot be limited in existence in any way.

4. There must be a Supreme Good

We perceive that some things in the universe are better than others (good, noble, true). We could not have a scale of values, unless we implicitly recognize that there is something that is "best" (most good, most noble, most true). Perfection depends upon being. A real hamburger is infinitely more valuable than the idea of a hamburger if someone is hungry and it is lunch time. Real money is more valuable than the idea of money. There must be a real being, in whom all the perfections are one (true, beautiful, and good), and by whom all perfection is communicated to lesser beings. Every judgment about the true, the beautiful, or the good implicitly appeals to the scale of value established by the highest truth, the most beautiful reality, or the greatest good.

5. There must be an Infinite Intelligence

Every thing in the universe is an example of order. Order does not happen by accident. According to the Second Law of Thermodynamics, entropy (disorder) increases. This means that the natural tendency of the physical universe is to become more disorderly. There must be an intelligent being who gave the universe the order we see in it. That being cannot be part of the universe of ordered things, and cannot be limited in intelligence.

No scientific discovery can overturn this argument. Every scientific discovery shows that being is intelligible. This is NOT a "God of the gaps" argument. It is an argument from the reality of human knowing. "If being is intelligible, then God exists."[11] If the universe is meaningful, there is a God. God is the meaning behind all meaning. Every time we make a knowledge claim, we affirm the order and intelligibility of the universe, even if the claim is that we know that we know very little of what can be known. *We know enough to know how little we know.*

The first three Ways all appeal to the idea that there cannot be an infinite regress of things-caused-by-other-caused-things. This insight is the key to the validity of those three arguments. I think this is definitely one of those things that people see at once, or never see at all. A simple example to help gain the insight is to compare the things we see being caused all around us to a chain of dominoes that are toppling in sequence, each one tipped over by the one that precedes it in the sequence. We could not see dominoes falling over, one after the other, unless someone set them up close enough to each other to be tipped over by the one before it, *and* tipped over the first domino in the sequence, to start the chain of events leading up to the cascade of falling dominoes that come later. Both the potential for acting on each other (the close arrangement of dominoes) and the action of starting the cascade of falling dominoes had to be given by something that wasn't a domino standing in line with the other dominoes.

Every thing we perceive in the universe around us was caused by other things in the universe. Science has studied this chain of causality, and tells us that the whole observable universe came forth from the Big Bang, somewhere in the neighborhood of 13 or 14 billion years ago. There is no physical record of what existed before, or apart from, the Cosmic Egg or God Particle that exploded in the Big Bang, because the physical record that exists to be read by scientists—the structure and state of the physical universe—is the product *of* the Big Bang. Even if there are many other universes, even infinitely many universes, that gave rise to the Big Bang, we may ask of all of them whether they are self-sufficient (uncaused causes), or caused by another (caused causes). The fact that we cannot observe them through physics does not prevent us from thinking about them metaphysically. An infinite number of Big Bangs trailing off into the past is not more self-explanatory than one solitary Big Bang—it is just a longer line of dominoes that needs to

---

[11] Bernard J. F. Lonergan, *Collected Works: Understanding and Being*, ed. Elizabeth A. Morelli and Mark D. Morelli (New York: Mellen, 1980), 242-246.

be set up in such a way that one thing can cause another thing, and that needs to be activated by some kind of being that is not stuck in the line of caused things-caused-by-other-caused-things.

The common conclusion of all Five Ways is "And this is what we mean by 'God.'" After outlining the Five Ways, Aquinas shows that there can be only one infinite, eternal being, and therefore, that the cause of motion, agency, contingent existence, truth, beauty, perfection, and order must be the same being. This pure Spirit is infinite, eternal, all powerful (omnipotent), all knowing (omniscient), all present (omnipresent), all good, all beautiful, all true, all just—in short, perfect in every way that we can imagine.

Anselm's Ontological Argument

St. Anselm of Canterbury (1033-1109 AD) proposed an argument for the existence of God, based on the meaning of the word itself. He defined "God" as the greatest conceivable being. A being that *exists* is greater than a being that does not exist. The greatest conceivable being is one that cannot not exist (a "necessary being," as in Aquinas's Third Way). If the greatest conceivable being cannot not exist, then God must exist.

As a general rule, most philosophers do not think this is a sound argument. In their view, the idea that God must exist really only leads to the *idea* that God must exist. My first teacher of medieval philosophy spent six months thinking about nothing but Anselm's argument; he said that he believed it on Mondays, Wednesdays, and Fridays but doubted it on Tuesdays, Thursdays, and Saturdays. On Sunday, he did his level best to stop thinking about it.

I love Anselm's definition of "God," and think that we cannot get very far in natural theology without using some version of it. Using Newman's terminology, apprehending the definition of the word "God" only leads to the notion that God *ought* to exist (notional apprehension and notional assent), but still leaves open the question of whether God does, in fact, exist (real apprehension and real assent).

Theological Anthropology: Who Do We Think We Are?

So what? What difference does it make if there is a God? The answer depends on how we *imagine* God's relationship to the world in general, and to humanity in particular.

All action comes from the imagination. That is why advertisers spend tens of billions of dollars each year. They know that if they can get the audience to imagine their product bringing them happiness, the sales made will more than cover the costs of the ad campaign. *The one who conquers the imagination rules the whole person.*

The way that we imagine God directly affects the way that we imagine ourselves. The Hindu image that we are gods and goddesses (Saguna Hinduism), or aspects of the one God (Nirguna

Hinduism), is very different from the view of the Abrahamic religions: that we are not God and not part of God, but creatures living in a covenant relationship with God.

The first chapter of Genesis (1:26-27) says that humans are made in the "image and likeness" of God. "What are humans that you are mindful of them, mere mortals that you care for them? Yet you have made them little less than a god, crowned them with glory and honor" (Ps 8:5-6). We have to be careful in drawing the right lessons from these and similar passages. We are like God, but God is not like us. God is not just a human figure writ large in the heavens. We resemble God most closely in our intelligence, in our desire for infinite happiness, in the unspeakable mystery of our personhood, and in our free will. From what we know of our existence and nature, we gain some insight into God's existence and nature, but we are finite, created, and oriented toward bodily existence in the physical universe, while God is infinite, uncreated, and utterly free from the constraints of space and time.

If we mistakenly imagine that God's mind is like ours, then it follows logically that we are too small for God to pay attention to each one of us personally. Astronomers love to play games with perspective, showing that the earth is far less than a speck of dust compared to the universe as a whole. When the astronomer's camera pans back far enough to comprehend the area of 40 to 50 billion light years spanned by the universe, the earth vanishes entirely from the frame; it is so small that it doesn't affect one pixel in the final image.

God is not like us. He does not have to back away physically to see everything in one glance. Because God is pure spirit, he is not limited to the field of space-time/matter-energy as we are; he does not do astronomy with telescopes or biology with microscopes. All of our language begins with, and is rooted in, our experience of the physical universe. There is no spatial preposition that cannot, in some sense, be used of God, and there is no spatial preposition that does not, in some sense, mislead our understanding of God if it is pushed too hard.

> God is *above* us. He is infinitely greater than everything else that is.
> God is *below* us. He is the ground of all being.
> God is *beside* us. He is our loving partner in life.
> God is *within* us. He dwells within us, both as Creator and as Redeemer.
> God is *behind* us. He is the Alpha (the "A") of all Creation.
> God is *before* us. He is the Omega (the "Z") of all Creation.
> God is *outside* the universe. He is Totally Other—the most alien of all imaginable aliens.
> God is *inside* the universe. He is the Cause of all causes. He is **omnipresent** (present everywhere).
> God is *beyond* all telling. He is too meaningful for us to define Him exhaustively.
> God is *in* every truth. His light illuminates all minds.

The problem with *metaphorical language* is that it can mislead us into thinking things like "God is watching us—from a distance" or "God is an absentee landlord." God is supremely **transcendent** (way *beyond* us) and supremely **immanent** (deep *within* us—closer to us than we are to ourselves). God knows us from the inside out. He knows us better than we know ourselves. He does not grow tired of paying attention to each one of His children personally, and He (very much unlike us!) does not suffer from a broken heart or unconscious conflicts in His psyche. Because He is infinite, He can give each one of us infinite attention, without taking anything away from any of his other creatures.

God is not stuck in time the way that we are. He is not 13 or 14 billion years away from us, setting the machinery of creation in motion and letting it work itself out apart from Him. Creation is not something that happened a long time ago in a faraway place. Creation is something happening here and now. God is "**I AM**", not "I WAS."

For Catholics, the conviction that we can recognize philosophically that there is an infinite and omnipresent God opens the door to the possibility of revelation from that God. If it is reasonable to think that there is a God, it is reasonable to think that that God might want to make Himself known to us.

Types of Religions: Is There a God There?

Depending on the definitions used, one might count tens of thousands to hundreds of thousands of religions that exist today, or have existed in the world. Simply listing all of the variants recognized by Religious Studies scholars would be very dull indeed. For my purposes, I hold that there are only a finite number of *types* of religions—just four. The box below exhausts all of the possible combinations of views about the existence of God and the existence of the universe.

I consider nihilism to be self-contradictory and utterly irrational, and yet there seem to be nihilists who are not troubled by asserting their own nonexistence and the nonexistence of others. Although I consider rationality to be a defining feature of human nature—and one of our most God-like attributes—people seem to be free to be irrational.

Some thinkers have coined a word that does not appear in the logic box. They call themselves "panentheists," in order to emphasize the fact that all things (Greek, *pan*) exist in God (Greek, *en* = "in" and *theos* = "God"). This term can be given an orthodox theist interpretation as a corrective to the misleading picture of God coming "into" the universe from some kind of space "outside" the universe. Theistic panentheism reminds us that God is not a creature in "outer space" who invades our universe, but the one *in Whom* all things exist. The danger of the term is that it is more easily identified with pantheism, which destroys the traditional Abrahamic distinction between uncreated being (God) and created being (the universe).

There are many other ways of grouping religions so they can be treated as members of the same type. Religious Studies scholars employ many different methods (sociology, anthropology, psychology, history, economics, linguistics, literary analysis, philosophy, theology, etc.) to call attention to interesting patterns in the data collected about religious beliefs and practices.

Unlike biology, which has a relatively well-established system for classifying forms of life (kingdom, phylum, class, order, family, genus, species), there is no common system to classify types of religions. There is some rough agreement that we may distinguish between smaller and larger religions, but every characterization of the difference between the two groups runs afoul of someone's sensitivities. The smaller religions might be called savage, primitive, local, native, indigenous, or tribal, while the larger religions might be called sophisticated, civilized, developed, international, or global. As a general rule, the local and tribal religions, such as those found in the indigenous peoples of Africa, the Americas, the Pacific Islands, and Australia do not seek converts, while the global religions, such as Buddhism, Christianity, and Islam have gone beyond ethnic and regional boundaries, precisely because their message is directed to the whole of humanity. Judaism does fit neatly into either classification. On the one hand, it is a family religion, meant for the descendants of Abraham, Isaac, and Jacob, but it is found all around the world because of the ability of the Jews to adapt to other cultures, while preserving their religious identity.

Some scholars skirt these problems of classifying religions by focusing instead on rituals, spirituality, ethics, or social customs, without using any kind of scale of size or sophistication. Some treat religions as evolutionary realities, surviving and developing when they serve human needs, but withering and decaying when they do not.

Those students who wish to continue in Religious Studies will have to grapple with these, and many similar, issues. They must take a stance, and inform their readers of the meaning of the terms they use in their speaking and writing; playing the definition game (p. 9) is an obligation within the Tribe of Religious Studies Scholars. The rest of us, I trust, can get along, for the most part, without developing clear and distinct ideas about theory and method in Religious Studies.

Types of Christianity: Sibling Rivalry

Ecumenism is a movement that began among non-Catholic Christians in the 19th century to strengthen and promote Christian unity. The World Council of Churches was founded in 1937, and represents a coalition of almost half a billion believers. In 1962-1965, Vatican II encouraged Catholics to ponder how much all Christians have in common, rather than focusing on the issues that divide us, because all "who believe in Christ and have been truly baptized are in communion with the Catholic Church even though this communion is imperfect."[12] As Paul says, there is

---

[12] Vatican II, "Unitatis Redintegratio: Decree on Ecumenism," 3. I will abbreviate this as UR in the remainder of my references to this document.

only "one Lord, one faith, one baptism; one God and Father of all, who is over all and through all and in all" (Eph 4:6; UR 1). This means that all who are baptized are members of the same Body of Christ as Catholics, and are truly brothers and sisters in the Lord.

From the standpoint of the Catholic Church, anyone who is baptized with water and the Trinitarian formula, regardless of who the minister is, is as baptized as if they were baptized by the Pope. There is no such thing as being "baptized Catholic" or "baptized Protestant." By the grace of Baptism, we are all filled with the life of the Trinity, and joined as one in Jesus (UR 22).

Vatican II encouraged Catholics to recognize how God's grace is poured out on our brothers and sisters in the Lord:

> Catholics must gladly acknowledge and esteem the truly Christian endowments from our common heritage which are to be found among our separated brethren. It is right and salutary to recognize the riches of Christ and virtuous works in the lives of others who are bearing witness to Christ, sometimes even to the shedding of their blood. For God is always wonderful in His works and worthy of all praise.
>
> Nor should we forget that anything wrought by the grace of the Holy Spirit in the hearts of our separated brethren can be a help to our own edification. Whatever is truly Christian is never contrary to what genuinely belongs to the faith; indeed, it can always bring a deeper realization of the mystery of Christ and the Church. (UR 4)

The Church's recognition that the Body of Christ and the grace of the Holy Spirit can be found "outside the visible boundaries of the Catholic Church" (UR 3) came as a shock to me. When I was a boy, I thought that all Protestants were going to Hell—and many of my Protestant friends thought the same of me and my fellow Catholics. The Council called Catholics to repent of that kind of mind-set:

> There can be no ecumenism worthy of the name without a change of heart. For it is from renewal of the inner life of our minds, from self-denial and an unstinted love that desires of unity take their rise and develop in a mature way. We should therefore pray to the Holy Spirit for the grace to be genuinely self-denying, humble, gentle in the service of others, and to have an attitude of brotherly generosity towards them. St. Paul says: "I, therefore, a prisoner for the Lord, beg you to lead a life worthy of the calling to which you have been called, with all humility and meekness, with patience, forbearing one another in love, eager to maintain the unity of the spirit in the bond of peace." (Eph 4:1-3; UR 7)

When St. Paul heard of conflict and divisions among Christians in Philippi, he gave advice about how to heal the rifts: "Finally, brothers, whatever is true, whatever is honorable, whatever is just, whatever is pure, whatever is lovely, whatever is gracious, if there is any excellence and if there is anything worthy of praise, think about these things" (Phil 4:8).

Recognizing Truth Wherever It Is Found

Although ecumenism, strictly speaking, is about unity among Christians, Vatican II also taught that Catholics should recognize the love of God poured out upon all of humanity, at all times and in all places.

> Religions found everywhere try to counter the restlessness of the human heart, each in its own manner, by proposing "ways," comprising teachings, rules of life, and sacred rites. The Catholic Church rejects nothing that is true and holy in these religions. She regards with sincere reverence those ways of conduct and of life, those precepts and teachings which, though differing in many aspects from the ones she holds and sets forth, nonetheless often reflect a ray of that Truth which enlightens all men. Indeed, she proclaims, and ever must proclaim Christ "the way, the truth, and the life" (John 14:6), in whom men may find the fullness of religious life, in whom God has reconciled all things to Himself. (2 Cor. 5:18-19)[13]

Just as Catholics should recognize all that is honorable, pure, lovely, gracious, excellent, and worthy of praise among other Christians (Phil 4:8), so, too, should they "recognize, preserve and promote the good things, spiritual and moral, as well as the socio-cultural values" found in non-Christian religions (NA 2). The document mentions Hinduism, Buddhism, Judaism, and Islam in particular (NA 2-4), but expects that the principle of open-hearted admiration of all that is good in our non-Christian brothers and sisters will extend to the whole human family—even to the good that is to be found among atheists:

> Nor does Divine Providence deny the helps necessary for salvation to those who, without blame on their part, have not yet arrived at an explicit knowledge of God and with His grace strive to live a good life. Whatever good or truth is found amongst them is looked upon by the Church as a preparation for the Gospel. She knows that it is given by Him who enlightens all men so that they may finally have life.[14]

---

[13] "Nostra Aetate: Declaration on Non-Christian Religions," 2. I abbreviate this as NA.
[14] "Lumen Gentium: Dogmatic Constitution on the Church," 16.

The Latin playwright, Terence (circa 195-159 BC) said, "Nihil humanum a me alienum"—"Nothing human is alien to me." This seems to be the attitude that the Church wants its members to develop. God loves all of His creation, and leaves no one out of His loving-kindness.

The Beauty of Selflessness

For me, self is the ground of all blessing. It is "I" to whom God gives all things as a free and unmerited gift. My self is what I know best, because it is through self-consciousness that I know all else around me. My self is also one of the greatest mysteries in my life. The self that I can put into words is not the real me.

Self is also the greatest obstacle to happiness (page 185). The Western religions all affirm that I am not self-sufficient; only God has no origin other than Himself, and I am not God. I have a longing to love, and to be loved without limit by other selves. What I give in love is my self, the greatest gift that I have been given; what I receive in love is the self of the other, their greatest treasure in life. Selfless self-giving is the form of every act of love.

It is possible to recognize the affirmation of the beauty of selflessness in all of the religions we have considered here.

Hinduism: **sannyasa, moksha**
Buddhism: **nirvana**
Confucianism: **jen, second nature**
Taoism: **wu wei**
Judaism: **obedience to the Torah**
Christianity: **death to self**
Islam: **Aslama**

No religion has a monopoly on love. Wherever humans live together, we find some who love, and some who refuse to love. In the end, I think there will be only one question on the final exam that we all have to take. The Selfless Self, from whom all other selves derive, will ask us, "What did you do with what I gave you?" I hope and pray that we all may pass that test with flying colors.

BIBLIOGRAPHY

• • • • • •

Augustine. *Confessions*, R. S. Pine-Coffin, trans. London: Penguin Books, 1961.

Bailey, Lee W., and Mary Pat Fisher. *An Anthology of Living Religions*. Upper Saddle River, NJ: Prentice Hall, 2000.

Catechism of the Catholic Church, 2nd ed. Washington, DC: United States Catholic Conference, 1997 (1992).

Cunningham, Lawrence S., and John Kelsay. *The Sacred Quest: An Invitation to the Study of Religion*. Upper Saddle River, NJ: Prentice Hall, 2006 (1991), 4th ed.

Davies, Brian. *An Introduction to the Philosophy of Religion*. Oxford: Oxford University Press, 2004 (1982), 3rd ed.

Deming, Will. *Rethinking Religion: A Concise Introduction*. Oxford: Oxford University Press, 2005.

Ellwood, Robert S., and Barbara A. McGraw. *Many Peoples, Many Faiths: Women and Men in the World Religions*. Upper Saddle River, NJ: Prentice Hall, 2009 (1992), 9th ed.

Freud, Sigmund. *Civilization and Its Discontents*, trans. James Strachey. New York: Norton, 1961 (1930).

Huff, Margaret C., and Ann K. Wetherilt. *Religion: A Search for Meaning*. Boston: McGraw-Hill, 2005.

Kessler, Gary E. *Studying Religion: An Introduction through Cases*. Boston: McGraw Hill, 2003.

Kreeft, Peter. *Fundamentals of the Faith: Essays in Christian Apologetics*. San Francisco: Ignatius Press, 1988.

Lewis, Clive Staples. *Abolition of Man, or Reflections on Education, with Special Reference to the Teaching of English in the Upper Forms of Schools*. New York: Macmillan, 1955 (1947).

———. *The Problem of Pain*. New York: Touchstone, 1996.

Livingston, James C. *Anatomy of the Sacred*. Upper Saddle River, NJ: Prentice Hall, 2009 (1998), 6th ed.

Lonergan, Bernard J. F. *Insight: A Study of Human Understanding*. New York: Harper and Row, 1978 (1957).

Martin, Richard C. *Islamic Studies: A History of Religions Approach*. Upper Saddle River, NJ: Prentice Hall, 1996, 2nd ed.

Modschiedler, John C., Kent E. Richter, Eva M. Räpple, and R. Dean Peterson. *Understanding Religion in a Global Society*. Belmont, CA: Thomson Wadsworth, 2005.

Moleski, Martin X. *Michael Polanyi: Scientist and Philosopher*, with William T. Scott. Oxford University Press, 2005.

————. *Personal Catholicism: The Theological Epistemologies of John Henry Newman and Michael Polanyi*, with foreword by Avery Dulles. Washington, DC: The Catholic University of America Press, 2000.

Newman, John Henry. *Apologia pro Vita Sua: Being a History of His Religious Opinions*. Edited and with introduction by Martin J. Svaglic. Oxford: Clarendon Press, 1967.

————. *Essay on the Development of Christian Doctrine*. New York: Sheed and Ward, 1960.

————. *An Essay in Aid of a Grammar of Assent*, edited and with introduction by Nicholas Lash. Notre Dame: University of Notre Dame Press, 1979.

Olson, Carl. *Theory and Method in the Study of Religion: A Selection of Critical Readings*. Belmont, CA: Wadsworth, 2003.

Polanyi, Michael. *Personal Knowledge: Towards a Post-Critical Philosophy*, corrected edition. Chicago: University of Chicago Press, 1962 (1958).

————. *The Tacit Dimension*. New York: Doubleday and Company, 1966.

Sagan, Carl. *The Demon-Haunted World: Science as a Candle in the Dark*. New York: Random House, 1996.

————. *Billions and Billions: Thoughts on Life and Death at the Brink of the Millennium*. New York: Ballantine, 1997.

————. *The Dragons of Eden: Speculations on the Evolution of Human Intelligence*. New York: Ballantine, 1977.

Smart, Ninian. *The Religious Experience*. Upper Saddle River, NJ: Prentice Hall, 1996, 5th ed.

Smith, Huston. *The World's Religions: Our Great Wisdom Traditions*. San Francisco: Harper Collins, revised and updated, 1991 (1958).

Stark, Rodney. *For the Glory of God: How Monotheism Led to Reformations, Science, Witch-Hunts, and the End of Slavery*. Princeton: Princeton University Press, 2003.

————. *The Victory of Reason: How Christianity Led to Freedom, Capitalism, and Western Success*. New York: Random House, 2006.

Waley, Arthur, trans. *The Analects of Confucius* (New York: Vintage, 1989).

Wilson, William Griffith, et al. *Alcoholics Anonymous: The Story of How Many Thousands of Men and Women Have Recovered From Alcoholism*. New York: Alcoholics Anonymous World Services, 1976 (1939); Third edition.

Appendix
The Development of Writing

• • • • • •

The early **Semitic languages**, Hebrew and Aramaic, originally lacked vowels. They developed from the Phoenician system which, in turn, seems to have derived from the use of some special Egyptian hieroglyphs that were used to represent sounds, rather than whole words or phrases. The Egyptian glyph used for the sound "a" seems to have been a bird. The Phoenicians used a picture of an ox's head for that sound. The horns of the ox resembled the horns of the crescent moon, so the letter became associated with the moon. From the Phoenician symbol came the alpha in Greek (α—look at it sideways to see the ox's head!), the aleph in Hebrew (א), and the "a" in Latin and English.

The brilliance of the shift from picture-writing to representation of sounds cannot be overstated. Imagine how hard it would be to draw pictures that said, "There are not enough pictures available to represent the 500,000 words in the English lexicon." Once the change was made, then the whole realm of thought could, in principle, be written down. If you could put something into words, you could put the words into writing, even if the concept deals with things like metaphysics, epistemology, philosophy, theology, literature, history, art, architecture, and the like.

The Semitic alphabets seem to have developed around 1700 BC. The oldest Hebrew inscription found so far comes (not surprisingly) from around 1000 BC, the time of the kingship of David in Jerusalem. Whatever writing the wandering tribes of Israel may have done between the time of the patriarch, Abraham, and the establishment of Jerusalem as the capital of the United Kingdom of Israel, it probably was not engraved in stone, and has now turned to dust. The story of Moses and the tablets engraved by God suggests that the authors of TNK believed that the alphabet existed in Moses's day.

What I have done with these examples is to work backward from our system of writing to something like what our texts would look like if we didn't have vowels, spaces, capitalization, and punctuation, all of which were later developments and refinements.

- **Y cn d th sm thng wth nglsh, srt f, lthgh t s prtty dffclt t wrt nd rd.**
  "You can do the same thing with English, sort of, although it is pretty difficult to write and read."
- **NdthHbrwsrgnllywrtwthnspcsbtwnwrds. Thtmdtvnmrdffclttrd!**
  "And the Hebrews originally wrote with no spaces between words. That made it even more difficult to read!"
- **ndthyddnthvcptlttrsrpncttnswd**
  "And they didn't have capital letters or punctuation as we do!"

I thank God for the unnamed geniuses who invented our system for representing language!

Timeline

• • • • • •

Prehistory

Tribal (local) religions. Probably forms of polytheism or polytheistic animism. Burial of the dead. Totems. Ritual magic (blessings and curses). Oral tradition preserved by elders, shamans, priests, pilgrimage sites, annual festivals. Various kinds of sacrifice (sometimes including human sacrifice). Astrology (religious interpretation of sun, moon, stars, planets, comets, meteors).

	Western Religions	**Eastern Religions**
	BC = "Before Christ" = "Jesus is *the* Christ"	
AKA "Before Common Era," "Before Present"		
~4000	Egyptian hieroglyphs.	
3761	Date of creation in Jewish calendar.	
2700	24 Egyptian unilateral (hieroglyphs for specified sounds).	
1850	Proto-Canaanite (Phoenician) alphabet.	
1700	The patriarchs: **Abraham, Isaac, and Jacob** (AKA **Israel**).	
1290-1200	**Moses, Passover, Exodus** from Egypt, conquest of Promised Land, Yhwhism, Torah.	
1200		Chinese writing; Sanskrit.

	Western Religions	**Eastern Religions**
1200-1000	**Judges**, animal sacrifice, early psalter. The Hebrew alphabet reaches the form we know today.	
1000	Oldest known Hebrew text.	
1010-970	**David** displaces Saul as king of Israel.	
970-930	Solomon (son of David and Bathsheba), builds **the first Temple**.	
922	**Northern Kingdom (Israel; 10 tribes)** divides from **Judah (Southern Kingdom; two tribes)**.	
753	Legendary date for the founding of the city of Rome.	
722	Northern Kingdom destroyed by the Assyrians (Syrians); "Israel" eventually becomes a religious title, while "Judah" becomes an ethnic title (hence, "**Jews**"—*the Jews are all that is left of the Israelites*).	
700	Deuteronomic tradition well established in this century. Rise of prophets criticizing hollow observance of law and infidelity to God.	
604		Earliest conjectured date for Lao Tzu. Contemporary of Kung Fu-tzu?
600	**Classical Period**—Greco-Roman civilization (*Hellenism*).	
586	**Babylonian Captivity**—destruction of First Temple; loss of kingship: *no more* **Messiahs**!	

• Timeline •

	Western Religions	Eastern Religions
563-483		Siddhartha Gautama of the Sakyas.
551-479		Kung Fu-tzu.
~534		"The four passing sights."
515	Building of the Second Temple in Jerusalem.	
~528		Siddhartha becomes "the Buddha."
470-399	Socrates.	
427-347	Plato.	
384-322	Aristotle.	
356-323	Alexander the Great.	
148	Rome defeats Macedonia (~Greece).	
63	Rome takes direct control of Judea.	
4	Probable date for birth of Jesus.	
	AD = Anno Domini = "Jesus is Lord" AKA "Common Era" and "Present"	
30 or 31	Probable dates for death of Jesus.	
30-90 (?)	**Apostolic era:** ends with death of last apostle ("the beloved disciple?").	
66-73	Jewish revolt against Rome. Jerusalem and the Temple were destroyed in 70 AD.	
90 (?)-735	**Patristic era:** "fathers of the Church."	
325	Council of Nicaea: first ecumenical (worldwide) council of the Church.	
381	Christianity made the official religion of the Roman Empire.	
476-1000	**Dark Ages.** "Fall of the city of Rome" (the Roman Empire continued in the East!).	

213

	Western Religions	**Eastern Religions**
520		Bodhidharma takes Lotus Flower Buddhism to China (Ch'an).
525	Dionysius Exiguus (AKA "Denny the Dwarf") invented BC/AD system; equated 1 AD with 754 UC (***"Ab Urbe Condita"***— "after the founding of the city").	
571-632	**Muhammad**, "Seal of the Prophets."	
610	Night of Power.	
622	**Hijra**: escape from Mecca to Medina; by his death in 632, Muhammad ruled most of Arabia.	
733	Muslims repelled at Battle of Tours; their empire extends from Spain to India.	
~800 AD		Ch'an becomes Zen in Japan.
1000-1400	**Middle Ages.** Scholasticism.	
1054	**Schism** between **Eastern Orthodox** churches and the Roman Catholic Church.	
1095-1291	Series of crusades (Christian holy wars) against Muslims. Muslims call their holy war a "jihad."	
~1200		Koans develop within Zen Buddhism.
1348	Black Death reaches Europe. Killed 50% in two years, 75% over 20 years!	
1453	Turks conquer Constantinople; later renamed Istanbul.	
1469-1539		Guru Nanak Dev—first of 10 Sikh gurus.

• TIMELINE •

	Western Religions	**Eastern Religions**
1492	Moors (Spanish Muslims) driven out of Spain by Ferdinand and Isabella.	
1400-1700	**Renaissance.** "Rebirth" of Greco-Roman civilization.	
1517	October 31: Martin Luther posts 95 theses (ideas, judgments). Birth of **Protestantism**.	
1529	Suleiman the Magnificent besieges Vienna.	
1683	Second Siege of Vienna by Muslims; John Sobieski rides to the rescue.	
1700 to present	**Enlightenment.**	
1776-1917	**Age of Revolutions** against Christian royal families.	
1914-1969	**Modernity.**	
1935		Birth of the 14th Dalai Lama (affirmed at age two, but not formally installed until 1950—apparently under Chinese rule).
1939-1945	WWII and the Holocaust.	
1947	Modern state of Israel created by unilateral action on the part of the United Nations. Fulfillment of the ideal of the Crusades to take the Holy Land away from the Muslims.	
1959		Dalai Lama flees Tibet to escape Chinese Communist government.
1970 to present	**Postmodernity.**	
1972	Jesus didn't return in glory!	
1988	Jesus didn't return in glory!	
1996	Jesus didn't return in glory!	
2000	Jesus didn't return in glory!	
2001	Jesus didn't return in glory!	
2025-2033	Maybe Jesus will return in glory!	

Index

Abraham 55, 57, 58, 64, 65, 66, 67, 68, 70, 74, 78, 87, 91, 96, 107, 108, 136, 156, 158, 161, 175, 202, 209, 211
Abrahamic religions 55, 64–68
Age of Revolutions 148
agnostic 186
agnosticism 186
Al Aqsa Mosque 161, 174–175
Alexander the Great 71, 93, 213
Allah 155, 156, 159, 160, 161, 162
Alms 161
anachronism 67, 148
Analects of Confucius 3, 38, 42, 208
ananda 28, 32, 34, 142
Anatta 34, 52
animism 37, 42, 49, 62, 186, 211
Apocalypticism 150
apocrypha 95
Apologetics 116
apostasy 127
apostolic era 124, 136, 138, 164
apostolic succession 127, 130, 164
apotheosis 114
Aquinas 9, 15, 72, 163, 195, 199

Arabs 66, 156, 172, 173, 175, 176
arhats 35
Arian heresy 138
Aristotle 93
Arjuna 26, 27
Aslama 156
Atheism 185, 186, 190
Atheism, methodological 62
atman 28, 34, 142, 143
Atonement 150
augury 43
Augustine 12, 64, 207
avatar 26, 36

Babylon 81, 91, 92, 99, 136, 151, 174
Babylonian Captivity 89, 90, 94, 103, 212
Baptism 102, 106, 109, 126, 137, 141, 144, 146, 167, 203
Baptism of Jesus 102
Bar Mitzvah 67
Bathsheba 86, 212
Battle of Tours 162, 214
Bhagavad-Gita 26, 79
bhakti 27, 29, 35

BIBLE 67, 71, 74, 75, 94, 122, 124, 125, 131, 132, 146, 166, 167, 174, 194
BIBLE, MOLESKI'S CONJECTURE ABOUT THE 125
BIG BANG 58, 187, 198
bishop 130, 146, 164
BISHOPS 127, 128, 129, 130, 131, 137, 138, 139, 150, 158, 164, 167, 168, 182, 184
BODHI 31, 33, 35
BODHIDHARMA 51, 214
BODHISATTVA 36
BOOK OF REVELATION 101, 120, 150, 151, 152
BO TREE 33
BRAHMA 26, 29
BRAHMAN 28, 34
BRAHMIN 25
BUDDHA 28, 29, 31, 32, 33, 34, 35, 41, 51, 52, 53, 213
BYZANTIUM 139, 149, 164

CALENDAR X, 65, 153, 157, 187
CANAAN 65, 73, 79
CANON 95, 101, 114, 119, 120, 121, 122, 124, 146, 158
CANON OF THE NEW TESTAMENT 100–101, 113, 121–124, 145
CANON OF THE OLD TESTAMENT 95, 123–124, 142, 146, 158
CARL SAGAN 4, 186, 187, 196
CASTE SYSTEM 25, 169
CATHOLICISM 2, 3, 12, 128, 131, 150, 158, 159, 163, 164, 165, 166, 168, 183, 208
CATHOLICISM, ROMAN 131, 163–164
CHI 42, 149
CHIT 28, 32, 34, 142
CHOSEN PEOPLE 65, 78, 80, 89, 91, 99, 103, 136, 145
CHRIST X, 72, 81, 82, 83, 84, 85, 86, 89, 90, 91, 95, 96, 102, 103, 104, 105, 106, 107, 108, 110, 111, 112, 113, 114, 115, 118, 126, 128, 129, 131, 132, 134, 135, 136, 137, 140, 142, 146, 147, 148, 149, 150, 152, 160, 202, 203, 204, 211
CHUANG TZU 47, 49
CHUN-TZU 39, 40
CHURCH AND STATE 148, 158, 165, 189–190. SEE ALSO THEOCRACY
CIRCUMCISION 66, 77, 132
CLASSICAL ERA 94, 149, 165
CLASSICS, THE 38, 42
CONFUCIUS 3, 28, 38, 39, 40, 41, 42, 43, 45, 51, 208
CONSTANTINOPLE 139, 148, 149, 150, 162, 163, 164, 214
CONTRADICTION 15–16, 50–51
COUNCIL OF JERUSALEM 134
COUNCIL OF NICAEA 136, 139, 142, 213
COVENANT 74, 77, 78, 84, 85, 87, 89, 91, 93, 94, 96, 102, 103, 106, 107, 108, 109, 126, 175
COVENANT, NEW 95–96, 106–108, 126–127
CREATION EX NIHILO 58, 63
CREATION STORIES X, 57–64, 113, 124, 139, 199–200, 204
CREED 14, 30, 34, 78, 139, 155, 159
CRUSADES 162, 173, 215

DALAI LAMA 36, 215
DALIT 25
DARK AGES 149, 150, 163, 213
DAVID 74, 80, 81, 83, 84, 85, 86, 87, 88, 89, 90, 91, 93, 96, 99, 102, 103, 104, 105, 106, 107, 108, 115, 157, 174, 209, 212
DAVID KORESH 91
DEACON 130, 146
DECALOGUE 75, 169, 171
DEFINITION GAME 11, 12, 14, 15, 43, 202
DEISM IX
DEITY IX, X, 62
DE-LITERALIZATION 135

democracy 94, 158, 173
demythologization 61, 117
Deposit of Faith 127, 128, 131, 136, 137, 138, 158, 168
Descartes 9, 13, 14
deuterocanonical 95, 142
Dhammapada 33
dharma 33, 35
Dialectics 27
Dialectics of Desire 27
diaspora 136, 174
divination 43
Divine Name 71, 72, 73, 80, 113, 114
divinization 33
doctrine, development of 138–139, 145–146
dogma 2, 79, 103, 127, 139, 142, 143, 144, 182, 186, 188, 195
Dome of the Rock 174
dukkha 33

Eastern Orthodox 75, 131, 164, 214
ego 28, 33, 72, 113, 114
Eightfold Path 33, 53
Elijah 90, 96, 103
Emancipation of the Jews 170
Enlightenment (Eastern) 31–33, 49–53
Enlightenment (Western) 13, 50–51, 158, 169–170, 187
epistemology 9, 16, 17, 185, 209
error-correcting protocols 125, 137
Esau 68, 69
Essenes 135
ethics 59, 202
Etymology ix
evil, problem of 63–64, 193. *See also* sin; *See also* Sin, Original; *See also* theodicy
evolution 58, 130, 194, 195
exegesis 74, 124, 132, 147

Exile 89, 91, 93, 94, 99, 136, 174
Exodus 70, 73, 74, 77, 99, 171, 211

fall of Rome 150, 163, 164
Fathers of the Church 122, 136, 150
fatwa 159
feng shui 42
Five Ways of Aristotle and Aquinas 195
forest dweller 30, 32, 34
Four Noble Truths 33
Four Passing Sights 31, 32

Gautama 31, 53, 213
genocide 66, 79, 182
genre 90, 124, 150
Gentile 90
Gentile 132, 133, 135, 147, 171
gnosis x
gnostic x
Golden Rule 39
gospel 6, 94, 95, 100, 101, 102, 103, 105, 108, 109, 113, 114, 115, 116, 117, 118, 119, 121, 122, 123, 127, 128, 133, 137, 174
gospel of John 100, 105, 108, 109
Granth Sahib 169
Great Schism 163
Greco-Roman civilization 60–61, 93–94, 99, 150, 163, 163–164, 169
Greek mythology 60–61
guru 36, 49, 167, 169

Hadith 158, 159
Hagar 66
Hajj 161
hajji 161
halal 159
Hanukkah 77
Haram 174, 175

HEAVEN 65, 72, 88, 102, 112, 113, 114, 132, 140, 141, 152, 153, 187, 195
HEBREW, etymology 55
HEBREW LANGUAGE 70–71, 209–210
HELL 142–143
HELLENISM 94, 139, 212
HENOTHEISM 78
HERESY 127, 138, 140, 143
HERMENEUTICS 124, 132
HIJRA 156, 157, 161, 214
HINAYANA 35
HISTORY, WORTH OF 119
HOLOCAUST 67
HOLOCAUST, THE 172
HOLY ORDERS 127, 129, 130, 146, 150
HUSTON SMITH vii, 39, 49
HYPERBOLE 73

ILLAH 155, 156
IMAM 159
INCARNATION 8, 114, 116, 139, 140, 141, 142, 150, 164
INDIFFERENTISM 185
INFALLIBILITY 127, 164
INFANCY NARRATIVES 100
INRI 105
ISAAC 66, 67, 68, 69, 70, 74, 80, 87, 108, 136, 202, 211
ISHMAEL 66, 156, 161
ISLAM, ETYMOLOGY OF 156
ISRAEL, ETYMOLOGY 68
ISRAEL, KINGDOM OF 81–91
ISRAEL, RESTORATION OF 171–175
ISTANBUL 162, 214

JACOB 45, 68, 69, 70, 74, 103, 108, 202, 211
JEHOVAH 72
JEN 39, 205

JERUSALEM, DESTRUCTION OF 89–91, 135–136
JERUSALEM HOLY TO MUSLIMS 160
JESUS OF NAZARETH 6, 99, 105, 140
JESUS THE CHRIST 114
JIHAD 161
JINNI 155
JIVA 25, 34, 145
JOHN HENRY NEWMAN 3, 5, 12, 128, 137, 208
JOHN THE BAPTIST 100, 102, 103, 135
JOSHUA 79, 80, 111
JUDAH, KINGDOM OF 89
JUDAISM, CONTEMPORARY VARIETIES OF 170–171
JUDAISM, SECOND TEMPLE 91–96, 99, 136, 174
JUDAIZERS 132
JUDAS FACTOR 127, 184
JUDGES 79–81
JUDGMENT DAY 111, 152, 181
JUSTICE 24, 59, 76

KARMA 24, 25, 26, 28, 29, 30, 31, 39, 64, 143, 145
KAUR 169
KETHUBIM 74
KORESH 91
KOSHER 77, 133, 159
KRISHNA 26, 27, 79, 169
KUNG FU TZU 37, 38, 51

LAO TZU 12, 45, 46, 47, 48, 49, 51, 52, 212
LAST TESTAMENT 76
LI 40–41
LOGIC ix, 3, 9, 13, 15–16, 46–51, 57, 113, 170, 188, 190–191. *See also* DESCARTES; *See also* ENLIGHTENMENT (WESTERN); *See also* NON-CONTRADICTION; *See also* THINKING, CRITICAL
LONERGAN 2, 16, 185, 198, 207
LONG TREK 38
LOTUS FLOWER SERMON 51

LXX 90, 95, 96, 106, 107, 113, 114, 141, 142, 158

Mahatma Gandhi 26
Mahayana 35
mandalas 36
mantras 36
maya 26, 28, 29, 31, 34, 50, 58
Messiah 81, 82, 83, 84, 85, 86, 89, 90, 91, 102, 103, 104, 105, 106, 107, 108, 111, 112, 113, 115, 126, 140, 146, 153, 160, 174
messianic expectations 90
Messianic Secret 103
metaphysics 4–5, 15, 25, 34, 37, 42, 62, 140, 188, 192–201. *See also* Aquinas; *See also* philosophy; *See also* science; *See also* theology, natural; *See also* saganism; *See also* theism
Michael Polanyi 12, 19, 119, 185, 208
Middle Ages 2, 15, 144, 158, 159, 163, 164, 214
Middle Way 32, 41
Mishnah 136, 158
Modernism 167, 168
Mohists 41
moksha 28, 29, 32, 34, 35, 59, 205
monotheism ix, 29, 60, 67, 75, 78, 92, 93, 140, 155, 160, 169, 186, 196
Moors 162, 215
Moses 28, 70, 73, 74, 75, 76, 77, 78, 79, 87, 92, 96, 107, 108, 113, 114, 209, 211
Moses, Books 74
Mount Moriah 87, 174
mudras 36
Muhammad 28, 96, 119, 155, 156, 157, 158, 159, 160, 161, 162, 172, 174, 175, 214
Muslim, etymology of 156
mythology, Greco-Roman 60–62

natural theology 192, 193, 195, 199

Nebi'im 74
New Covenant 106, 107, 108, 126
Nicene Creed 139, 140, 153
Night of Power 156, 161, 214
Nirguna 26, 29, 50, 78, 199
nirvana 52, 143, 205
non-contradiction, principle of 15, 50–51
Northern Kingdom 212
Notional Apprehension 5
Notional Assent 5

ordination 128, 167, 168
Organic Model of Revelation 138
Original Sin 63, 64, 140, 160, 189

pagan 62, 77, 134, 148, 195
Palestine 80, 138, 172, 173, 176
Palestinian refugee problem 171–174
panentheism 201
pantheism ix, 29, 60, 186, 201
pantheon ix, 28, 37
papacy 127, 130, 131, 138, 150, 164
pariah 25, 26
Passover 72, 73, 77, 90, 107, 108, 109, 110, 111, 118, 131, 211
patriarch 66, 69, 164, 209
Patristic Era. See Church, Fathers of the
Pentateuch 74, 75, 77, 132, 136
Pentecost 77, 107, 133
People of the Book 162
Pharisees 115, 135, 136, 181
Philistines 80, 172
philosophy 2–3, 13, 15, 19, 24, 27, 34–35, 43, 49, 59, 92, 92–93, 119, 124, 163, 170, 195–196, 201. *See also* Ethics; *See also* Hermeneutics; *See also* metaphysics; *See also* theology, natural; *See also* saganism
Pillars of Islam 159

Plato 12, 93, 163, 195, 213
polygamy 66, 93, 158, 169
polytheism ix, 55, 60, 62, 92, 155, 186, 211
priest vii, 3, 67, 83, 112, 113, 128, 130, 146, 175
priests, sins of. See Judas Factor
primacy 131, 164
Promised Land 65, 73, 74, 79, 136, 172, 174, 211
prophets 74, 96, 103, 114, 129, 141, 153, 155, 158, 175, 212
Prophets, Seal of 96, 155–158, 175
Protestantism 117, 164, 165, 166, 167, 190, 215
Providence 69, 204
Purgatory 4, 142, 143, 144, 166

Quran 66, 95, 114, 119, 156, 157, 158, 159, 160, 161, 167, 175

rabbi 95, 101, 115, 159
Rabbinic Judaism 135–136
Ramadan 161, 169
Ramakrishna 30, 185
real apprehension 4–9, 18, 32–33, 47–48, 63, 199
real assent 4–6, 11, 63, 181, 199
realism, philosophy of 15
Realists 41
Reformation 165, 166
reincarnation 25, 27–28, 35, 58, 145, 169
Relativism 1
Renaissance 150, 163, 164, 165, 166, 169, 170, 215
resurrection 6, 67, 105, 106, 107, 108, 110, 112, 115, 117, 118, 124, 128, 129, 133, 135, 136, 139, 140, 141, 142, 152, 174, 185
retortion 16
revelation 27, 90, 114, 125, 131, 138, 142, 150, 160, 163, 175, 192, 201

Sabbath 77, 115, 170, 171
Sacrament 146
Sadducees 135
saganism 196
Saguna 29, 199
Sakyamuni 33
Sakyas 31, 33, 53, 213
salaam 156
samadhi 28
samsara 25, 26, 28, 30, 33, 34, 35, 58, 59
Samson 80, 81
Samuel 45, 81, 82, 83, 84, 96, 102
sangha 35, 52
sannyasa 27, 28, 30, 31, 205
sanzen 52
Sarah 66
sat 28, 32, 34–35
satori 52, 53
Saul 81, 82, 83, 84, 86, 102, 212
schismatics 117
scholasticism 163
science 6–8, 19, 62, 169, 187–188, 191–194, 196. *See also* Enlightenment, Western; *See also* evolution
science fiction 191
seal of 149
Second Temple 92, 93, 95, 96, 97, 99, 107, 113, 135, 136, 174, 213
Semites 55
Semitic 55, 66, 80, 121, 156, 209
Septuagint 95, 96, 113, 142
Shahada 155, 156, 158, 159, 160
Shang Ti 43
Sharia 158, 159, 175
Shema 78
Shiites 159
Shinto 52
Shiva 26, 29

Index

Siddhartha. *See* Buddha
Siege of Vienna 215
Sikh religion 167, 169
Singh 169
sin, Jewish concept of 64
slavery 69, 74, 91, 109, 150, 158, 163
Socrates 11, 93, 186, 195, 213
sola fide, sola gratia, sola scriptura 165
Solomon 74, 81, 86, 87, 88, 89, 90, 92, 105, 106, 115, 157, 212
spirituality 14–15, 30, 35, 41, 46, 49–53, 59–60, 176, 182, 189
spirituality, Eastern 49–53
spirituality of the Exile 91
stages of life 30, 32, 34
Stark, Rodney 62, 150
stories, truth of 24, 46, 49, 57–61, 64–65, 79, 93, 95, 109–110. *See also* demythologization
sublimation 76
Sufis 159
Sunni 159
synoptics 103, 109, 110, 113

Talmud 136, 158
tanha 33, 34
tantrism 36, 53
Tao 12, 38, 45, 46, 47, 48, 49, 51, 76
Taoism, forms of 49
Tao of the Ancients 38
Tathagata 32, 35
te 37, 41, 45, 46, 49, 51
telephone game 125
Temple, destruction of 89–91, 135–136
Temple of Solomon 77, 83, 86–87, 91
Ten Commandments. *See* Decalogue; *See also* ethics; *See also* justice; *See also* Torah
Testament, New 95, 103–108, 126. *See also* canon of the New Testament; *See also* Covenant
Testament, Old 95, 106–107. *See also* LXX; *See also* TNK; *See also* Covenant
testimony essential to historical knowledge 119
theism ix, 186, 190
the mean 41
theocracy 158
Theodor Herzl 84, 171
theology ix, 3, 34, 42, 110, 116, 159–160, 163, 199. *See also* animism; *See also* Atonement; *See also* Aquinas; *See also* Church, Fathers of the; *See also* Catholicism; *See also* creed; *See also* demythologization; *See also* doctrine, development of; *See also* dogma; *See also* ethics; *See also* Incarnation; *See also* monotheism; *See also* philosophy; *See also* polytheism; *See also* revelation; *See also* Sacrament; *See also* Trinity
theology, natural 192–202
theophany 27, 75
Theravada 34
Thomas Aquinas 9, 15, 72, 163, 195
Ti 37
TNK 74, 77, 78, 82, 90, 91, 92, 93, 95, 96, 106, 107, 112, 113, 114, 141, 142, 158, 161, 209
Torah 62, 71, 74, 75, 77, 78, 79, 86, 91, 92, 93, 94, 95, 96, 99, 107, 115, 126, 132, 133, 134, 135, 136, 170, 171, 174, 205, 211
tradition, deliberate 38
tradition, oral 76–77, 121, 126–127
Trent, Tridentine 122–123, 145–146, 166
Tridentine 166
Trinity 8, 29, 139, 141, 150, 164, 203
Turks 162, 163, 172, 214

TWELVE TRIBES OF ISRAEL 68

UPANISHADS 23
URIAH 86, 87

VAJRAYANA 35, 36, 53
VEDAS 23, 169
VIRGINAL CONCEPTION 60
VIRTUE 24, 39
VISHNU 26, 29
WEN 39, 42, 53
WU WEI 45, 205

YIN-YANG 49, 53
YOGA, FORMS OF 29–30
YOGI 29
YOM KIPPUR 77, 175

ZAZEN 52
ZEALOTS 135
ZION 84, 171
ZIONISM 84, 171